The Climate Cartel

Money Managers, Energy Companies, and the Politics of ESG

snova
New York

Government Procedures and Operations Series

The Woke Agenda: Defending America's Economy, Bureaucracy, and Military
Benjamin W. Liddell (Editor)
ISBN: 979-8-89530-895-0
eBook ISBN: 979-8-90134-029-5

Constitutional Amendments: Perspectives on Equality and Reform
Andrea Como (Editor)
ISBN: 979-8-89530-862-2
eBook ISBN: 979-8-89530-963-6

The Future of the Clean Water Act: Policy, Funding, and Regulatory Perspectives
Gerald C. Lawrence (Editor)
ISBN: 979-8-89530-795-3
eBook ISBN: 979-8-89530-920-9

Addressing the Debt Limit: Legislative Insights and Economic Impacts
Chad D. Reed (Editor)
ISBN: 979-8-89530-770-0
eBook ISBN: 979-8-89530-922-3

Reproductive Rights in Post-Roe America: Barriers, Policies, and Advocacy
Clarence J. Hinton (Editor)
ISBN: 979-8-89530-855-4
eBook ISBN: 979-8-89530-907-0

Protecting Social Security for Future Generations
Shayne Nielsen (Editor)
ISBN: 979-8-89530-639-0
eBook ISBN: 979-8-89530-647-5

The National Flood Insurance Program (NFIP): Background, Reforms and Affordability
Jolene Rivera (Editor)
ISBN: 979-8-89530-612-3
eBook ISBN: 979-8-89530-635-2

Social Security Insights: Legislation, Coverage, and Financial Health
Gina P. King (Editor)
ISBN: 979-8-89530-483-9
eBook ISBN: 979-8-89530-511-9

More information about this series can be found at
https://novapublishers.com/product-category/series/government-procedures-and-operations/

Gabriel A. Darrick
Editor

The Climate Cartel

Money Managers, Energy Companies, and the Politics of ESG

snova
New York

Library of Congress Cataloging-in-Publication Data

ISBN: 979-8-90134-148-3 (Hardcover)
ISBN: 979-8-90134-158-2 (eBook)

Published by Nova Science Publishers, Inc. † New York

Contents

Preface

This book provides an examination of the intersection between corporate governance, climate policy, and financial influence in the United States. It investigates how institutional investors and money managers have shaped the strategies and decision-making of major energy companies through Environmental, Social, and Governance (ESG) initiatives. Chapters explore alleged coordination among financial actors, the role of public pension funds, and antitrust inquiries aimed at understanding potential collusion in the energy sector. By analyzing the legal, political, and economic dimensions of ESG-driven corporate activism, this book offers an in-depth perspective on the mechanisms, implications, and debates surrounding corporate influence in climate governance.

Chapter 1

Sustainability Shakedown: How a Climate Cartel of Money Managers Colluded to Take Over the Board of America's Largest Energy Company*

U.S. House of Representatives

Executive Summary

In U.S. antitrust law, competition is always favored over collusion.[1] The largest money managers—however powerful they may be—cannot collude to "pre-empt the working of the market by deciding for [themselves] that . . . customers do not need that which they demand."[2] This is especially true when their conspiracy shrinks the production of the affordable energy products relied upon by millions of Americans. The Committee on the Judiciary is entrusted with the "[p]rotection of trade and commerce against unlawful restraints and monopolies," including anticompetitive agreements that restrict products available to American consumers.[3]

In the 118th Congress, the Committee has investigated the adequacy of U.S. antitrust laws in light of increasing commitments among left-wing environmental activists and major institutional investors to impose

---

* This is an edited, reformatted and augmented version of Interim Staff Report of the Committee on the Judiciary, U.S. House of Representatives, dated December 13, 2024.

[1] *See Nat'l Cotton Oil Co. v. Texas*, 197 U.S. 115, 129 (1905) ("[C]ompetition, not combination, should be the law of trade.").

[2] *FTC v. Ind. Fed'n of Dentists*, 476 U.S. 447, 462 (1986).

[3] Rules of the House of Representatives R. X(1)(l)(16) (2023).

In: The Climate Cartel
Editor: Gabriel A. Darrick
ISBN: 979-8-90134-148-3

environmental, social, and governance (ESG) goals on the U.S. economy. The Committee's oversight has revealed substantial evidence that a "climate cartel" of financial institutions—from the "Big 3" asset managers to "blue-state" public pensions to the proxy advisor duopoly—collude to pressure American businesses to commit to "net zero" and scale down disfavored production.[4] Through climate coalitions—including the Glasgow Financial Alliance for Net Zero (GFANZ), the Net Zero Asset Managers initiative (NZAM), Ceres, and Climate Action 100+— investors form coordinated pressure campaigns to target U.S. companies and demand that they disclose, reduce, and enforce "net-zero" climate commitments.[5] When companies refuse to surrender and comply, the climate cartel colludes to fire company board members and replace them with climate cartel-aligned members.[6]

Building off of the Committee's prior reports, this report primarily focuses on the climate cartel's "net-zero" pressure campaign against America's largest energy producer: ExxonMobil Corporation. As part of its climate crusade to "[s]hrink and pivot the oil and gas sector to clean energy,"[7] the climate cartel targeted the U.S. oil and gas giant using its predictable pressure campaign sequence:

- *Target Disfavored Companies.* The climate cartel branded ExxonMobil as a "focus company" on its climate blacklist, grading it against a "net-zero" benchmark and signaling investors to organize a barrage of shareholder pressure campaigns—more than any other company in the world;[8]
- *Force Disclosures.* Through "name and shame" engagements, the climate cartel demanded that ExxonMobil make immaterial climate disclosures that "obscure material information" by "distort[ing] markets" with speculative, climate-related guesswork;[9]

---

[4] *See generally* H. COMM. ON THE JUDICIARY, 118TH CONG., CLIMATE CONTROL: EXPOSING THE DECARBONIZATION COLLUSION IN ENVIRONMENTAL, SOCIAL, AND GOVERNANCE (ESG) INVESTING (June 11, 2024).

[5] *Id.*

[6] *Id.*

[7] CERES53737 at CERES53741.

[8] *Shareholder Proposal Database*, CERES, https://engagements.ceres.org/ (last visited Dec. 6, 2024).

[9] HIS MARKIT, CLIMATE-RELATED FINANCIAL RISK AND THE OIL AND GAS SECTOR 11, 15 (2017), https://legacy-assets.eenews.net/open_files/assets/2017/05/17/document_cw_01.pdf.

- *Force Reductions.* The climate cartel launched "Trojan Horse"[10] campaigns, calling for emission reduction "targets" that require steep declines in ExxonMobil's production and use of affordable, carbon-based energy; and
- *Enforce Demands.* When ExxonMobil refused to surrender to its "net-zero" demands, the climate cartel colluded to "vote no" against its board of directors to "show that engagement can have teeth—and that investors are willing to escalate pressure against companies that refuse to act."[11]

In 2021, after repeated attempts to force ExxonMobil to adopt "net-zero" climate goals, the climate cartel conspired to "refresh" the ExxonMobil board by removing and replacing its directors. The Committee has uncovered evidence that shows the climate cartel believed, in the words of Anne Simpson, the Climate Action 100+ Steering Committee Chair, "Exxon's board members should have hell to pay" for opposing the cartel's crusade.[12] As a result, the cartel "buil[t] a war room" to escalate its pressure campaign.[13] Critically, this effort included the climate cartel threatening BlackRock and State Street Global Advisors to join Climate Action 100+ even after both asset managers expressed concerns that the initiative's "collusion" and "collaborative engagement" may violate federal law.[14] In May 2021, the climate cartel successfully removed and replaced three of ExxonMobil's board members. Evidence produced to the Committee shows the climate cartel's elaborate and collusive scheme over the prior year to gut ExxonMobil's board to secure "net-zero" climate commitments. For example:

- The Biden-Harris Administration emboldened and recruited investors for the climate cartel. In early 2021, the climate cartel "look[ed] to capitalise on the momentum created by the [Biden-Harris Administration's] . . . climate policy"[15] and worked with Biden-Harris

---

[10] *For Investors*, FOLLOW THIS, https://www.follow-this.org/for-investors/ (last visited Dec. 6, 2024).

[11] CERES13570 at CERES13571; *see also* Transcribed Interview of Andrew Logan, Senior Director, Ceres, (Sept. 9, 2024) at 34:14–35:16.

[12] CERES24135 at CERES24137.

[13] CERES45367 at CERES45374.

[14] *See* CERES1561 at CERES1561; BLK-HJC-100207 at BLK-HJC-100207.

[15] GFANZ13103 at GFANZ13171.

"senior staff in key regulatory agencies" to advance its agenda.[16] In particular, the Biden-Harris Administration's Special Presidential Envoy for Climate, John Kerry, "help[ed] recruit investors for" Ceres, an activist nonprofit organization and leading member of the climate cartel.[17]

- Climate Action 100+ "conceived" an intricate plan and received $4.7 million from climate cartel affiliates to partner with an activist hedge fund to gut the ExxonMobil board. The climate cartel's lead investors "conceived the idea of partnering with [an] activist fund" to "refresh" the ExxonMobil board.[18] In March 2020, Climate Action 100+ received $4.7 million to "implement[] an unprecedented effort to replace board members at one of the world's very largest companies . . . . Exxon"[19] in order "to get new people—[its] people—added to the Exxon board."[20]
- The climate cartel positioned activist fund Engine No. 1 as the public face of the campaign to maintain credibility and mask its "net-zero" agenda. The cartel reasoned that if the "board campaign[] [were] CA100+ originated, that may . . . shift the tone of the entire initiative and make it more difficult for some signatories to support or remain involved."[21] As a result, climate cartel investors colluded with one-year-old activist fund Engine No. 1, which held 0.02% of ExxonMobil's shares, to advance its agenda publicly.[22]
- The climate cartel colluded with European investment firms and "blue-state" pensions to advance the "refreshment" campaign. In early 2020, the climate cartel conducted an "EU roadshow" and secured critical foreign support, including from foreign entities Federated Hermes, Legal & General, and Aviva Investors—with roughly a combined $2.3 trillion in assets under management.[23] The

---

16 CERES2871 at CERES2873 ("Ceres is now communicating with 40 members of the Biden Administration's transition team—which includes top-tier climate advocates who are well known to Ceres.").

17 CERES63255 at CERES63257.

18 CERES58560 at CERES58561.

19 CERES58560 at CERES58561.

20 CERES45367 at CERES45373.

21 CERES1260 at CERES1263.

22 Matt Phillips, *Exxon's Board Defeat Signals Rise of Social-Good Activists*, N.Y. TIMES (June 9, 2021), https://www.nytimes.com/2021/06/09/business/exxon-mobil-engine-no1-activist.html.

23 *Results, Presentations and Reports*, AVIVA INVESTORS, https://www.aviva.com/investors/results-presentations- reports-2021/ (last visited Dec. 6, 2024); *Federated Hermes (FHI)*

cartel also engaged "blue-state" public pensions such as California Public Employees' Retirement System (CalPERS), New York State Common Retirement Fund (NYS), California Teachers' Retirement System (CalSTRS), and the Minnesota State Board of Investment (MSBI). Notably, the MSBI was the deciding vote that secured the election of the climate cartel's third board candidate to ExxonMobil's board.[24]

- Before the ExxonMobil board "refreshment," the climate cartel threatened BlackRock and State Street Global Advisors to join Climate Action 100+. After the asset managers initially refused to join Climate Action 100+ because they were "concerned with collusion"[25] and believed that "engaging alongside other investors may trigger regulatory issues,"[26] climate cartel members threatened to pull multi- billion-dollar contracts, which led BlackRock and State Street Global Advisors to join the initiative and its pressure campaign against ExxonMobil.[27]
- The climate cartel colluded with the "Big 3" asset managers to secure a "critical mass" of votes for the ExxonMobil board "refreshment." BlackRock stated that it could "engage [ExxonMobil] in parallel" but told the climate cartel that the "notion of not in the same room is key."[28] After regular engagement from the climate cartel,[29] BlackRock, State Street Global Advisors, and Vanguard all voted to remove and replace members of the ExxonMobil board.[30]
- The climate cartel "flagged" for investors the ExxonMobil board "refreshment" to signal them to support the campaign. Climate Action 100+ publicly "flagged" the vote to "buil[d] momentum,"[31] put its

---

Q2 Earnings Top Estimates, AUM Rise, YAHOO! FINANCE (July 26, 2024), https://finance. yahoo.com/news/federated-hermes-fhi-q2-earnings-124200811. html; *H1 2021 Results: Strong Financial Performance – 14% Growth in Operating Profit and 22% ROE*, LEGAL & GEN. (Aug. 4, 2021), https://group.legalandgeneral. com/media/ pqvbebib/hy21-press-release_analyst-pack.pdf.

24 MINN. STATE BD. OF INV., ENVIRONMENTAL, SOCIAL, GOVERNANCE REPORT 1 (2021), https://msbi.us/sites/default/files/2021-08/msbi_esg_report_-_august_2021.pdf.

25 CERES1561 at CERES1561.

26 BLK-HJC-100207 at BLK-HJC-100207.

27 CERES14474 at CERES14476; CERES50191 at CERES50195.

28 CERES40303 at CERES40304.

29 CERES62869 at CERES62959.

30 *See* CERES15811.

31 CERES4013.

members "under significant pressure to vote affirmatively,"[32] and avoid "giving the green light to Blackrock et al to not be supportive of the slate."[33] The climate cartel believed that the "flagging of [the] director vote" was a "critical strategic move on [the] part of CA100+" to communicate to investors that they are "being scrutinized on how [they] vote."[34]

- The climate cartel collaborated with the proxy advisor duopoly to recommend in favor of the board "refreshment" and broadcast the campaign to its clients. After the climate cartel engaged ISS and Glass Lewis to support its "iconic" vote,[35] both proxy advisors recommended in favor of three of the cartel's favored board candidates.[36] Glass Lewis also collaborated with the climate cartel to "develop[] and launch[] in advance of the 2021 Proxy Season a CA100+ Alert Mechanism"[37] to "ensure that CA100+ flagged resolutions rise to the top of the voting queue for all investors crucially bringing added attention to a wider audience of investors."[38]

In the end, the climate cartel secured "three climate activists" on the ExxonMobil board of directors.[39] In the year following the campaign, ExxonMobil made a series of "net-zero" commitments for the first time.[40] While publicly the world thought the 2021 ExxonMobil board "refreshment" campaign was advanced by a small activist hedge fund from San Francisco, "behind the scenes,"[41] the climate cartel knew that it was the "engine behind Engine 1."[42] After its board "refreshment" at ExxonMobil, the climate cartel emphasized that "[t]he job . . . [had] only just begun."[43] It continues to leverage

---

32 Press Release, CLIMATE ACTION 100+, In Stunning Vote, Shareholders Elect Two New Directors Put Forth by Shareholders at ExxonMobil, Seeking Climate Expertise and Action, https://www.climateaction100.org/news/in-stunning-vote-shareholders-elect-two-new-directors-put-forth-by-shareholders-at-exxonmobil-seeking-climate-expertise-and-action/ (May 26, 2021).

33 CERES17169 at CERES17171.

34 CERES9645 at CERES9645.

35 CALPERS_13337 at CALPERS_13337.

36 CALPERS_4388 at CALPERS_4401.

37 CERES57272 at CERES57276.

38 *Id.*

39 CERES29333 at CERES29337.

40 *ExxonMobil: One Year Later*, ENGINE NO. 1 (May 25, 2022), https://engine1.com/transforming/articles/exxon- mobil-one-year-later/.

41 CERES1260 at CERES1263.

42 CERES9645 at CERES9645.

43 CALPERS_4585 at CALPERS_4587.

what it calls "[t]he Exxon effect"—that is, "the idea that this could happen to you"—to pressure other U.S. companies to surrender to its "net-zero" climate agenda.[44]

The Biden-Harris Administration failed to investigate the climate cartel and enforce U.S. antitrust law despite clear evidence of collusion. In contrast, as of the date of this report, the Committee has received and reviewed 278,553 documents and 2,596,401 pages of non-public information in response to letters and subpoenas sent to climate cartel members. It has also completed transcribed interviews or depositions of five key players within the cartel's ranks.

Following the Committee's investigative efforts, at least 70 investors have withdrawn from Climate Action 100+[45] for reasons including obligations under "antitrust and competition laws."[46] Nevertheless, the climate cartel remains committed to advancing its "net-zero" agenda, supporting U.S. companies that it deems to be "on the right side of climate history" and, as it did in 2021 at ExxonMobil, waging a climate crusade against those who are not.[47] The Committee remains committed to continuing its investigation of the climate cartel's anticompetitive conduct to inform potential legislative reforms.

---

[44] CERES62869 at CERES62940.

[45] *Compare Investor Signatories*, CLIMATE ACTION 100+ (Nov. 14, 2022), https://web.archive.org/web/2022111418 4301/https://www.climateaction100.org/whos-involved/investors/, *with Investor Signatories*, CLIMATE ACTION 100+, https:// www.climateaction100.org/whos-involved/investors/ (last visited Dec. 6, 2024); *see also* Letters from former Climate Action 100+ investor signatories to Comm. (on file with the Comm.).

[46] Letter from BlackRock Inc. to the Climate Action 100+ Steering Committee 1 (Feb. 2, 2024), https://www.blackrock.com/corporate/literature/publication/2024-our-participation-in-climate-action-100.pdf.

[47] Transcribed Interview of Mark Carney, Co-Chair, GFANZ (Apr. 17, 2024) at 105:2–109:10. The Big 3 asset managers were scrutinized recently because of their efforts to impose "net-zero" climate goals on U.S. companies. On November 27, 2024, 11 state Attorneys General filed a complaint alleging that BlackRock, State Street, and Vanguard violated federal and state antitrust laws by "leverag[ing] their holdings and voting of shares to facilitate an output reduction scheme." Compl. ¶ 6, *Texas v. BlackRock*, No. 6:24-cv-00437 (Nov. 27, 2024). Significantly, as an example of the Big 3's anticompetitive behavior, the complaint names the climate cartel's Engine No. 1-led campaign to remove and replace members of the ExxonMobil board of directors. *Id.* ¶ 90(b).

I. A Cartel Colludes to Impose Left-wing Climate Policy Goals

Under U.S. antitrust law, competitors may not self-regulate markets through "private governance" designed to reduce the output of disfavored products.[48] Section 1 of the Sherman Act outlaws agreements "in restraint of trade or commerce"[49] where competitors collude to form "an extra-governmental agency, which prescribes rules for the regulation and restraint of interstate commerce . . . and thus 'trenches upon the power of the national legislature.'"[50] It does so because "it is not the prerogative of private parties to act as self-constituted censors of business ethics, to install themselves as judges and guardians of the public welfare, and to enforce by drastic measures their conceptions thus informed."[51]

Cartels that impose market standards meant to reduce disfavored production to "net zero" not only destroy competition but also interfere with democracy. In the United States, the Constitution empowers the people's representatives to "regulate Commerce . . . among the several States."[52] Thus, if there are to be "departures from the notion of a free-enterprise system as it was originally conceived in this country," it must be "the product of congressional action and the will of the people" rather than that of "private forces."[53]

A. The American People Have Rejected the Biden-Harris Administration's Left-Wing Climate Agenda

For decades, left-wing policymakers have tried and failed to enact radical "net-zero" climate laws designed to drain the U.S. economy of affordable, carbon-based energy. In 2009, the Democrat-led Congress failed to pass a "cap-and-trade" law to tax greenhouse gas (GHG) emissions that would have raised the

48 See, e.g., Fashion Originators' Guild v. FTC, 312 U.S. 457, 467 (1941); Nat'l Soc'y Pro. Eng'rs v. United States, 435 U.S. 679, 690, 695 (1978); Ind. Fed'n Dentists, 476 U.S. at 459.

49 See 15 U.S.C. § 1.

50 Fashion Originators' Guild, 312 U.S. at 465 (quoting Addyston Pipe & Steel Co. v. United States, 175 U.S. 211, 242 (1899)).

51 FTC v. Wallace, 75 F.2d 733, 737 (8th Cir. 1935).

52 U.S. CONST. art. I.

53 United States v. Topco Assocs., 405 U.S. 596, 612 (1972).

average American family's energy bill by $1,241.[54] In 2015, the Obama Administration unilaterally implemented its so-called "Clean Power Plan," which would have raised electricity prices by at least 12% over fourteen years.[55] In 2022, the Supreme Court struck the Clean Power Plan down, noting that "Congress considered and rejected [the Plan] multiple times."[56]

Most recently, President Joe Biden and Vice President Kamala Harris have continued left-wing efforts to impose "net-zero" climate mandates on the U.S. economy. In 2019, Democrats, including then-Senator Kamala Harris, voted in support of the "Green New Deal" that aimed to "get rid of farting cows and airplanes"[57] and meet "100 percent of the power demand in the United States" through "zero-emission energy sources."[58] On the campaign trail before the 2020 election, both Joe Biden and Kamala Harris vowed to implement a radical climate agenda. Biden promised to "end fossil fuels"[59] and put energy company executives "in jail."[60] Harris insisted that "[t]here's no question [she is] in favor of banning fracking."[61]

---

[54] Nicolas Loris & Ben Lieberman, *Cap and Trade: A Handout for Corporations and a Huge Tax on Consumers*, THE HERITAGE FOUND. (June 10, 2009), https://www.heritage.org/environment/report/cap-and-trade-handout- corporations-and-huge-tax-consumers.

[55] Nicolas Loris, *The Many Problems of the EPA's Clean Power Plan and Climate Regulations: A Primer*, THE HERITAGE FOUND. (July 7, 2015), https://www.heritage.org/environment/report/the-many-problems-the-epas-clean-power-plan-and-climate-regulations-primer#_ftnref7; *West Virginia v. EPA*, 597 U.S. 697, 731 (2022).

[56] *West Virginia*, 597 U.S. at 731 (cleaned up).

[57] Amanda Radke, *Green New Deal Proposes Eliminating "Farting Cows"* (Feb. 10, 2019), BEEF MAGAZINE, https://www.beefmagazine.com/cattle-health/green-new-deal-proposes-eliminating-farting-cows-; *see also* Recognizing the Duty of the Federal Government to Create a Green New Deal, H.R. 109, 116th Cong. (2019).

[58] Matthew Daly, *McConnell Wields Green New Deal as Bludgeon Against Dems*, AP NEWS (Feb. 12, 2019), https://apnews.com/article/a3153729c1aa4805a47161026d5d638a.

[59] Steve Peoples, *In Intimate Moment, Biden Vows to 'End Fossil Fuel,'* AP NEWS (Sept. 6, 2019), https://apnews. com/united-states-presidential-election-9dfb1e4c381043 bab6fd0fa6dece3974?utm_medium=email&utm_source=ncl_amplify&utm_campaign=230907-agenda47_america_must_have_the_1_lowest_cost_energy_and_electricity_on_earth&utm_content=ncl-hf2SjmjQbB&_nlid=hf2SjmjQbB&_nhids=KwrTVAq.

[60] Katelyn Caralle, 'We Should Put Them in Jail!' Joe Biden Wants to Prosecute Fossil Fuel Executives for Environmental Damage—but Doesn't Mention Son Hunter Who Helped Run Ukrainian Natural Gas Giant, DAILYMAIL (Dec. 30, 2019), https://www.dailymail.co.uk/news/article-7837265/We-jail-Biden-wants-prosecute-fossil-fuel-executives-environment-damage.html?utm_medium=email&utm_source=ncl_amplify&utm_campaign=230907-agenda47_america_must_have_the_1_lowest_cost_energy_and_electricity_on_earth&utm_content=ncl-k9K7Y9vG3e&_nlid=k9K7Y9vG3e&_nhids= KwrTVAq.

[61] Kevin D. Roberts, *Kamala Harris Would Destroy Pennsylvania Energy Jobs*, THE HERITAGE FOUND. (Aug. 26, 2024), https://www.heritage.org/energy/commentary/kamala-harris-would-destroy-pennsylvania-energy-jobs.

On their first day in office in 2021, the Biden-Harris Administration rejoined the Paris Climate Agreement to reach "net-zero" emissions by 2050 and limit warming to "1.5 degrees Celsius."[62] If implemented, the Paris Agreement's demands would cost the U.S. economy nearly

$3 trillion in reduced production and more than 9 million industrial and manufacturing jobs.[63] However, because the Biden-Harris Administration has failed to secure Senate support for ratification, the Paris Agreement continues to have "no substantive, legal obligations for the United States."[64] In short, the American people and their democratically elected representatives' response to two decades of left-wing climate policy has been consistent and clear: "No."

B. The Climate Cartel Is Committed to Left-wing "Net-zero" Climate Goals

In recent years, a climate cartel of money managers has attempted to impose through market power what left-wing policymakers have for decades failed to accomplish through legislation or administrative fiat.[65] Through various climate coalitions, institutional investors and environmental activists collude

---

[62] Press Release, U.S. DEP'T OF STATE, *The United States Officially Rejoins the Paris Agreement*, https://www.state.gov/the-united-states-officially-rejoins-the-paris-agreement/ (Feb. 19, 2021). The Paris Agreement's goal is to limit global warming to only 1.5 degrees Celsius above pre-industrial levels. Paris Agreement to the United Nations Framework Convention on Climate Change, Dec. 12, 2015, T.I.A.S. No. 16-1104, 3156 U.N.T.S. 54113, art. 2(1) ("This Agreement, in enhancing the implementation of the Convention, including its objective, aims to strengthen the global response to the threat of climate change . . . including by . . . pursuing efforts to limit the temperature increase to 1.5°C above pre-industrial levels, recognizing that this would significantly reduce the risks and impacts of climate change.").

[63] NERA Economic Consulting, Impacts of Greenhouse Gas Regulations on the Industrial Sector 11–15 (2017), https://accf.org/wp-content/uploads/2017/03/170316-NERA-ACCF-Full-Report.pdf.

[64] Jane A. Leggett, Cong. Rsch. Serv., IF11746, United States Rejoins the Paris Agreement on Climate Change: Options for Congress 1 (2021).

[65] American Clean Energy and Security Act of 2009, H.R. 2454, 111th Cong. (2009) (2009 legislation to "Cap and Trade" GHG emissions dies in the Senate); H.R.J. Res. 109, 116th Cong. (2019) (House resolution calling for the "Green New Deal" dies in committee); *see also West Virginia*, 597 U.S. at 730, 735 (finding that the EPA lacked a statutory basis to cap emissions through the Obama administration's "Clean Power Plan"); *see also supra* Part I (discussing failed left-wing climate campaigns); *see generally* H. COMM. ON THE JUDICIARY, 118TH CONG., CLIMATE CONTROL: EXPOSING THE DECARBONIZATION COLLUSION IN ENVIRONMENTAL, SOCIAL, AND GOVERNANCE (ESG) INVESTING (June 11, 2024) (introducing the climate cartel and explaining its plot to decarbonize the global economy).

to make American businesses' "access to finance dependent on the transition to net-zero."[66] These entities are united by a common commitment: eliminate GHG-emitting investments in their portfolios to "net zero by 2050."[67] This "net-zero" goal requires the total negation of greenhouse gases produced by human activity,[68] which necessitates dramatic reductions in affordable, carbon-based energy.[69]

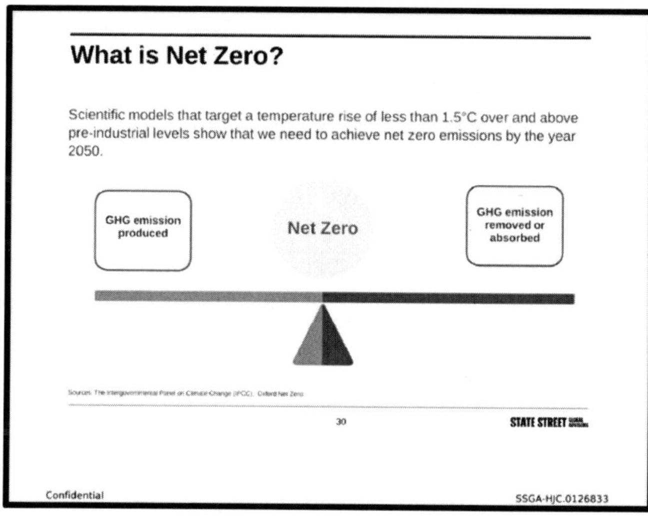

---

[66] CERES37663 at CERES37668.

[67] GFANZ34869 at GFANZ34876. *See, e.g.*, NET-ZERO ASSET OWNER ALLIANCE, COMMITMENT DOCUMENT FOR PARTICIPATING ASSET OWNERS 2 ("My Organisation commits to transitioning its investment portfolios to net-zero GHG emissions by 2050 consistent with a maximum temperature rise of 1.5°C above pre-industrial levels."); *Paris Aligned Asset Owner Commitment Statement*, PARIS ALIGNED ASSET OWNERS, https://www.parisalignedasset owners.org/commitment/ (last visited Dec. 6, 2024) ("[M]y institution commits to . . . [t]ransitioning our investments to achieve net zero portfolio GHG emissions by 2050, or sooner."); GFANZ34 at GFANZ39 ("[M]y organisation commits to support the goal of net zero greenhouse gas (GHG) emissions by 2050, in line with global efforts to limit warming to 1.5°C. It also commits to support investing aligned with net zero emissions by 2050 or sooner."); CLIMATE ACTION 100+, CLIMATE ACTION 100+ SIGNATORY HANDBOOK 7 (2023), https://www.climate action100.org/wp-content/uploads/2023/06/Signatory-Handbook-2023-Climate-Action-100.pdf ("[W]e will work with the companies in which we invest to encourage them to work towards the global goal of halving GHG emissions by 2030 and delivering net zero GHG emissions by 2050, in line with the goals of the Paris Agreement to pursue efforts to limit warming to 1.5°C.").

[68] *See Net Zero*, OXFORD ENGLISH DICTIONARY, https://www.oed.com/dictionary/net-zero_n?tab=meaning_and_use (last visited Dec. 6, 2024).

[69] *See* Transcribed Interview of Danielle Fugere, President & Chief Counsel, As You Sow (Jan. 18, 2024) at 163:4– 6.

The climate cartel's "net-zero" goal demands a complete negation of GHG emissions by 2050.[70]

1. The Climate Cartel's Conspirators

The climate cartel is a cabal of financial institutions that broadly fall into five categories. First, its ranks include the world's largest institutional investors, such as the "Big Three" asset managers—BlackRock, Inc.,[71] State Street Global Advisors,[72] and The Vanguard Group[73]— which collectively manage $23.8 trillion in assets and together are the largest shareholder of 88% of all companies in the S&P 500.[74] The Big Three also control over a quarter of the voting shares in the S&P 500.[75] These institutional investors are often called "universal owners" because their portfolios are so vast and diversified that they include sizable shares in the whole U.S. economy.[76]

---

[70] SSGA-HJC.126804 at SSGA-HJC.126833.

[71] BlackRock is a member of GFANZ, NZAM, and—until February 2024—Climate Action 100+. *Signatory Disclosure: BlackRock*, NET ZERO ASSET MANAGERS INITIATIVE, https://www.netzeroassetmanagers.org/signatories/blackrock/ (last visited Dec. 6, 2024).

[72] State Street Global Advisors is a member of GFANZ and NZAM, and it was a member of Climate Action 100+ until February 2024. *Signatory Disclosure: State Street Global Advisors*, NET ZERO ASSET MANAGERS INITIATIVE, https://www.netzeroassetmanagers.org/signatories/state-street-global-advisors-2/ (last visited Dec. 6, 2024).

[73] *An Update on Vanguard's Engagement with the Net Zero Asset Managers Initiative (NZAM)*, VANGUARD (Dec. 7, 2022), https://corporate.vanguard.com/content/corporatesite/us/en/corp/articles/update-on-nzam-engagement.html.

[74] JAN FICHTNER ET AL., HIDDEN POWER OF THE BIG THREE? PASSIVE INDEX FUNDS, RE-CONCENTRATION OF CORPORATE OWNERSHIP, AND NEW FINANCIAL RISK 313 (Cambridge U. Press 2017), https://www.cambridge.org/core/services/aop-cambridge-core/content/view/30AD689509AAD62F5B677E916C28C4B6/S1469356917000064a.pdf/hidden-power-of-the-big-three-passive-index-funds-re-concentration-of-corporate-ownership-and-new-financial-risk.pdf.

[75] LUCIAN A. BEBCHUK & SCOTT HIRST, THE SPECTER OF THE GIANT THREE 18 (2019), https://papers.ssrn.com/sol3/Delivery.cfm/SSRN_ID3557142_code1664187.pdf?abstractid=3385501&mirid=1&type=2.

[76] *See* Amelia Miazad, *Prosocial Antitrust*, 73 HASTINGS L.J. 1637, 1692 (2022).

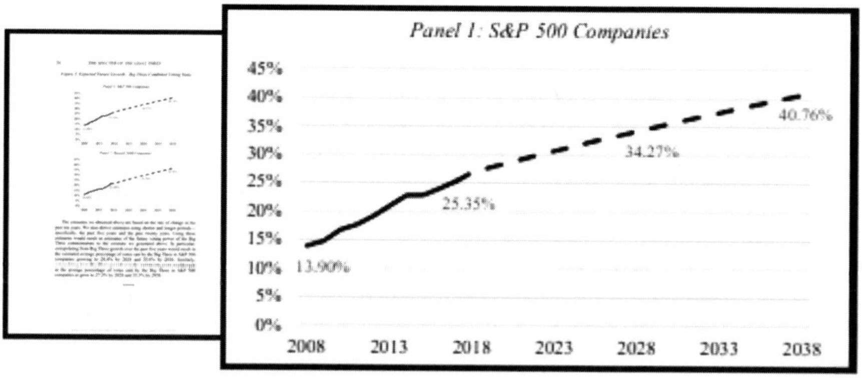

The "Big 3" combined voting share in the S&P 500 is expected to rise to 40.76% by 2038.[77]

Second, the climate cartel's most aggressive and influential investors include "blue-state" public pension funds. These state funds—including the Minnesota State Board of Investment (MSBI),[78] the California Public Employees' Retirement Fund (CalPERS),[79] the California State Teachers' Retirement System (CalSTRS),[80] the New York State Common Retirement Fund (NYS),[81] and the New York City Employees' Retirement System

---

[77] BEBCHUK & HIRST, *supra* note 75, at 20.

[78] *Investor Signatories*, CLIMATE ACTION 100+, https://www.climateaction100.org/whos-involved/investors/?search_investors=Minnesota+State+Board+of+Investment&investor_type=All(last visited Dec. 6, 2024).

[79] *CalPERS*, UNITED NATIONS ENV'T PROGRAMME – FINANCE INITIATIVE, https://www.unepfi.org/member/calpers/ (last visited Dec. 6, 2024); *Investor Signatories*, CLIMATE ACTION 100+, https://www.climateaction100.org/whos- involved/investors/? search_investors=calpers&investor_type=All (last visited Dec. 6, 2024).

[80] *Investor Signatories*, CLIMATE ACTION 100+, https://www.climateaction100.org/whos-involved/investors/? search_investors=calstrs&investor_type=All (last visited Dec. 6, 2024).

[81] *Signatory Disclosure: New York State Common Retirement Fund (CRF)*, PARIS ALIGNED ASSET OWNERS, https:// www.parisalignedassetowners.org/signatories/new-york-state-common-retirement-fund-crf/ (last visited Dec. 6, 2024); *Investor Signatories*, CLIMATE ACTION 100+, https://www.climateaction100.org/whos-involved/investors/? search_ investors=New+York+State+Common+Retirement+Fund&investor_type=All (last visited Dec. 6, 2024).

(NYCERS)[82]—"are [leaders] on ESG in the U.S."[83] Chaired by Governor Tim Walz, the MSBI, for instance, uses the retirement savings of teachers, nurses, police officers, and firefighters in Minnesota to "participate in ESG coalitions and engage with corporations on ESG-related issues."[84]

Third, the climate cartel is populated with European investment firms like London-based Aviva Investors, which takes a "radical and active approach"[85] to pressure American companies to "transition to net-zero emissions."[86] Notably, many European firms are legally required to engage with their portfolio companies on environmental issues, often leading them to pressure American companies to adopt ESG goals.[87] In the United Kingdom, for example, trust-based pensions are required to integrate ESG goals into their investment decisions.[88] As a result, as financial services firm Morningstar explained, "in the US firms must justify ESG by explaining why, while in Europe they must explain why not."[89]

Fourth, the climate cartel contains self-described "gadfly" activist groups, like As You Sow and Engine No. 1, that buy small shares in U.S. companies solely to launch radical climate- related shareholder campaigns "to change corporations from the inside out."[90] Since 2010, As You Sow alone has filed 778 ESG-related shareholder resolutions.[91] In the 2024 proxy season, it filed a staggering eighty-nine.[92]

---

[82] *Signatory Disclosure: New York City Employee's Retirement System (NYCERS)*, PARIS ALIGNED ASSET OWNERS, https://www.parisalignedassetowners.org/signatories/new-york-city-employees-retirement-system-nycers/ (last visited Dec. 6, 2024); *Investor Signatories*, CLIMATE ACTION 100+, https://www.climateaction100.org/whos-involved/investors/?search_investors=new+york+city&investor_type=All.

[83] CERES30849 at CERES30854.

[84] *Environmental, Social and Governance (ESG) Stewardship*, MINN. STATE BD. OF INV., https://msbi.us/ESG-stewardship (last visited Dec. 6, 2024). As detailed in the Committee's interim staff report of October 24, 2024, the MSBI has colluded with other climate cartel members to pressure U.S. utilities to adopt net-zero climate goals and shut down affordable carbon-based energy sources, which raised electricity prices for American consumers. *See generally* H. COMM. ON THE JUDICIARY, 118TH CONG., HOW GOVERNOR TIM WALZ'S STATE PUBLIC PENSION FUND COLLUDES WITH THE CLIMATE CARTEL TO RAISE ENERGY PRICES FOR AMERICAN CONSUMERS (Oct. 24, 2024).

[85] AV11 at AV82.

[86] GFANZ3499 at GFANZ3551.

[87] AV23803 at AV23809.

[88] *Id.*

[89] *Id.*

[90] *About Us*, AS YOU SOW, https://www.asyousow.org/about-us (last visited Dec. 6, 2024).

[91] *Current Resolutions*, AS YOU SOW, https://www.asyousow.org/resolutions-tracker (last visited Dec. 6, 2024).

[92] *Id.*

Finally, the climate cartel includes the proxy advisory market's duopoly: Institutional Shareholder Service (ISS) and Glass, Lewis & Co ("Glass Lewis"). These two proxy advisors control 97% of the industry[93] and hold contracts with investors managing $26.8 trillion and $23.6 trillion, respectively.[94] Together, they act as "de facto corporate governance regulators" by providing shareholder voting recommendations to institutional investors.[95] Significantly, the proxy advisor duopoly frequently bases its recommendations on data and analysis provided by the climate cartel.[96] These highly influential recommendations can swing shareholder votes anywhere between 10% and 30%.[97] The climate cartel's investor members also "routinely encourag[e] proxy advisory firms to recommend to all investors to support certain [climate] resolutions."[98]

2. The Climate Cartel's Coalitions

The climate cartel coordinates its ESG efforts through a network of climate coalitions.

The Glasgow Financial Alliance for Net Zero (GFANZ) is the largest coalition of net-zero- committed financers.[99] It joins together "more than 675 firms across the global financial sector"[100] responsible for approximately 40% of global private finance.[101] Founded in April 2021, GFANZ is designed to "accelerate the world's transition to net zero" and "[u]nite the financial sector to commit to net zero, set high ambition targets, and transform the financial infrastructure to support the net-zero transition."[102] Financial institutions join

---

[93] David F. Larcker et al., The Big Thumb on the Scale: An Overview of the Proxy Advisor Industry, HARV. L. SCH.F. CORP. GOVERNANCE (June 14, 2018), https://corpgov.law.harvard.edu/2018/06/14/the-big-thumb-on-the-scale-an-overview-of-the-proxy-advisory-industry/.

[94] Chong Shu, *The Proxy Advisory Industry*, 154 J. FIN. ECON. 103810, 6 (2024).

[95] Letter from Wachtell, Lipton, Rosen & Katz to Elizabeth M. Murphy, Sec'y, Sec. & Exch. Comm'n 6 (Oct. 19, 2010), http://www.sec.gov/comments/s7-14-10/s71410-129.pdf.

[96] *See infra* Part III.

[97] *See infra* Part III.

[98] CERES55720 at CERES55720.

[99] *About Us*, GLASGOW FIN. ALL. FOR NET ZERO, https://www.gfanzero.com/about (last visited Dec. 6, 2024) [hereinafter "*About Us*, GFANZ"].

[100] *The Alliances and GFANZ*, GLASGOW FIN. ALL. FOR NET ZERO, https://www.gfanzero.com/membership/ (last visited Dec. 6, 2024).

[101] GFANZ6704 at GFANZ6704.

[102] GFANZ40972 at GFANZ40973.

GFANZ by "joining one of eight sector-specific alliances."[103] Three of them are for investors: the Net Zero Asset Managers Initiative (NZAM), the Net Zero Asset Owner Alliance, and the Paris Aligned Asset Owners.[104] All three investor alliances require their members to pledge and implement rigorous net-zero commitments, with the Paris Agreement's "1.5C goal . . . wired into the founding documents of the component alliances."[105]

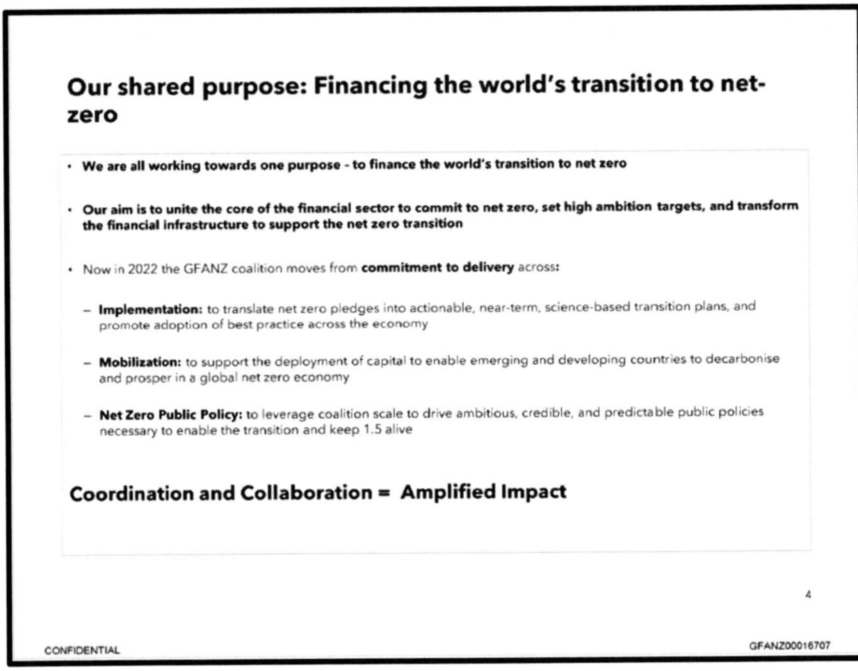

Our shared purpose: Financing the world's transition to net-zero

- **We are all working towards one purpose - to finance the world's transition to net zero**
- **Our aim is to unite the core of the financial sector to commit to net zero, set high ambition targets, and transform the financial infrastructure to support the net zero transition**
- Now in 2022 the GFANZ coalition moves from **commitment to delivery** across:
  - **Implementation:** to translate net zero pledges into actionable, near-term, science-based transition plans, and promote adoption of best practice across the economy
  - **Mobilization:** to support the deployment of capital to enable emerging and developing countries to decarbonise and prosper in a global net zero economy
  - **Net Zero Public Policy:** to leverage coalition scale to drive ambitious, credible, and predictable public policies necessary to enable the transition and keep 1.5 alive

Coordination and Collaboration = Amplified Impact

4

CONFIDENTIAL GFANZ00016707

GFANZ alliances facilitate coordination and collaboration towards "net zero."[106]

NZAM expects its investor signatories to reduce GHG-emitting investments by conducting shareholder "engagements" with U.S. companies in their portfolio to adopt "net- zero" goals.[107] In shareholder engagements, NZAM investor signatories are directed to "explain their expectations of investees and the sanctions that they will apply" so that "[w]hen [net-zero]

[103] *The Alliances and GFANZ*, *supra* note 100.
[104] *Id.*
[105] BLK-HJC-176222 at BLK-HJC-176222.
[106] GFANZ16704 at GFANZ16707.
[107] CERES37663 at CERES37676.

targets are missed, a transparent escalation strategy should be followed, including financial sanctions, with full divestment and litigation as the strongest sanctions."[108]

To shore up the ranks of the climate cartel, NZAM warns its investor signatories that "net-zero" targets that "[do] not meet the commitment's minimum requirements" will be "rejected by the initiative,"[109] and NZAM investor signatories that fail to meet their "net-zero" commitments for more than a year "will be delisted from the initiative."[110]

Ceres, an activist environmental nonprofit, also convenes and coordinates "powerful networks of investors and companies" to "chang[e] markets and sectors from the inside out."[111] Ceres's investor network is its largest program and is "at the heart of Ceres' work,"[112] containing more than 200 investors managing $44 trillion in assets—roughly 1.5 times the U.S. GDP.[113] The central goal of Ceres's "net-zero" campaign is to "spur[] widespread changes in capital flows (and emissions)" and "a fundamental rewrite of the rules for capital formation."[114]

---

[108] GFANZ6575 at GFANZ6576; *see also* VAN_HJC_31168 at VAN_HJC_31168 ("When we aligned to NZAM, we committed to clear escalation policy to support the transition.").

[109] GFANZ34 at GFANZ45.

[110] *Id.* at GFANZ42.

[111] *About Us*, CERES, https://www.ceres.org/about (last visited Dec. 6, 2024).

[112] CERES37663 at CERES37675.

[113] *Gross Domestic Product (Third Estimate), Corporate Profits (Revised Estimate), and GDP by Industry, Second Quarter 2024 and Annual Update*, BUREAU OF ECON. ANALYSIS U.S. DEP'T OF COM. (Sept. 26, 2024), https://www. bea.gov/news/2024/gross-domestic-product-fourth-quarter-and-year-2023-advance-estimate.

[114] CERES37663 at CERES37670.

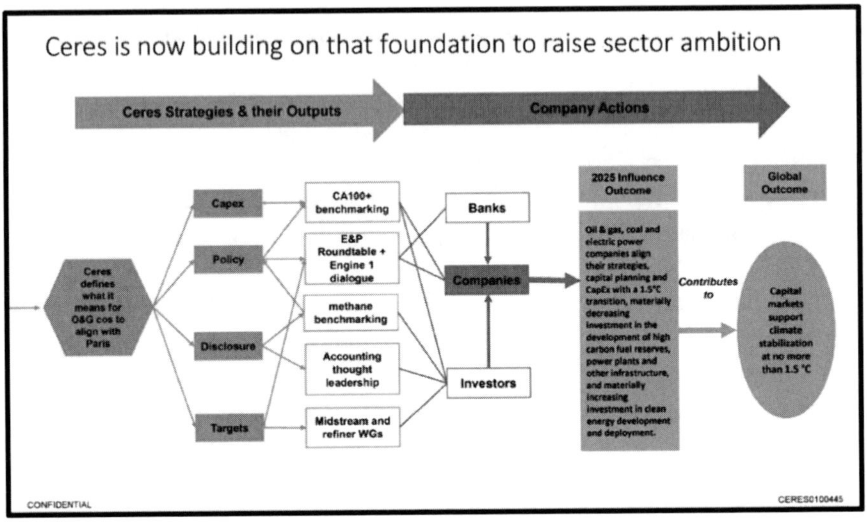

Ceres aims to pressure companies to achieve "net zero" by reducing carbon-based energy and infrastructure investments.[115]

Ceres's largest initiative is Climate Action 100+, a coalition of "the most influential global institutional investors,"[116] formed in 2017 to "engag[e] with companies about setting net- zero targets."[117] Like NZAM, Climate Action 100+ pressures U.S. companies to commit to "net- zero" goals through shareholder engagement.[118] Ceres clearly states that Climate Action 100+ "is not simply a sign-on statement—it requires all Participating signatories to actively engage with companies to pursue clear and ambitious decarbonization. Investors and companies are held accountable."[119]

Climate Action 100+ transforms the cartel's climate crusade from disjointed, individual engagements into a collective enterprise. It does so by streamlining campaigns against U.S. businesses into a strict, hierarchical

---

115 CERES100440 at CERES100445.

116 *About Climate Action 100+*, CLIMATE ACTION 100+, https://www.climateaction 100.org/about/(last visited Dec. 6, 2024).

117 CERES61210 at CERES61224.

118 *See, e.g.*, CERES92777; CERES62869; CERES98951; CALPERS_18545; CERES73116; CERES60773; CERES60136; CERES58376; CERES60571; CERES58091; CERES58904; CERES57032; CERES57386; CERES59255; CERES7029; CERES34253; CERES62824; CERES42438; CERES57427; CERES58513; CERES58327; CERES73223; CERES57932; CERES67272; CERES61893; CERES62179; CERES60332; CERES60267; CERES42136; CERES1188; CERES39292; CERES79993; CERES41396; CERES76393; CERES73288; CERES33243; CERES1279.

119 CERES57687 at CERES57687.

structure "spearheaded by a lead investor or co-lead investors, who work with several contributing investors."[120] Within Climate Action 100+, lead investors set the climate cartel's strategic objectives, signal investors to execute those objectives through the initiative's "flagging" process, and rely on the Ceres investor network apparatus to coordinate support for shareholder votes.[121]

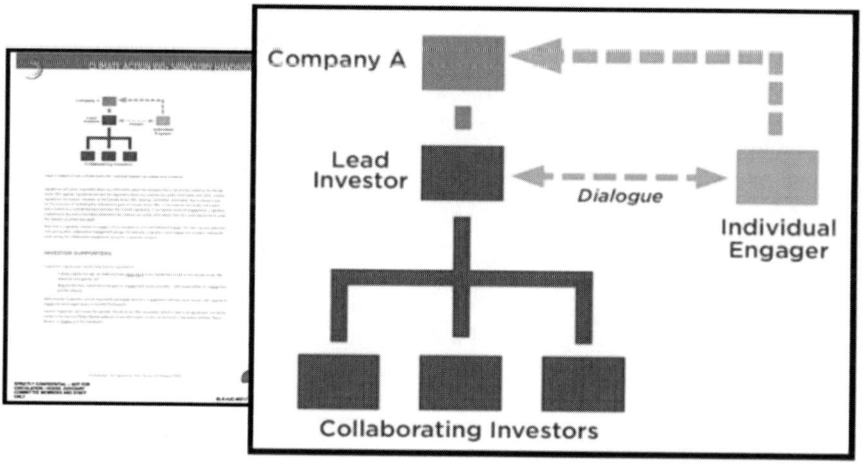

Climate Action 100+ engagement groups organize into a disciplined, hierarchical structure.[122]

3. The Climate Cartel's "Net-zero" Commitment Is Designed to Cut U.S. Energy Production

To achieve its "net-zero" objectives, the climate cartel "chang[es] the criteria and requirements for the provision of finance, investment, and other financial products/services" so that "access to capital . . . will increasingly be contingent on performance against climate-related metrics."[123] GFANZ expects its investor signatories to measure their portfolio companies against several endorsed "assessment tools" that "evaluate the credibility of [net-zero]

---

[120] *Engagement Process*, CLIMATE ACTION 100+, https://www.climateaction100.org/approach/engagement-process/ (last visited Dec. 6, 2024).

[121] *2024 Proxy Season & Flagged Shareholder Votes*, CLIMATE ACTION 100+, https://www.climateaction100.org/ approach/proxy-season/ (last visited Dec. 6, 2024).

[122] BLK-HJC-217700 at BLK-HJC-217725.

[123] GFANZ1 at GFANZ5; GFANZ462 at GFANZ465.

transition plans."[124] The most influential GFANZ-endorsed "net-zero" standard is the Climate Action 100+ Net Zero Company Benchmark.[125] This 11-point Benchmark scores a "focus list" of 170 of the world's largest businesses with $10.3 trillion in market capitalization[126] against standards for "emissions reduction, governance, and climate-related disclosure on the implementation of net zero transition plans."[127]

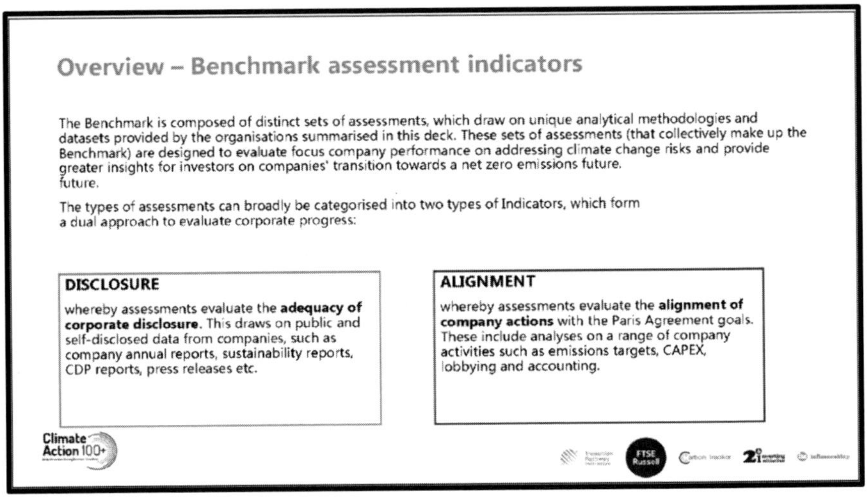

Climate Action 100+ uses its Benchmark to grade companies against its "net-zero" agenda.[128]

The climate cartel uses standards like the Net Zero Company Benchmark to hold "focus companies" accountable for their "commitment to the . . . goals of the Paris Agreement (i.e., limiting global warming to 1.5°C)."[129] This standard is notable not only because the United States has not ratified the Paris Agreement and, therefore, it is not binding on companies operating in the United States,[130] but also because the Paris Agreement's goal of "limiting

---

[124] GFANZ462 at GFANZ483.

[125] GFANZ1 at GFANZ10.

[126] *Companies*, CLIMATE ACTION 100+, https://www.climateaction100.org/whos-involved/companies/ (last visited Dec. 6, 2024).

[127] *Frequently Asked Questions: Net Zero Company Benchmark*, CLIMATE ACTION 100+ (Oct. 2024), https://www. climateaction100.org/net-zero-company-benchmark/questions/.

[128] CERES58936 at CERES59002.

[129] *Frequently Asked Questions: Net Zero Company Benchmark*, *supra* note 127.

[130] *See supra* Section I.A; CERES57210 at CERES57212 ("Theoretical risk until policy landscape aligns with what CA100 and others are telling companies."). Because the Paris Agreement has not been ratified by the Senate, it has no legal effect on businesses operating

global warming to 1.5°C" requires dramatic reductions in the production of efficient carbon-intensive energy.[131] According to the Carbon Tracker initiative, which conducts the Net Zero Company Benchmark's data analytics, "[w]ithout a response sufficient to prematurely close existing [oil & gas] projects, a warming of 1.5°C is already effectively locked in, and no new projects are compliant with the low end of the Paris goals."[132] Similarly, according to a report prepared for GFANZ by management consulting firm McKinsey & Company,

> Achieving a 1.5°C pathway *will require managed phaseout* of existing carbon-intensive assets[.] . . . Local communities and economies that are dependent on carbon-intensive assets may face *significant economic and social impacts[.]* Asset operators and owners may face loss of *future cash flows and high costs to develop low-carbon alternatives* . . . with oil & gas and hard-to- abate sectors facing continued product demand and limited low- carbon alternatives.[133]

The economic and social costs of implementing the Paris Agreement's 1.5°C goal are so high, in fact, that Climate Action 100+-affiliated "lawyers do not think 1.5C is feasible[,] and they do not believe it aligns with the fiduciary duty" that asset managers owe to their asset owner clients.[134] Nevertheless, the Paris Agreement's 1.5°C standard, as measured by the Climate Action 100+ Net Zero Company Benchmark, forms the climate cartel's "foundation for ongoing engagement discussions as it collates what [Climate Action 100+] expect[s] companies to produce to align with [its] expectations."[135] The Benchmark "inform[s] escalation decisions including voting, specifically for CA100+ engagements but also more generally."[136] It

---

in the United States. Richard A. Epstein, *Biden's Unlawful Re-Entry into Climate Accord*, HOOVER INST. (Feb. 1, 2021), https://www.hoover.org/research/bidens-unlawful-re-entry-climate- accord.

[131] ExxonMobil CEO Darren Woods recently said that President-elect Trump should remain in the Paris Climate Agreement to prevent the "stops and starts" and "uncertainty" of pulling out of the Agreement for the second time. Collin Eaton & Benoît Morenne, *Exxon Says Trump Should Keep U.S. in Paris Climate Pact*, WALL ST. J. (Nov. 12, 2024), https://www.wsj.com/business/energy-oil/exxon-says-trump-should-keep-u-s-in-paris-climate-pact- 3d8de471. Notably, ExxonMobil did not comment on whether the Paris Agreement has benefited the company or the energy industry. *See id.*

[132] AV18990 at AV18990.

[133] GFANZ42731 at GFANZ42738.

[134] CERES73347 at CERES73370.

[135] CERES24301 at CERES24304.

[136] *Id.*

is also "key for investors to decide what they do . . . with unresponsive/poor performing firms. For example, some investors will divest unresponsive firms" and "others will vote against directors as standard."[137] In sum, "the CA100+ Benchmark establishes a high bar for companies—and for the first time ever, will define a consistent standard for what companies need to do, and thus for investor pressure on companies that are falling short."[138]

II. The Climate Cartel Colluded to Take over America's Largest Energy Producer

In its climate crusade, the cartel's primary target is the American energy industry. While not as flashy as Silicon Valley or Wall Street, American oil, gas, and coal silently power the world's largest economy. Every year, affordable, carbon-based fuels supply 80% of America's energy and provide 12.3 million American jobs.[139] Natural gas in the United States, for instance, provides heat for 60% of American households,[140] gasoline fuels 265.7 million vehicles on America's roads and highways,[141] and jet fuel keeps 45,000 flights with 2.9 million Americans aloft every day.[142] American carbon-based fuels

---

137 *Id.*

138 CERES10442 at CERES10448.

139 *The Economic Benefits of Oil and Gas*, U.S. DEP'T OF ENERGY, https://www.energy.gov/articles/economic-impact-oil-and-gas (last visited Dec. 6, 2024).

140 *Natural Gas Explained: Use of Natural Gas*, U.S. ENERGY INFO. ADMIN. (Apr. 28, 2023), https://www.eia.gov/ energyexplained/natural-gas/use-of-natural-gas.php#.

141 *New Registrations of Gasoline Vehicles Are Still Growing Despite the EV Push*, INST. FOR ENERGY RSCH. (Dec. 21, 2023), https://www.instituteforenergyresearch.org/fossil-fuels/gas-and-oil/new-registrations-of-gasoline-vehicles-are-still-growing-despite-the-ev-push/.

142 *Air Traffic by the Numbers*, FED. AVIATION ADMIN. (Sept. 9, 2024), https://www.faa.gov/air_traffic/by_the_ numbers.

account for 60% of all U.S. electricity generation[143]—powering data centers,[144] automotive factories,[145] and all American life in between.[146]

Despite America's reliance on affordable oil and gas, the climate cartel's objective is to "[s]hrink and pivot the oil and gas sector to clean energy."[147] To this end, the climate cartel has launched a barrage of "net-zero" pressure campaigns against American energy producers intended to reduce their production. For energy companies that refuse to surrender to activist investor pressure, the climate cartel "will coordinate strategic investor engagement to move companies to downsize."[148] Within the energy sector, its top target is America's largest oil and gas business: ExxonMobil.

A. Target: The Climate Cartel Branded ExxonMobil as a "Focus Company"

The ExxonMobil Corporation is one of America's most storied businesses. For more than 160 years, its products have powered American transportation and industry.[149] Thomas Edison used ExxonMobil's lubricates in his first central generating system; the Wright brothers used its fuel to take flight from Kitty Hawk, North Carolina; and Charles Lindbergh relied on its oil on his historic flight across the Atlantic.[150] Over the 20th century, ExxonMobil's growth closely paralleled that of the U.S. economy, as it has helped provide the energy needed to sustain America's economic rise.[151] Today, ExxonMobil is America's seventh-largest company and its largest energy company

---

143 *Electricity Explained: Electricity in the United States*, U.S. ENERGY INFO. ADMIN. (Mar. 26, 2024), https://www. eia.gov/energyexplained/electricity/electricity-in-the-us.php.

144 Lakshmi Varanasi, *AI Execs Who Urgently Need More Energy to Power Their Tech Revolution Are Turning to Fossil Fuels*, BUS. INSIDER (Mar. 24, 2024), https://www. businessinsider.com/ai-energy-electricity-data-centers- fossil-fuels-tech-revolution-2024-3.

145 *Michigan State Energy Profile*, U.S. ENERGY INFO. ADMIN. (Aug. 17, 2023), https://www.eia.gov/state/print.php? sid=mi; *see also* JASON HAYES, ELECTRICITY IN MICHIGAN: A PRIMER (Mackinac Cent. for Pub. Pol'y 2021), https:// www.mackinac. org/archives/2021/s2020-03.pdf.

146 *Electricity Explained: Use of Electricity*, U.S. ENERGY INFO. ADMIN. (Dec. 18, 2023), https://www.eia.gov/energyexplained/electricity/use-of-electricity.php.

147 CERES53737 at CERES53741.

148 CERES43806 at CERES43819.

149 *Our History*, EXXONMOBIL (Feb. 9, 2023), https://corporate.exxonmobil.com/who-we-are/our-global- organization/our-history.

150 *Id.*

151 Joseph A. Pratt, *Exxon and the Control of Oil*, 99 J. AM. HIST. 145, 145, 148–49, 154 (2012).

overall,[152] selling more than 5.4 million barrels of petroleum products daily and fueling American transportation with 11,000 fuel stations sprinkled throughout the United States.[153]

In recent years, however, ExxonMobil's prominent position in America's oil and gas industry has attracted the attention of the climate cartel. In 2017, Climate Action 100+ branded ExxonMobil as a "Focus Company,"[154] adding it to a "climate blacklist" of 170 businesses with $10.3 trillion in market capitalization targeted by its "net-zero" engagements.[155] Ceres describes the Climate Action 100+ "focus list" as "the trigger and the start of the [engagement] process."[156] As a "focus company," Climate Action 100+ regularly grades ExxonMobil against its Net Zero Company Benchmark and coordinates investor pressure campaigns to demand that the company comply with the Benchmark's requirements.[157] Since the climate cartel branded it a "focus company," ExxonMobil has been the target of seventy-one climate-related shareholder campaigns—more than any company in the world.[158]

By targeting ExxonMobil in particular, the climate cartel sought to send a warning to other "Focus Companies" that it would not hesitate to enforce its "net-zero" demands. It saw ExxonMobil's refusal to comply with its Net Zero Company Benchmark as hurting Climate Action 100+'s "credibility" and "believe[d] strongly that if [it] d[id]n't push the most laggard companies very hard," it would "signal[] to all other focus companies that [Climate Action 100+] has no teeth[] and is not actually the powerful entity that companies at first thought it was."[159] When it comes to "laggard" companies most deserving engagement escalation, the climate cartel considered "Exxon . . . generally top of the list."[160] As a result, the climate cartel has sought to make an "example" out of ExxonMobil to perpetuate what it refers to as the "Exxon effect" as it

---

152 *ExxonMobil*, FORTUNE, https://fortune.com/company/exxon-mobil/ (last visited Dec. 6, 2024).

153 *A Look Inside Downstream*, EXXONMOBIL, https://corporate.exxonmobil.com/who-we-are/our-global-organization/business-divisions/downstream/a-look-inside-downstream (last visited Dec. 6, 2024).

154 *Company Assessment: ExxonMobil Corp.*, CLIMATE ACTION 100+, https://www.climate action100.org/company/ exxon-mobil-corporation/ (last visited Dec. 6, 2024).

155 *Net Zero Company Benchmark*, CLIMATE ACTION 100+, https://www.climateaction 100.org/net-zero-company- benchmark/ (last visited Dec. 6, 2024).

156 CERES62869 at CERES62952.

157 *Id.*

158 *Shareholder Proposal Database*, *supra* note 8 (noting that ExxonMobil has been targeted by 65 climate-related shareholder campaigns since the end of 2017).

159 CERES62497 at CERES62497.

160 CERES57222 at CERES57222.

engages with other focus companies—"the idea that this could happen to you."[161]

Over the last decade, the climate cartel has waged its largest-ever pressure campaign against ExxonMobil to dramatically reduce the company's oil and gas production. Climate cartel investors maintained that "[w]ithout a commitment to reduce production over time, [ExxonMobil's] GHG emissions will continue to rise,"[162] which was inconsistent with a "net- zero" future where there is "no need for any new oil."[163] In their view, ExxonMobil's continued investment in oil and gas production, therefore, "will need to decline at a pace that only allow[s] for development and maintenance of existing [oil] fields."[164]

To accomplish this output reduction, the climate cartel deployed a three-step strategy against ExxonMobil: disclose, reduce, and enforce. This approach is not unique to the climate cartel's campaign against ExxonMobil. In fact, it reflects the "three asks" of Climate Action 100+, which its investor signatories are required to adopt and impose as "a common high-level agenda for company engagement."[165] First, the climate cartel calls for target companies to make "corporate disclosure[s]" on a plethora of immaterial climate-related criteria, including GHG emissions.[166] Second, armed with that information, the climate cartel demands that target companies "[t]ake action to reduce [GHG] emissions across the value chain," including and especially "Scope 3" emissions.[167] Third and finally, to ensure that target companies follow through on their "net-zero" commitments, the climate cartel campaigns each company to "[i]mplement a strong governance framework" to enforce its "net-zero" goals.[168] If the company refuses to comply, the climate cartel is "willing to go to the top rung" of enforcement by "replac[ing] board members."[169]

---

161 CERES62869 at CERES62940.
162 CALPERS_38581 at CALPERS_38582.
163 *Id.*
164 *Id.* at CALPERS_38584.
165 *The Three Goals*, CLIMATE ACTION 100+, https://www.climateaction100.org/the-three-goals/ (last visited Dec. 6, 2024).
166 *Id.*
167 *Id.*
168 *Id.*
169 CERES66958 at CERES66963, CERES66964.

B. Disclose: The Climate Cartel Campaigned to Force ExxonMobil to Make Climate Disclosures That Are Immaterial to Investment Decisions

Since 2017, the climate cartel has targeted ExxonMobil with at least 20 shareholder campaigns calling for climate-related disclosures immaterial to investment decisions.[170] These efforts form the foundation of the climate cartel's pressure campaign against ExxonMobil.

According to GFANZ Co-Chair Mark Carney, who testified to the Committee in a transcribed interview, securing climate disclosures from U.S. companies is "important [for] the achievement of net zero" because it allows climate cartel members to "decide who to lend to or invest in and who to avoid."[171] The climate cartel uses the information gained through climate-related disclosure campaigns to score companies like ExxonMobil against the Climate Action 100+ Net Zero Company Benchmark and other GFANZ-endorsed "assessment tools."[172]

In 2017, led by the New York State Common Retirement Fund (NYS) and the European- based investment Church Commissioners and supported by Ceres investor engagement groups,[173] investors filed a shareholder resolution calling for ExxonMobil to publish a report on its business viability under a net-zero "scenario."[174] Like nearly all of the climate cartel's climate-related disclosure campaigns, the 2017 shareholder resolution was based on recommendations from the Task Force on Climate-related Financial Disclosures (TFCD).[175] Formed in 2016, the TFCD is a project chaired by former New York City Mayor and climate activist Michael Bloomberg that aims to create a framework to "speed the transition to a low- carbon economy"

---

170 *Shareholder Proposal Database*, *supra* note 8.

171 Transcribed Interview of Mark Carney, *supra* note 47, at 48:16–21.

172 GFANZ462 at GFANZ483.

173 CERES92232 at CERES92235.

174 EXXONMOBIL, NOTICE OF 2017 ANNUAL MEETING AND PROXY STATEMENT 62 (Apr. 13, 2017), https://d1io3yog0oux5.cloudfront.net/_6b72482e95300fbc394b26085db4c0df/exxonmobil/db/2301/21379/proxy_statement/2017_proxy_statement.pdf ("Shareholders request that . . . ExxonMobil publish an annual assessment of the long-term portfolio impacts of . . . global climate change policies . . . . The assessment . . . should analyze the impacts on ExxonMobil's oil and gas reserves and resources under a scenario in which reduction in demand results from carbon restrictions . . . adopted by governments."); *see also* ARJUNA19858 at ARJUNA19864.

175 Marianne Lavelle, *Exxon Shareholders Approve Climate Resolution: 62% Vote for Disclosure*, INSIDE CLIMATE NEWS (May 31, 2017), https://insideclimatenews.org/news/31052017/exxon-shareholder-climate-change-disclosure- resolution-approved/.

and support the "movement away from fossil fuel energy and related physical assets."[176]

Notably, under U.S. securities law, public companies operating in the United States must disclose all *material* information.[177] Material disclosures are intended to provide investors with the information necessary to make informed investment decisions.[178] In contrast, the climate cartel's 2017 shareholder resolution demanded that ExxonMobil publish speculative estimates of "the impacts on [its] oil and gas reserves and resources" under a theoretical, net-zero scenario "in which reduction in demand results from carbon restrictions . . . adopted by governments."[179]

Before and during this 2017 net-zero "scenario" shareholder campaign, ExxonMobil repeatedly warned that such speculative net-zero "scenario" reporting would confuse and mislead its investors. The company explained that its existing disclosures showed that—even withstanding increased government regulation—oil and gas will remain the primary and fastest-growing energy source through 2040.[180] Renewable energy, in contrast, will meet only 4% of energy demand within that same timeframe.[181] Considering these market realities, ExxonMobil believed its existing disclosures

[176] TASK FORCE ON CLIMATE-RELATED FIN. DISCLOSURES, RECOMMENDATIONS OF THE TASK FORCE ON CLIMATE-RELATED FINANCIAL DISCLOSURES i, ii (2016), https://assets.bbhub.io/company/sites/60/2020/10/16_1221_TCFD_ Report_Letter.pdf. In March 2023, the Biden-Harris U.S. Securities and Exchange Commission (SEC) issued a highly controversial climate-risk disclosure rule also based on the TFCD's recommendations. The Enhancement and Standardization of Climate-related Disclosures for Investors, 17 C.F.R. § 210, 229, 230, 239, 249 (2024). The initially proposed rule references Ceres 21 times as well as Ceres-coordinated networks, such as NZAM and Climate Action 100+. The Enhancement and Standardization of Climate-related Disclosures for Investors, 87 Fed. Reg. 21,334 (proposed Apr. 11, 2022). According to Ceres, its efforts to establish a "mandatory climate disclosure by the Securities and Exchange Commission" spanned "over a decade." CERES2871 at CERES2873 (emphasis omitted). The nonprofit believes a mandatory climate disclosure rule "will change the face of our economy and indicate that the US has joined with climate leaders around the globe." *Id.*

[177] *TSC Indus., Inc. v. Northway, Inc.*, 426 U.S. 438, 439 (1976) (defining material information as such that "there is a substantial likelihood that a reasonable shareholder would consider it important in deciding how to vote").

[178] *Id.* at 448.

[179] *Report on 2-degree Analysis and Strategy (XOM, 2017 Resolution)*, CERES, https://engagements.ceres.org/ceresengagementdetailpage?recID=a0l1200000Bn9eLAAR (last visited Dec. 6, 2024).

[180] Marianne Lavelle, *Exxon Shareholders Approve Climate Resolution: 62% Vote for Disclosures*, INSIDE CLIMATE NEWS (May 31, 2017), https://insideclimatenews.org/news/31052017/exxon-shareholder-climate-change-disclosure- resolution-approved/.

[181] *Id.*

"sufficiently test[ed] the portfolio to ensure long-term shareholder value and position[ed] the Company to maintain a leadership role in energy development."[182]

Likewise, leading industry expert Daniel Yergin, Vice Chairman of S&P Global, found that climate-related disclosures based on the TFCD's recommendations could "obscure material information and create a false sense of certainty around the financial implications of long-term scenario[s]" that "would distort markets, not enhance them."[183] These disclosures would require companies to speculate about climate change and environmental regulation outside their control and across a timeline dramatically longer than those used in financial disclosures under U.S. securities law.[184] As a result, TFCD climate reporting "could lead investors to misunderstand opportunities and risks, misprice assets, and forego future returns."[185]

Despite this, climate cartel members "worked together globally to get [an] Exxon majority vote."[186] "Ceres played a central role in [the] 2017 campaign"[187] by supporting the co- filing of the resolution by "more than 50 institutional investors from North America and Europe, with more than $5 trillion in assets," including CalPERS.[188] Ceres and its networks also supported "[i]nstitutional investors with an additional $5 trillion of assets," including Aviva Investors and Legal & General Investment Management, "declar[ing] that they will vote in favor of the proposal."[189] Critically, the Ceres-supported campaign also won the support of the proxy advisor duopoly ISS and Glass Lewis and the votes of the "Big 3" asset managers, BlackRock, Vanguard, and State Street Global Advisors, which held over 18% of

---

182 Cydney Posner, *Are Shareholder Proposals on Climate Change Becoming a Thing?*, HARV. L. SCH. F. CORP. GOVERNANCE (June 21, 2017), https://corpgov.law.harvard.edu/2017/06/21/are-shareholder-proposals-on-climate- change-becoming-a-thing/.

183 HIS MARKIT, *supra* note 9, at 11–15.

184 *Id.* at 11.

185 *Id.*

186 CERES73182 at CERES73186.

187 CERES92232 at CERES92235.

188 Memorandum from NYS to the ExxonMobil S'holders 1 (Apr. 21, 2017), https://ceres.my.salesforce.com/sfc/p/#A0000000ZqYY/a/1H000000UYIF/MBf9DGdbLLC3ZtTgXIpqP6mBeHKqyjYsogqN05498Uo.

189 *Id.*

ExxonMobil's shares at the time.[190] In total, the climate cartel's 2017 net-zero "scenario" resolution received 62.1% shareholder support.[191]

After the 2017 climate disclosure campaign's success at ExxonMobil, Ceres and its investor affiliates notified members of the climate cartel that "[o]ngoing engagement will be conducted under the Climate Action 100+ initiative announced in Paris."[192] NYS and the Church Commissioners, the campaign's lead investors, were anointed as lead investors for the newly minted Climate Action 100+ ExxonMobil engagement group.[193] From the outset, the Climate Action 100+ ExxonMobil engagement group resolved to "seek[], through the CA100+ initiative, to collectively engage with focus companies and achieve deep and lasting commitments to align with the goals of the Paris Agreement. Signatory investors [would] be deploying intervention strategies to accelerate action as needed."[194] The following year, the Climate Action 100+ ExxonMobil engagement group escalated to the next phase of its pressure campaign: it demanded that ExxonMobil set GHG-emission reduction targets designed to shrink its oil and gas production.

C. Reduce: The Climate Cartel Pressured ExxonMobil to Set Emission Reduction Targets Crafted to Reduce Output

The climate cartel's demand for GHG-emission reduction targets is the centerpiece of its "net-zero" strategy. Rather than outright calling for ExxonMobil to produce less oil and gas, the climate cartel disguised this goal in a self-described "Trojan Horse"[195] by pressuring ExxonMobil to reduce the GHG emissions resulting from consumers' use of its oil and gas products,

---

190 Posner, *supra* note 182. Gaining BlackRock, Vanguard, and State Street Global Advisors' support of the 2017 resolution was enough to win majority shareholder support, as these climate cartel members were the three largest shareholders of ExxonMobil. CALPERS_31652 at CALPERS_31652.

191 Lavelle, *supra* note 180. Interestingly, the New York State Common Retirement Fund had filed an almost identical shareholder proposal just one year prior. *Id.* But without the climate cartel coordinating its success, it failed with nearly half the amount of support that the 2017 proposal received. *See id.*

192 AV1175 at AV1175.

193 *See* CERES62869 at CERES62988.

194 CALPERS_42287 at CALPERS_42287.

195 *For Investors*, FOLLOW THIS, https://www.follow-this.org/for-investors/ (last visited Dec. 6, 2024).

known as "Scope 3" emissions.[196] In contrast to emissions that ExxonMobil produces directly from its operations and purchases (i.e., "Scope 1" and "Scope 2" emissions), "Scope 3" emissions refer to emissions that ExxonMobil did not produce but to which it contributed in some way indirectly.[197] For oil and gas companies like ExxonMobil, "Scope 3" emissions are almost exclusively those resulting from consumers using the products it sells—at some point in the future—in homes, cars, and planes.[198]

Because ExxonMobil has no control over consumers' post-sale use of its products, the only way for it to eliminate its "Scope 3" emissions is to reduce its own oil and gas production. According to ExxonMobil, its "ability to reduce the carbon intensity of [its] existing products is limited by their physical properties."[199] Therefore, "[s]ignificant reductions in carbon intensity will require a breakthrough in technology or a move away from [its] existing businesses."[200] In response, Ceres has vaguely suggested that "it might be probable" for ExxonMobil to "offset the emission from all of [its] production with carbon capture" but nevertheless admits that "whether [that] [is] the most economic approach is a different question."[201] Other members of the climate cartel, like As You Sow, are more transparent: "ultimately fossil fuel use has to be reduced."[202]

In 2018, the Climate Action 100+ ExxonMobil engagement group began coordinated efforts to push ExxonMobil to adopt Scope 1–3 GHG-emission reduction targets. On December 5, 2018, to "solicit [investor] support" for the campaign,[203] Ceres privately emailed all "CA100+ ExxonMobil collaborating investors," notifying them that the engagement group's lead investors, the NYS and the Church Commissioners, planned to "co-file[] a shareholder resolution with ExxonMobil which calls [on] the company to set targets on its operational and product [i.e., Scope 1, 2, & 3] emissions in line with the goals of the Paris Agreement."[204] Ceres told the ExxonMobil engagement group that

---

[196] *Yale Experts Explain Scope 3 Emissions*, YALE SUSTAINABILITY (Nov. 14, 2023), https://sustainability.yale.edu/explainers/yale-experts-explain-scope-3-emissions.

[197] *Id.* (defining Scope 1 emissions as "direct emissions from sources owned or controlled by an institution or company" and Scope 2 emissions as "indirect emissions from electricity an institution purchases").

[198] *Id.*

[199] BLK-HJC-2012 at BLK-HJC-2013.

[200] *Id.*

[201] Transcribed Interview of Andrew Logan, *supra* note 11, at 54:21–55:2 (emphasis added).

[202] Transcribed Interview of Danielle Fugere, *supra* note 69, at 163:4–6.

[203] CALPERS_26227 at CALPERS_26227.

[204] CALPERS_4893 at CALPERS_4894.

the resolution was "a key ask from the Climate Action 100+ initiative"[205] and its goal was "to ensure that pressure is kept on Exxon to act."[206]

To "signal . . . early support" from the engagement group, Ceres invited all investors via e-mail to "co-file" the 2018 resolution "[u]s[ing] the exact resolution text that [Ceres had] attached to [its] email."[207] Ceres boasted to the investors that "there is power behind broad and sustained investor collaboration on climate engagement."[208] Less than two weeks later, on December 17, 2018, over thirty investors—representing nearly $2 trillion in assets—joined the lead investors to co-file the shareholder resolution.[209] In the following months, Ceres and the lead investors worked to ensure that the rest of the climate cartel was regularly "kept informed about engagement with Exxon . . . through CA100+ calls and correspondence."[210]

Notably, the climate cartel took steps to centralize control over the pressure campaign in the hands of the Climate Action 100+ engagement group's lead investors. During the co-filing process, Ceres directed the engagement group to "delegate[] authority for [the resolution's] negotiated withdrawal to the lead filer."[211] This granted NYS and the Church Commissioners, as the lead filers, the sole power to negotiate with ExxonMobil and terminate the pressure campaign if their terms were met. It also reduced the likelihood of climate cartel "defectors" who may initially co-file the shareholder resolution but then attempt to withdraw their support and leave the engagement. Instead, with authority over the shareholder resolution vested solely in the lead investors, the climate cartel engaged ExxonMobil as a unified force.

With the support of the Climate Action 100+ engagement group, the lead investors petitioned ExxonMobil to directly engage its board of directors as if the climate cartel members were a single shareholder. As a practice, ExxonMobil "grants investor access at independent director level only to top 10 shareholders," which excluded nearly all of the climate cartel's investor signatories.[212] However, the climate cartel realized that, joined together, "the CA100+ engagement group [wa]s comfortably the equivalent of . . . Exxon's

---

205 *Id.*
206 CALPERS_26227 at CALPERS_26227.
207 CALPERS_4893 at CALPERS_4894.
208 *Id.* at CALPERS_4895.
209 CALPERS_16485 at CALPERS_16486.
210 CALPERS_4893 at CALPERS_4894.
211 *Id.*
212 CALPERS_31652 at CALPERS_31652.

4th largest shareholder."[213] As a result, ExxonMobil agreed to negotiate with the lead investors and investor signatory representatives on behalf of the unified Climate Action 100+ engagement group.[214]

In a February 2019 meeting, ExxonMobil explained to the Climate Action 100+ engagement group that it has an obligation as a global energy producer to provide the "modern energy [that] enables longer, healthier lives" but recognized that it must do so "while mitigating impacts on the environment."[215] Accordingly, ExxonMobil detailed to the engagement group its "serious and significant effort" to confront this "dual challenge of providing the energy society needs while mitigating climate change,"[216] including its work on "the biofuels that will be important for decarbonising heavy duty vehicles, gas that will help reduce emissions from power generation, [and] new [carbon capture and storage] technology that may become economic and scaleable [sic]."[217] Further, ExxonMobil stated, "[A] 'good portion' of [its] [research and development] spend" was going toward "lowering emissions," and the company had "set meaningful emissions reduction targets covering methane, flaring and oil sands operations."[218]

Nevertheless, the Climate Action 100+ engagement group "expressed disappointment" with the company's assertions and "pushed [ExxonMobil] on disclosure of Scope 3 emissions and the need for Scope 1–3 targets as requested in the shareholder proposal" filed in 2018.[219] In response, ExxonMobil stated it did not "believe in disclosing Scope 3 emissions because it is the responsibility of the emitter to do the disclosing," not the company that has no control over emissions from the products it has already sold.[220] Moreover, ExxonMobil was unwilling to set unachievable "net-zero" GHG-emission targets:

> [ExxonMobil] doesn't believe in setting targets when it doesn't have a clear line of sight on how to achieve them. It doesn't set aspirational goals. It thinks technology will become scaleable [*sic*] but it doesn't sufficiently exist yet. It won't set targets without the means and the policy signals from government. The solution-set needs to be in place. . . . We

---

[213] *Id.*
[214] *Id.*
[215] CALPERS_6988 at CALPERS_6988.
[216] *Id.*
[217] *Id.*
[218] *Id.*
[219] *Id.* at CALPERS_6989, CALPERS_6990.
[220] *Id.* at CALPERS_6989.

struggle to plan the business on the aspirations of the Paris Agreement rather than what we see in the market[.][221]

Based on those concerns, ExxonMobil challenged the climate cartel's shareholder resolution at the SEC.[222] In its SEC filings, Exxon argued that the resolution would force "[u]nilateral action by ExxonMobil" to reduce GHG emissions from its sold products, "limit[ing] the growth of ExxonMobil's businesses" and requiring it to "reduce its own production."[223] ExxonMobil explained that even if it were to unilaterally cut output as requested, the shareholder resolution would fail to reduce global GHG emissions levels because demand for oil and gas would remain unchanged.[224] Instead, "any market share ceded by ExxonMobil would simply be met by other producers . . . who may lack ExxonMobil's operational expertise, technological advantages and commitment to conducting its operations efficiently."[225] In such a case, "a reduction in production of oil and gas by ExxonMobil could result in an increase in actual energy-related CO2 emissions."[226] On April 2, 2019, the SEC, during the Trump Administration, agreed with ExxonMobil and granted its request to exclude the 2018 shareholder resolution from the ballot at the company's annual shareholder meeting.[227]

D. Enforce: The Climate Cartel Voted Against ExxonMobil's Board of Directors to Penalize Noncompliance with Climate Demands

Following ExxonMobil's opposition to the 2018 GHG-emission reduction targets shareholder proposal, the climate cartel sought to escalate its engagement by voting against the company's board of directors. The climate cartel believed that "the success and credibility of CA100+ is dependent on [its] ability to show that engagement can have teeth—and that investors are willing to escalate pressure against companies that refuse to act [P]ressuring boards remains one of the few avenues for investors to force companies to

---

[221] *Id.*
[222] *Id.* at CALPERS_6990.
[223] CALPERS_41281 at CALPERS_41284–85.
[224] *Id.* at CALPERS_41283–84.
[225] *Id.* at CALPERS_41284.
[226] *Id.*
[227] Letter from M. Hughes Bates, Special Counsel, SEC to Louis L. Goldberg, Davis Polk & Wardwell LLP 2 (Apr. 2, 2019), https://www.sec.gov/divisions/corpfin/cf-noaction/14a-8/2019/ncppr040219-14a8.pdf; *see also* AV23803 at AV23816.

act."[228] By voting against company directors who refuse to comply, the climate cartel seeks to enforce its "net-zero" goals.

In 2019, Anne Simpson, then-Chair of the Climate Action 100+ Steering Committee and CalPERS's Director of Board Governance & Sustainability, declared to Steering Committee members that "Exxon's board members should have hell to pay [T]here ought to be consequences of Exxon's decision to seek removal of the resolution through the SEC."[229] Ms. Simpson signaled the cartel's future steps:

> The next stage will be the [ExxonMobil annual general meeting] where the board of directors will be seeking those same shareowners' support for re-election. I've spoken to Liz Gordon [of New York State Common Retirement Fund, a lead investor of the engagement group], and she expects to have a planning call with CA100+ next Monday. We should also be thinking about outreach to the proxy advisers, and certainly updating the many investors who signed the letter of support. A Pyrrhic victory at best, for Exxon.[230]

Ceres's Senior Director Cynthia McHale bluntly replied to Ms. Simpson: "Yes, it's very disappointing but not surprising. The need for escalation at Exxon seems to have arrived."[231]

However, the climate cartel initially found coordinating voting action against the ExxonMobil board of directors difficult. In particular, in preparation for its 2019 campaign against the board, the climate cartel found "it tricky to develop guidelines for CA100+ investors" to vote against company board members because "[t]here are strict rules on what you can say when soliciting other investors' votes."[232] Under U.S. securities law, financial institutions must formally file a solicitation with the SEC and follow strict requirements for calling on other investors to support shareholder votes.[233] Nevertheless, Climate Action 100+ resolved to "tread[] the line between being coordinated and overstepping the mark" by "bringing information" to investors on pressure campaigns "with the implication that support would be

---

228 CERES13570 at CERES13571; *see also* Transcribed Interview of Andrew Logan, *supra* note 11, at 34:14–35:9.
229 CERES24135 at CERES24137.
230 CALPERS_26293 at CALPERS_26293.
231 *Id.*
232 CERES30849 at CERES30853.
233 *See* Solicitation Before Furnishing a Proxy Statement, 17 C.F.R. § 240.14a-12(b)–(c) (2024).

welcome."[234] In 2019 and 2020, the climate cartel's lead investors sent private emails to the Climate Action 100+ engagement group, disclosing their intent "to hold the board accountable for its governance failures in climate risk . . . [by] vot[ing] against the re-election of the entire board."[235] The lead investors further "call[ed] on shareholders to implement a strong voting stance on director election in line with their own voting policies."[236]

At the same time, the climate cartel collectively worked to adopt voting policies that allow for votes against board members for climate-related reasons. Ceres directs climate cartel investors to "use the CA100+ Net Zero Company Benchmark . . . to inform . . . voting as well as other forms of escalation at focus companies."[237] Similarly, "[a]s part of the NZAM initiative investors commit to align their stewardship activities with achievement of net zero emissions by 2050 (e.g. by voting against director reappointments of companies that are mis-aligned with this objective)." To that end, NZAM investor signatories are expected to alter their voting policies to allow for votes against company board members who fail to meet climate-related criteria.[238] For example, the proxy voting guidelines of State Street Global Advisors state, "We may vote against directors due to failure to demonstrate effective oversight in . . . [c]limate risk management at companies in carbon-intensive industries or companies receiving shareholder proposals that exhibit significant misalignment with our . . . disclosure assessment criteria."[239]

---

[234] CERES30849 at CERES30854.

[235] CALPERS_9774 at CALPERS_9775; *see also* CALPERS_49456.

[236] CALPERS_9774 at CALPERS_9775.

[237] CERES10442 at CERES10448.

[238] *See* GL2161 at GL2163.

[239] *Global Proxy Voting and Engagement Policy*, STATE STREET GLOB. ADVISORS 11, https://www.ssga.com/library-content/assets/pdf/global/asset-stewardship/proxy-voting-and-engagement-policy.pdf (last visited Dec. 6, 2024).

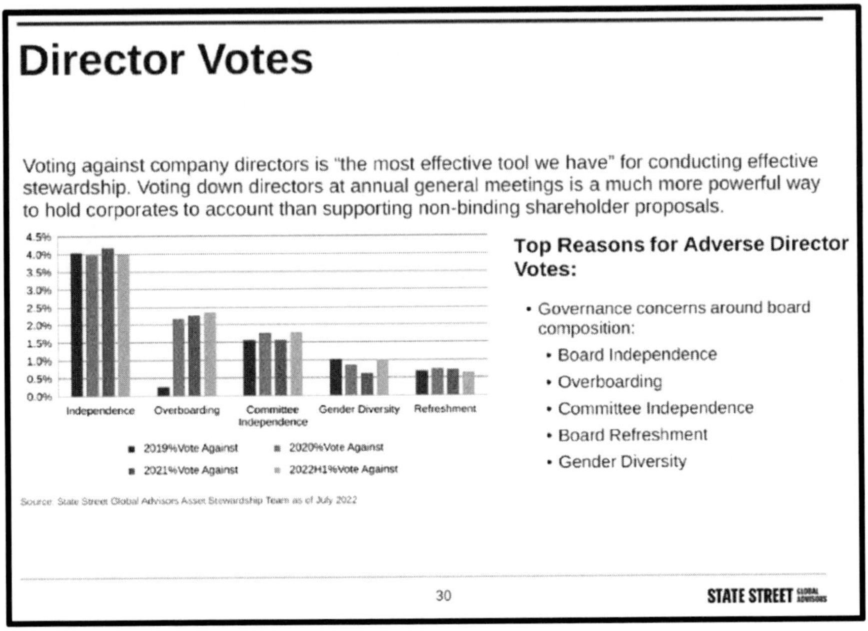

State Street Global Advisors votes against company directors for climate-related reasons, maintaining that it is "the most effective tool we have."[240]

In both 2019 and 2020, the Climate Action 100+ ExxonMobil engagement group worked "in conjunction with CERES efforts to build the vote" against ExxonMobil board members and "reach[ed] out directly to the largest shareholders."[241] Additionally, Ceres "offered to facilitate voting pre-declarations," allowing the investors to publicly signal to the rest of the climate cartel their support for the "vote no" campaigns before the ExxonMobil shareholder votes.[242]

These coordinated "vote no" campaigns at ExxonMobil led to significant declines in support for the board members in 2019 and 2020, including BlackRock voting against two board members in 2020.[243] Still, they did not result in any removals.[244] Instead, the climate cartel saw voting "no" against

---

240 SSGA-HJC.424879 at SSGA-HJC.424908.

241 CALPERS_9774 at CALPERS_9775.

242 CALPERS_49456 at CALPERS_49461.

243 *See* ExxonMobil Corporation, Current Report (Form 8-K) (June 5, 2018); ExxonMobil Corporation, Current Report (Form 8-K) (June 4, 2019); ExxonMobil Corporation, Current Report (Form 8-K) (June 2, 2020); ExxonMobil Corporation, Current Report (Form 8-K) (June 2, 2021).

244 *Id.*

the ExxonMobil board of directors as "a means of expressing . . . unhappiness with the board," but "rarely impactful" as a means "to change the makeup of the board."[245] That is because "vote no" campaigns "do[] not propose alternative candidates for the board and can be rejected by the board."[246] Instead, "[i]ncreasing votes against board members. . . are ***symbolic*** votes . . . so [board members] hopefully feel more personally responsible for exercising climate governance."[247]

Over time, however, the climate cartel's lead investors determined that rather than merely "voting no" against ExxonMobil board members, enforcing its "net-zero" goals required "vot[ing] to *replace* board members if it is unable to hold a board accountable."[248] In an interview titled "Reaching for the High Hanging Fruit to Drive Meaningful Corporate Decarbonisation," Mindy Lubber, CEO of Ceres, which holds leadership roles in GFANZ and Climate Action 100+, explained the shift in strategy:

> If companies aren't willing or able to respond to the challenge of moving towards a net zero transition, we will look for new leadership. It cannot be an option that we simply stand still, we need to move at pace and scale. There may be board directors who don't feel compelled or have the expertise to get this transition done—but they must then make way for those that do.[249]

E. Refresh: The Climate Cartel Orchestrated the 2021 Campaign to Remove and Replace ExxonMobil Board Members

As early as February 2020—amid its second "vote no" campaign against ExxonMobil in as many years—the climate cartel began developing a plan to remove and *replace* members of the company's board of directors. This was in part because, during the prior two years, the climate cartel had launched a barrage of 15 climate-related shareholder resolution campaigns, yet none received majority shareholder support, and the SEC granted no-action requests for seven of the shareholder resolutions for impermissibly interfering with

---

[245] Transcribed Interview of Andrew Logan, *supra* note 11, at 27:10–28:7.
[246] CERES45367 at CERES45372.
[247] CERES62745 at CERES62747.
[248] CERES1260 at CERES1263 (emphasis added); *see also* CERES45367 at CERES45367.
[249] CERES17681 at CERES17682.

ExxonMobil's "ordinary business."[250] As ExxonMobil continued to resist the climate cartel's pressure campaigns, the Climate Action 100+ engagement group began to view ExxonMobil as not only a climate "laggard" but as downright "recalcitrant."[251]

---

[250] *See Report on Environmental Health Impacts and Management (XOM, 2019 Resolution)*, CERES, https:// engagements.ceres.org/ceres_engagementdetailpage?recID=a0l1H00000CO4JfQAL (last visited Dec. 6, 2024); *Adopt Board Oversight of Climate Change (XOM, 2019 Resolution)*, CERES, https://engagements.ceres.org/ceres_ engagementdetailpage?recID=a0l1H00000CNyTYQA1 (last visited Dec. 6, 2024); *Adopt GHG Reduction Targets (XOM, 2019 Resolution)*, CERES, https://engagements.ceres.org/ceres_ engagementdetailpage?recID=a0l1H00000CN sY3QAL (last visited Dec. 6, 2024); *Report on Environmental Health Impacts and Management (XOM, 2019 Resolution)*, CERES, https://engagements.ceres.org/ceres_engagementdetailpage?recID=a0l1H00000CFGgwQAH (last visited Dec. 6, 2024); *Separate Chair/CEO (XOM, 2019 Resolution)*, CERES, https://engagements.ceres.org/ceres_engagementdetailpage?recID=a0l1H00000CFAPUQA5 (last visited Dec. 6, 2024); *Report on Lobbying (XOM, 2019 Resolution)*, CERES, https://engagements.ceres.org/ceres_engagementdetailpage?recID=a0l1H00000CEemhQAD (last visited Dec. 6, 2024); *Report on Environmental Health Impacts and Management (XOM, 2020 Resolution)*, CERES, https://engagements.ceres.org/ceres_engagementdetailpage?recID=a0l1H00000Cj0d5QAB (last visited Dec. 6, 2024); *Separate Chair/CEO (XOM, 2020 Resolution)*, CERES, https://engagements.ceres.org/ceres_engagementdetailpage?recID=a0l1H00000BZKMHQA5; *Report on Business Impacts to Sustainable Energy Access (XOM, 2019 Resolution)*, CERES, https://engagements.ceres.org/ceres_engagementdetailpage?recID=a0l1H00000CNylIQAT (last visited Dec. 6, 2024); *Report on Climate-related Transition Plan (XOM, 2019 Resolution)*, CERES, https://engagements.ceres.org/ceres_engagementdetailpage?recID=a0l1H00000CEmokQAD (last visited Dec. 6, 2024); *Report on 2-degree Analysis and Strategy (XOM, 2020 Resolution)*, CERES, https://engagements.ceres.org/ceres_engagementdetailpage?recID=a0l1H00000CjGJUQA3 (last visited Dec. 6, 2024); *Adopt Public Policy Advocacy Principles (XOM, 2020 Resolution)*, CERES, https://engagements.ceres.org/ceres_engagementdetailpage?recID=a0l1H00000CjCvhQAF (last visited Dec. 6, 2024); *Establish Board Committee on the Environment (XOM, 2020 Resolution)*, CERES, https://engagements.ceres.org/ceres_engagementdetailpage?recID=a0l1H00000CjCmQQ AV (last visited Dec. 6, 2024); *Report on 2-degree Analysis and Strategy (XOM, 2020 Resolution)*, CERES, https:// engagements.ceres.org/ceres_engagementdetailpage?recID=a0l1H00000BZU4yQAH (last visited Dec. 6, 2024); *Report on Corporate Climate Lobbying in Line with Paris Agreement (XOM, 2020 Res)*, CERES, https://engagements.ceres.org/ceres_engagementdetailpage?recID=a0l1H00000BZU2iQAH (last visited Dec. 6, 2024).

[251] Transcribed Interview of Andrew Logan, *supra* note 11, at 34:14–35:16, 127:20–130:9.

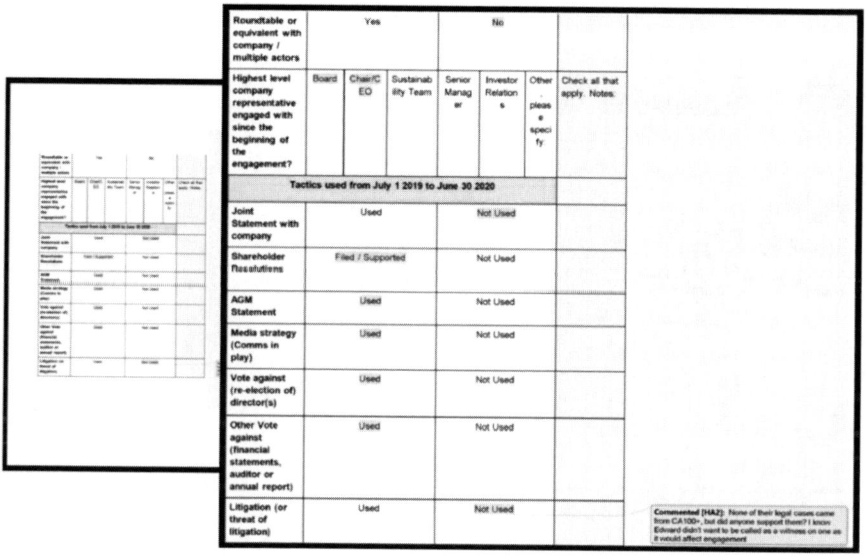

Roundtable or equivalent with company / multiple actors		Yes			No		
Highest level company representative engaged with since the beginning of the engagement?	Board	Chair/CEO	Sustainability Team	Senior Manager	Investor Relations	Other, please specify	Check all that apply. Notes:
Tactics used from July 1 2019 to June 30 2020							
Joint Statement with company		Used			Not Used		
Shareholder Resolutions		Filed / Supported			Not Used		
AGM Statement		Used			Not Used		
Media strategy (Comms in play)		Used			Not Used		
Vote against (re-election of) director(s)		Used			Not Used		
Other Vote against (financial statements, auditor or annual report)		Used			Not Used		
Litigation (or threat of litigation)		Used			Not Used		

Commented [HA2]: None of their legal cases came from CA100+, but did anyone support them? I know Edward didn't want to be called as a witness on one as it would affect engagement

Before 2021, the Climate Action 100+ engagement group had "[u]sed" a variety of engagement "[t]actics" to pressure ExxonMobil.[252]

On February 7, 2020, Ceres CEO Mindy Lubber expressed to Ceres staff her disappointment with the climate cartel pressure campaign: "Exxon Mobil is in fact unique (in every way) and perhaps we need to build a war room to discuss opportunities to ramp up yet further I assume this is a priority of CA100+ and the networks are fully engaged."[253] At"that point in time," the Climate Action 100+ engagement group's goal was to at least "get[] the company to set Scope 1 and 2 targets for its emissions . . . [and] make progress against the benchmark that Climate Action 100+ has set up to measure company performance," through, for instance, the disclosure of Scope 3 emissions.[254] However, the engagement group's lead investors grew increasingly "frustrated . . . that the investor engagement with Exxon was not really moving the company in any way."[255] The climate cartel's lead investors concluded that "engagement at Exxon has hit a wall, making it a candidate for board refreshment."[256]

---

[252] CALPERS_44739 at CALPERS_44741.
[253] CERES45367 at CERES45374.
[254] Transcribed Interview of Andrew Logan, *supra* note 11, at 62:11–15, 53:2–25.
[255] *Id.* at 61:17–20.
[256] CERES1260 at CERES1263.

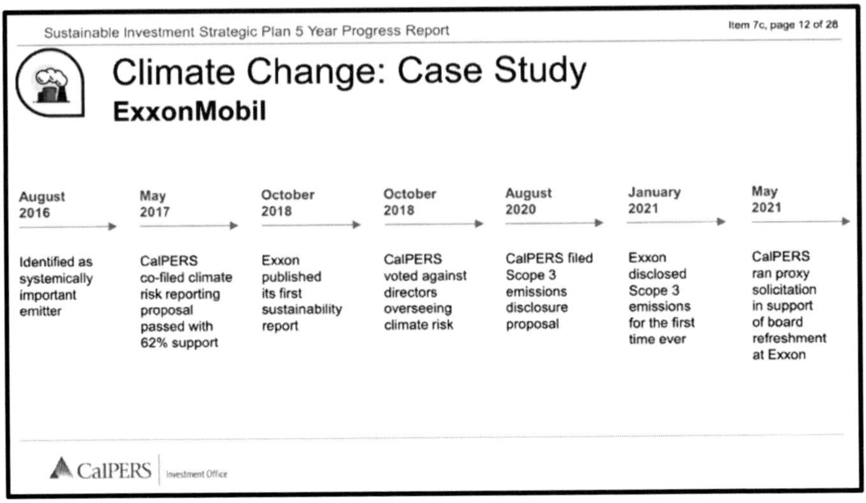

The 2021 board "refreshment" was the culmination of a multi-year pressure campaign against ExxonMobil.[257]

1. The Biden-Harris Administration Recruited for and Emboldened the Climate Cartel to Escalate Its Campaign

The likelihood of a Biden-Harris Administration taking office in early 2021 also made the timing right for the climate cartel to escalate its pressure campaign against ExxonMobil. During the Trump Administration, the SEC had raised the threshold for investors to file shareholder resolutions to protect American businesses from radical ESG campaigns.[258] The Trump Administration also marked an era of governmental reform and deregulation aimed at growing and expanding the American energy sector. Under President Trump, the United States left the Paris Climate Agreement[259] and became a net energy exporter for the first time in nearly 70 years,[260] producing over 12

---

[257] CALPERS_72 at CALPERS_83.

[258] Paul Kiernan, *SEC Raises Bar for Shareholder Resolutions*, WALL ST. J. (Sept. 23, 2020), https://www.wsj.com/articles/sec-raises-bar-for-shareholder-resolutions-11600877050?mod=article_inline.

[259] Press Release, THE WHITE HOUSE, *President Trump Announces U.S. Withdrawal from the Paris Climate Accord*, https://trumpwhitehouse.archives.gov/articles/president-trump-announces-u-s-withdrawal-paris-climate-accord/(June 1, 2017).

[260] Javier Blas, *The U.S. Just Became a Net Oil Exporter for the First Time in 75 Years*, BLOOMBERG (Dec. 6, 2018), https://www.bloomberg.com/news/articles/2018-12-06/u-s-becomes-a-net-oil-exporter-for-the-first-time-in-75-years?

million barrels of oil a day[261] and a historic 34.9 quads of natural gas in 2019.[262] At the end of President Trump's first term, not only had American families saved an average of $2,500 a year in lower electric and gas prices,[263] but the United States also led the world in GHG emission reductions.[264]

In contrast, a Biden-Harris White House represented a new era of environmental regulation fully aligned with the climate cartel's "net-zero" agenda. On November 7, 2020, a mere four days after the presidential election, Ceres CEO Mindy Lubber emailed Glass Lewis's Senior ESG Director, Courteney Keatinge, announcing that together with "President-elect Joe Biden and Vice President-elect Kamala Harris," Ceres would "work urgently to achieve a net- zero emissions future," through "the largest global investor engagement initiative, Climate Action 100+."[265] In a 2020 report sent to GFANZ, Climate Action 100+ stated that

> Joe Biden and Kamala Harris [are] likely to drive a significant shift in US climate policy Investors in the Climate Action 100+ engagement group will look to capitalize on the momentum created by the expected shift in domestic climate policy and use this to encourage more ambition from focus companies in the US.[266]

On the Biden-Harris Administration's first day in office, it began imposing its radical "net-zero" climate agenda. The Administration immediately rejoined the Paris Climate Agreement;[267] canceled the Keystone XL Pipeline, which was expected to produce 830,000 barrels of oil per day

---

[261] *U.S. Crude Oil Production Grew 11% in 2019, Surpassing 12 Million Barrels per Day*, U.S. ENERGY INFO. ADMIN. (Mar. 2, 2020), https://www.eia.gov/todayinenergy/detail.php?id=43015&.

[262] *U.S. Net Natural Gas Exports Remain Flat in First Half of 2024*, U.S. ENERGY INFO. ADMIN. (Sept. 25, 2024), https://www.eia.gov/todayinenergy/detail.php?.

[263] Ronald Stein, *Biden's 'We Are Going to Get Rid of Fossil Fuels' Is a Primary Cause for Shortages and Inflation*, THE HEARTLAND INST. (Mar. 10, 2022), https://heartland.org/opinion/bidens-we-are-going-to-get-rid-of-fossil-fuels-is-a-primary-cause-for-shortages-and-inflation/.

[264] *Latest Inventory of U.S. Greenhouse Gas Emissions and Sinks Shows Long-term Reductions, with Annual Variation*, U.S. ENV'T PROT. AGENCY (Apr. 13, 2020), https://www.epa.gov/newsreleases/latest-inventory-us-greenhouse-gas-emissions-and-sinks-shows-long-term-reductions?.

[265] GL2067 at GL2067, GL2068.

[266] GFANZ13103 at GFANZ13171.

[267] *Paris Climate Agreement*, THE WHITE HOUSE (Jan. 20, 2021), https://www.whitehouse.gov/briefing-room/statements-releases/2021/01/20/paris-climate-agreement/.

and create 71,000 jobs;[268] banned drilling on America's largest oil fields in Alaska;[269] and ordered federal agencies to measure and regulate the "social cost of carbon," costing the U.S. economy as much as an estimated $561 billion in regulatory compliance costs.[270] In a January 22, 2021, email to climate cartel supporters, Ceres celebrated the Biden- Harris Administration's climate agenda, writing:

> What a difference a week can make. Ceres congratulates President Joe Biden and Vice President Kamala Harris for their swift action to reenter the U.S. into the global Paris Agreement and restore a number of critical environmental regulations. They included placing a moratorium on drilling in the Arctic National Wildlife Refuge, revising fuel economy and emission standards and methane emission standards, and revoking the permit for the Keystone XL Pipeline.[271]

The Biden-Harris Administration did more than shift "climate policy" in the cartel's favor; it worked directly with the climate cartel to recruit investors and escalate its agenda. Ceres "deeply engaged with key financial regulators and the Biden Administration" as well as "senior staff in key regulatory agencies" to "set crucial changes in motion due to the Biden Administration's commitment to ambitious climate action."[272] In particular, the Biden-Harris Administration's Special Presidential Envoy for Climate, John Kerry, "help[ed] recruit investors for" Ceres.[273]

---

[268] Valerie Richardson, *House Republicans Bring Bill to Authorize Keystone XL Pipeline, Cut Biden out of Process*, THE WASH. TIMES (Feb. 2, 2021), https://www.washingtontimes.com/news/2021/feb/2/house-republicans-bring-bill- reauthorize-keystone-/.

[269] Arctic National Wildlife Refuge, 1002 Area, Petroleum Assessment, 1998, Including Economic Analysis, U.S. GEOLOGICAL SURV. (last modified Nov. 29, 2016), https://pubs.usgs.gov/fs/fs-0028-01/fs-0028-01.htm?; Jillian Ambrose, Biden Suspends Trump-era Oil Drilling Leases in Alaska's Arctic Refuge, THE GUARDIAN (June 2, 2021), https://www.theguardian.com/us-news/2021/jun/01/biden-suspends-oil-drilling-leases-alaska-arctic-refuge-trump-era.

[270] Decl. of Prof. David E. Dismukes ¶¶ 14–26, *Louisiana v. Biden*, No. 2:21-cv-1074 (W.D. La. 2022), ECF No. 57.

[271] CERES11071 at CERES11071.

[272] CERES2871 at CERES2872, CERES2873.

[273] CERES63255 at CERES63257.

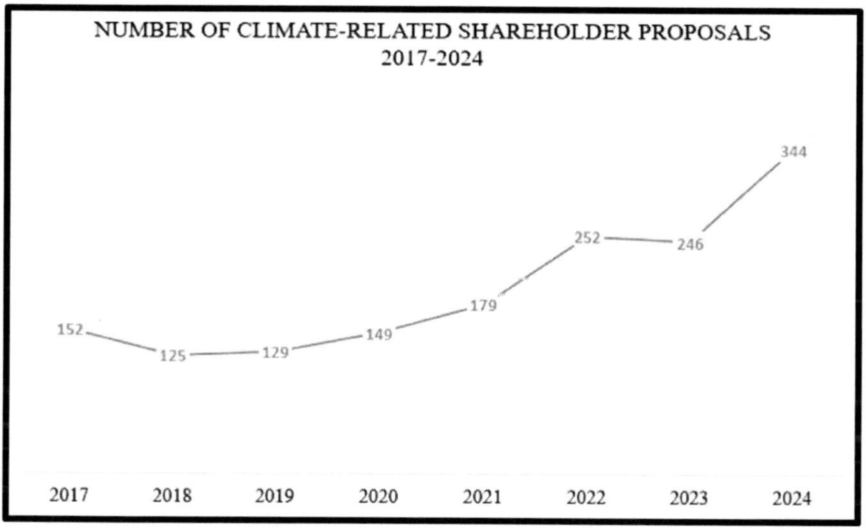

Under the Biden-Harris Administration, climate-related proposals more than doubled.[274]

The Biden-Harris Administration's closest left-wing allies also partnered with the climate cartel. Climate activist Michael Bloomberg's nonprofit, Bloomberg Philanthropies, promised to pour millions of dollars into Ceres which is used to "support [the] Biden climate agenda"[275] as well as NZAM[276] and Climate Action 100+.[277] From 2020 to 2021, during which the climate cartel executed its plan to "refresh" the ExxonMobil board of directors, the left-wing Foundation to Promote Open Society and Open Society Institute delivered a combined $1.7 million to Ceres- affiliate As You Sow for shareholder activism.[278] The Bezos Earth Fund granted Ceres $3 million for its climate finance programs that focus on "mov[ing] private equity out of fossil fuels."[279] With the support of these "key tailwinds," including the "Biden [A]dministration and Ceres key relationships," Ceres and its investor

---

[274] Company Results: Proposals on Climate Change, Energy, and Other Environmental Jan. 2017 to SEP. 2024, DILIGENT MKT. INTELL. (on file with the Comm.).
[275] *Id.* at CERES63258.
[276] *See* CERES85309 at CERES85312–13.
[277] *See* CERES27898 at CERES27898.
[278] *Awarded Grants*, OPEN SOC'Y FOUNDS., https://www.opensocietyfoundations.org/grants/past?filter_keyword= as+you+sow (last visited Dec. 6, 2024).
[279] CERES63255 at CERES63257.

networks resolved to "shift more resources to strategies focused on driving accountability for corporate progress against climate commitments."[280]

2. The Climate Cartel Crafted an Intricate "Exxon Strategy" to "Refresh the Board

In 2020, the climate cartel's lead investors began to put "100% of [their] focus . . . on teeing up an activist strategy for [2021] that would nominate a slate of directors to replace the existing [ExxonMobil] board."[281] Edward Mason, Head of Responsible Investment at the Church Commissioners and NZAM Advisory Group member,[282] "conceived the idea of partnering with [an] activist fund" to "refresh" the ExxonMobil board, and the newly appointed ExxonMobil engagement group lead investor "CalPERS . . . expressed interest in leading [it]."[283]

In March 2020, Climate Action 100+ funder, the Children's Investment Fund Foundation (CIFF)—a climate activism nonprofit known for funding "climate litigation" against U.S. energy companies[284]—"conditionally offered $3.7m over two years for CA100+" to orchestrate the "[r]apid escalation of engagement to fire directors who fail to deliver transition plans alignedwith Paris, with a vanguard of activist investors taking the lead."[285] Additionally, a "funder (not CIFF) who is a strong champion for CA100+ . . . made a time-limited offer of an additional $1m . . . toward costs of an Exxon board-refreshment campaign."[286]

In spring 2020, the climate cartel considered the funders' proposal and began to craft an "Exxon Strategy" to "refresh" ExxonMobil's board of directors. In email communications, Ceres "point[ed] out [that] there . . . ha[d] not been one single corporate member replaced at any company globally in the past decade for reasons that include climate [so] the idea of replacing board members at every climate-lagging company [wa]s tremendously far from current reality."[287] Instead members of the Climate Action 100+ Steering

---

[280] CERES91503 at CERES91508.

[281] CERES45367 at CERES45367; *see also* CERES89544.

[282] *Partners*, Net Zero Asset Managers, https://www.netzeroassetmanagers.org/partners-participants/ (last visited Dec. 6, 2024).

[283] CERES58560 at CERES58561.

[284] *Children's Investment Fund Foundation (CIFF)*, INFLUENCE WATCH, https://www.influencewatch.org/non-profit/childrens-investment-fund-foundation-ciff/(last visited Dec. 6, 2024).

[285] CERES60818 at CERES60818, CERES60822 (emphasis omitted).

[286] CERES62497 at CERES62498.

[287] CERES58560 at CERES58560.

Committee noted that "[t]he spirit of the [funders'] request [wa]s [that] CA100+ [would] go to the next level, using board seat challenges to advance its goals."[288] To achieve this aim, the Climate Action 100+ Steering Committee resolved to "[e]stablish a credible threat of board member refreshment[] by implementing an unprecedented effort to replace board members at one of the world's very largest companies. Instead of going at every lagging company, all [of] the CA100+[would] go at one: Exxon."[289] In the "Exxon Campaign—HIGHLY CONFIDENTIAL" section of a 2020 report prepared for CIFF, the climate cartel declared:

> When recalcitrant companies demonstrate that other escalation tactics are not working, it is crucial for investors to take concerted action to refresh the board of directors. . . . [I]t is important to demonstrate that investors are willing to go to the top rung, with activist investor(s) who do board refreshment on a regular basis. Doing this with even a limited number of companies will send a powerful signal to other major GHG emitting companies around the world.[290]

As part of its ambitious ExxonMobil "strategy," the Climate Action 100+ ExxonMobil engagement group planned to "partner with a mainstream activist hedge fund to go after the Exxon board."[291] As initially outlined, the activist fund to lead the charge would be JANA Partners, an asset manager operated by "a bunch of cutthroats" specializing in activist campaigns.[292] Because "under proxy access, shareholder[s] can nominate one-quarter of the board," and ExxonMobil had a twelve-person board of directors,[293] the activist fund would identify four candidates to form "a slate of climate competent directors."[294] This allowed the climate cartel to craft the campaign's appearance so that it would "be perceived and run as a mainstream activist campaign, rather than something driven by foundations and climate advocates."[295]

---

[288] CERES1260 at CERES1263.
[289] CERES58560 at CERES58561 (emphasis omitted).
[290] CERES46032 at CERES46038.
[291] CERES45367 at CERES45373.
[292] *Id.*
[293] *Board of Directors*, EXXONMOBIL, https://corporate.exxonmobil.com/corporate-governance/board-of-directors (last visited Dec. 6, 2024).
[294] CERES1260 at CERES1263.
[295] CERES57222 at CERES57223.

Ceres and its coordinating investor networks understood that "[t]he real challenge . . . [would] be to make voting against the [ExxonMobil] board a priority for the larger CA100+ members."[296] Accordingly, while it recognized that its "behind the scenes role [wa]s critical,"[297] the activist nonprofit planned to "circulate information from lead investors and/or investor signatories" to proxy advisors and large institutional investors.[298] Ceres believed that if investors knew that "one fund ha[d] chosen to go down a particular path, [it] ma[de] it more likely that another [investor] would be willing to consider it."[299] By broadcasting "collective lists" of investors voting in favor of the board "refreshment" campaign, it aimed to "highlight[] momentum around the Exxon board vote."[300]

Climate Action 100+ followed a disciplined and coordinated plan to ensure the board "refreshment" campaign had the "greatest chance of success."[301] Its efforts included "[s]upport[ing] the recruitment and vetting of board candidates . . . to advance the climate agenda," "[e]ngaging major asset managers," and coordinating "build-the-vote" efforts "within and beyond the Climate Action 100+ orbit."[302] The climate cartel's goal was simple: "get new people—[its] people—added to the Exxon board."[303]

---

296 CERES45367 at CERES45374; *see also* CERES89974; CERES110282.
297 CERES1260 at CERES1263.
298 CALPERS_5004 at CALPERS_5005.
299 Transcribed Interview of Andrew Logan, *supra* note 11, at 58:1–7.
300 CALPERS_3188 at CALPERS_3188, CALPERS_3191.
301 CERES46032 at CERES46039.
302 *Id.*
303 CERES45367 at CERES45373.

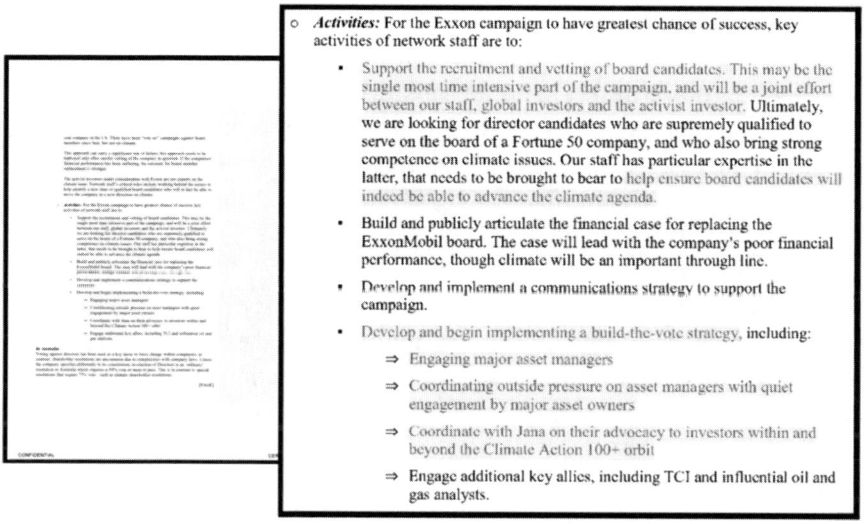

o *Activities:* For the Exxon campaign to have greatest chance of success, key activities of network staff are to:

- Support the recruitment and vetting of board candidates. This may be the single most time intensive part of the campaign, and will be a joint effort between our staff, global investors and the activist investor. Ultimately, we are looking for director candidates who are supremely qualified to serve on the board of a Fortune 50 company, and who also bring strong competence on climate issues. Our staff has particular expertise in the latter, that needs to be brought to bear to help ensure board candidates will indeed be able to advance the climate agenda.
- Build and publicly articulate the financial case for replacing the ExxonMobil board. The case will lead with the company's poor financial performance, though climate will be an important through line.
- Develop and implement a communications strategy to support the campaign.
- Develop and begin implementing a build-the-vote strategy, including:
  - ⇒ Engaging major asset managers
  - ⇒ Coordinating outside pressure on asset managers with quiet engagement by major asset owners
  - ⇒ Coordinate with Jana on their advocacy to investors within and beyond the Climate Action 100+ orbit
  - ⇒ Engage additional key allies, including TCI and influential oil and gas analysts.

The climate cartel developed and implemented a coordinated "Exxon campaign."[304]

3. The Climate Cartel Enlisted Engine No. 1 as the Public Face of the "Exxon Strategy"

From the beginning, the climate cartel took careful steps to ensure that "CA100+ play[ed] a behind the scenes role" in driving the "Exxon campaign" forward.[305] While "[o]n one hand, having a public association with CA100+ is important for sending a strong signal to other recalcitrant companies on the CA100+ focus list,"[306] the climate cartel believed that if it became public that "board campaigns are CA100+ originated, that may also shift the tone of the entire initiative and make it more difficult for some signatories to support or remain involved."[307]

Ceres was also concerned that its "relationships" with other U.S. companies "could be adversely affected by a visible association between Ceres and efforts to replace board members within the corporate arena,"[308] because "oil and gas companies don't want an activist slate run on them."[309]

---

[304] CERES46032 at CERES46039.
[305] CERES1260 at CERES1263.
[306] CERES58560 at CERES58561.
[307] CERES1260 at CERES1263.
[308] CERES58560 at CERES58560.
[309] Transcribed Interview of Andrew Logan, *supra* note 11, at 146:8–147:5, 148:9–149:10.

To abate these concerns, Ceres believed it was "important that [an] activist hedge fund be positioned as the lead for this effort, with investor networks [i.e., Climate Action 100+] in particular staying behind the scenes."[310] JANA Partners, an investment firm "specializ[ing] in activism across a range of issues," initially expressed interest in leading the climate cartel's efforts.[311] In particular, Charlie Penner, a partner at JANA Partners, who had previously led activist campaigns along with CalSTRS against other large U.S. companies,[312] had researched a potential activist takeover of ExxonMobil since 2019.[313] Like the climate cartel, Mr. Penner believed that ExxonMobil's business strategy did not consider the "fighting chance the world decides not to blow itself up."[314] In December 2019, Ceres staff and Climate Action 100+ lead investors began "an information sharing . . . set of conversations" with Mr. Penner to plan "a campaign at Exxon [that] would include . . . climate related concerns."[315]

However, "JANA Partners ultimately did not lead the campaign to replace the ExxonMobil board[]."[316]After receiving pushback from his colleagues, Mr. Penner determined that JANA Partners would not provide the support "necessary for [the campaign] to be successful."[317] As a result, Mr. Penner left JANA Partners and joined environmentalist Chris James to start a small investment fund in San Francisco, California, called Engine No. 1.[318]

Engine No. 1 opened its doors in 2020 to "seek opportunities to employ its active ownership beliefs."[319] The core of its mission was actively "measur[ing] the investment made by companies in [their] employees, communities, customers and the environment, including through the use of financial, operational, and environmental, social and governance ('ESG')

---

310 CERES58560 at CERES58561.

311 Transcribed Interview of Andrew Logan, *supra* note 11, at 32:1–32:17.

312 Derek Brower & Ortenca Aliaj, *Engine No 1, the Giant-Killing Hedge Fund, Has Big Plans*, FIN. TIMES (June 3, 2021), https://www.ft.com/content/ebfdf67d-cbce-40a5-bb29-d361377dea7a.

313 CALPERS_4388 at CALPERS_4391.

314 Saijel Kishan, *Charlie Penner, the Investor Reshaping Exxon from the Inside*, BLOOMBERG (Dec. 1, 2021), https://www.bloomberg.com/news/features/2021-12-01/charlie-penner-engine-no-1-investor-reshaping-exxon- bloomberg-50-2021.

315 Transcribed Interview of Andrew Logan, *supra* note 11, at 31:12–34:10.

316 *Id.* at 72:5–74:20.

317 *Id.* at 31:12–34:10.

318 *See* CALPERS_4388 at CALPERS_4391.

319 *Engine No. 1: The Power of Active Ownership*, RIA CHANNEL (Mar. 28, 2022), https://www.riachannel.com/ engine-no-1-the-power-of-active-ownership-engine-1-3-28-22/.

metrics."[320] Its focus was "to create value by helping companies transform their businesses to be sustainable."[321] To instigate this sort of transformation, Engine No. 1 believed that "[c]oordination by activists appears to be a determinant of successful engagements."[322] Compared to JANA Partners, Mr. Penner found Engine No. 1 to "be a better platform" for the ExxonMobil board "refreshment" campaign.[323] Thus, as Ceres's Senior Director Andrew Logan testified to the Committee, "the plan to refresh the ExxonMobil board followed [Mr. Penner] to Engine No. 1."[324]

In addition to its coordination with Engine No. 1, the climate cartel also worked outside of the Climate Action 100+ initiative to form a more radical "parallel group" of investors.[325] In self-described "good cop/bad cop" engagements,[326] the climate cartel generally "bring[s] in a parallel group of more ambitious investors, outside [the] CA100[+] working group, to escalate" when the "CA100[+] engagement [doesn't] move fast enough."[327] In 2020, members of the climate cartel formed such a group in "CURE, [the] Coalition United for a Responsible Exxon."[328] Led by As You Sow and supported by over 145 investors with $2.4 trillion in assets,[329] CURE publicly advocated for the climate cartel's board "refreshment" strategy and called for ExxonMobil to establish "capital discipline," which entails "cutting investment in oil and gas production."[330]

On December 7, 2020, Engine No. 1 sent a letter to ExxonMobil announcing its nomination of four directors to the company's board.[331] The letter opened, "No company in the history of oil and gas has been more influential than Exxon Mobil Corporation It is clear, however, that the industry and the world it operates in are changing and that ExxonMobil must change as well."[332] That same day, CURE announced its support for Engine No. 1's

---

320 *Id.*

321 *Shareholder Voting*, Engine No. 1, https://engine1.com/transforming/shareholder-voting/ (last visited Dec. 6, 2024).

322 ENGINE NO. 1, A NEW WAY OF SEEING VALUE 13 (June 2021), https://www.shareholderforum.com/access/ Library/20210916_Engine1.pdf.

323 Transcribed Interview of Andrew Logan, *supra* note 11, at 72:5–74:11.

324 *Id.*

325 *See* CERES85006 at CERES85008, CERES85011; *see also* CERES62869 at CERES62952.

326 CERES62869 at CERES62952.

327 CERES85006 at CERES85008.

328 Deposition of Andrew Behar, Chief Executive Officer, As You Sow (Mar. 28, 2024) at 86:10–92:18.

329 *About CURE*, CURE (May 6, 2021), https://curexxon.org/about/.

330 Deposition of Andrew Behar, *supra* note 328, at 86:10–92:18.

331 *See* ENGINENO1-118HJC-PROD-54 at ENGINENO1-118HJC-PROD-55.

332 *Id.*

activist slate.[333] Three days later, Climate Action 100+'s lead investor, the Church Commissioners, likewise publicly announced its support.[334]

Over the next six months, as the climate cartel worked "behind the scenes"[335] to build support, Engine No. 1 publicly campaigned and argued that ExxonMobil must be transformed from the top down to survive in a low-carbon future. "Clinging to strategy until forced to change is not a coherent strategy," Engine No. 1 told investors in a Climate Action 100+-hosted webinar.[336] For ExxonMobil to be "[r]e-energiz[ed]," investors must elect a board determined "to set long-term total emissions reduction targets that are truly Paris consistent."[337]

ExxonMobil responded to Engine No. 1 by highlighting that its total shareholder returns had "outperformed peers by 25 to 30 percentage points over the six months, one year, two years, and three years" before April 15, 2021.[338] Moreover, rather than transitioning to "net zero," ExxonMobil pointed out that global demand for oil and gas would continue to grow in the future, "requiring $12 trillion of additional investment in new exploration and production to meet the demand."[339] Nevertheless, after the announcement of Engine No. 1's campaign to "refresh" the board, ExxonMobil unilaterally decided to add three new directors to address any corporate governance concerns.[340]

Still, Engine No. 1 and the rest of the climate cartel refused to suspend the board "refreshment" campaign. Engine No.1 founder Chris James viewed ExxonMobil's decision to add three new directors to the board as a "promise[] made at gunpoint," which he believed is "rarely kept."[341] As an "active owner," Engine No. 1 believed it needed its director candidates to win seats for ExxonMobil to chart a better course.[342] At the time of its board refreshment campaign, the investment firm held $40 million worth or 0.02% of ExxonMobil's shares.[343] It also was only one year old.[344]

---

333 *Id.*
334 *Id.*
335 CERES1260 at CERES1263; *see also* CERES95803.
336 ENGINENO1-118HJC-PROD-2314 at ENGINENO1-118HJC-PROD-2356.
337 *Id.* at ENGINENO1-118HJC-PROD-2376.
338 CALPERS_4388 at CALPERS_4398.
339 *Id.*
340 See id.
341 Jessica Aguirre, The Little Hedge Fund Taking Down Big Oil, N.Y. TIMES (June 15, 2021), https://www.nytimes. com/2021/06/23/magazine/exxon-mobil-engine-no-1-board.html.
342 See generally ENGINENO1-118HJC-PROD-2314.
343 CALPERS_4388 at CALPERS_4388; Phillips, supra note 22.
344 Id.

4. The Climate Cartel Coordinated with European Investors and "Blue-State" Pensions to Secure Early Support for the Board "Refreshment"

Engine No. 1, however, did not act alone. Well before Engine No. 1's December 2020 letter to ExxonMobil nominating four new board members, the climate cartel worked to secure the support of European-based investment firms and the three largest pensions in the United States and CA100+ investor signatories: CalPERS, CalSTRS, and NYS.[345]

The climate cartel began by recruiting support from European investment firms, which comprise most of GFANZ and Climate Action 100+'s investor membership.[346] European investment firms are also generally more willing to engage U.S. companies aggressively.[347] Aviva Investors, for example, a London-based asset manager with $213 billion under management[348] and leadership roles in both GFANZ and CA100+,[349] views "[c]limate change [a]s the biggest systemic challenge of our time"[350] and believes that "there is clearly a moral imperative to act."[351] Central to its engagement strategy, Aviva promises to "[v]ote against companies on the list of Climate Action 100+ that do not have a science-based target" and "as an escalation of a failed engagement."[352]

In March 2020, the ExxonMobil engagement group lead investors conducted an "EU roadshow" in Europe to gauge "potential appetite for a campaign to nominate . . . an alternate set of directors at Exxon."[353] Edward

---

345 CERES57222 at CERES57223; see also CERES89277.

346 See The Alliances and GFANZ, supra note 100; see also Investor Signatories, Climate Action 100+, https://www. climateaction100.org/whos-involved/investors/ (last visited Dec. 6, 2024).

347 In 2019, the top six institutional investor supporters of climate-related shareholder resolutions—voting in favor almost 85% of the time on average—were all based in Europe. See AV23803 at AV23806. That same year, 56% of European firms were involved in shareholder engagements compared to 18% in the United States. See id. at AV23809.

348 *Aviva PLC 2023 Full Year Results Announcements*, AVIVA INVS. (Mar. 7, 2024), https://www.aviva.com/newsroom/news-releases/2024/03/FY2023-results-announcement/.

349 *See* GFANZ7148 at GFANZ7165; *see also* AV6692 at AV6695.

350 *This Is What Climate Action Looks Like*, AVIVA INVS., https://www.avivainvestors.com/en-us/responsibility/climate-action/[https://web.archive.org/web/20240224101619/ https://www.avivainvestors.com/en-us/responsibility/ climate-action/].

351 *Translating Climate Ambition into Action*, AVIVA INVS., https://www.avivain vestors.com/ en-us/responsibility/our-climate-approach/[https://web.archive.org/web/20240413023848/https://www.avivainvestors.com /en-us/responsibility/our-climate-approach/].

352 AV11 at AV50.

353 Transcribed Interview of Andrew Logan, *supra* note 11, at 69:16–70:18; *see also* CERES57222 at CERES57223.

Mason of the Church Commissioners "set up a series of meetings in Europe with European investors . . . to get some initial responses to their thinking."[354] Mr. Mason reported to Ceres staff that the "EU roadshow . . . went quite well, and . . . (the activist fund) is eager to move ahead with the campaign to replace the [ExxonMobil] board."[355] After engagement with European investment firms, Mr. Mason was "confident that there [would] be a multi-national coalition driving [the] campaign."[356] Ultimately, European- based Climate Action 100+ and NZAM investor signatories Federated Hermes, Legal & General, and Aviva Investors—with roughly a combined $2.3 trillion in assets under management[357]— publicly declared support in advance of the ExxonMobil board "refreshment."[358]

Additionally, the climate cartel secured the early support of the largest "blue-state" public pensions in the United States, which were all members of the climate cartel.[359] Moreover, CalPERS and NYS served as lead investors of the Climate Action 10+ ExxonMobil engagement group.[360] In the months before the ExxonMobil board of directors election, the climate cartel worked to position the "campaign . . . [as led by] CalSTRS/NYS in the US."[361] Accordingly, in its December 7, 2020, letter to ExxonMobil, Engine No. 1 announced that its slate of directors was publicly supported by CalSTRS, "the second largest pension fund in the U.S. whichowns over $300 million in value of [ExxonMobil's] stock."[362] In addition, CalPERS, the largest state public pension fund in the United States with over $495 billion in assets under management, pledged to "use its vote to replace [ExxonMobil] board members."[363] NYS also announced public support of the Engine No. 1 slate of directors, and thus Ceres was able to "highlight CalPERS, NYS and CalSTRS' support of the slate" in its outreach to climate cartel members.[364]

---

[354] Transcribed Interview of Andrew Logan, *supra* note 11, at 69:16–70:18.

[355] CERES57222 at CERES57223.

[356] *Id.*

[357] Results, Presentations and Reports, supra note 23; Federated Hermes (FHI) Q2 Earnings Top Estimates, AUM Rise, supra note 23; H1 2021 Results: Strong Financial Performance – 14% Growth in Operating Profit and 22% ROE, supra note 23.

[358] CALPERS_4105 at CALPERS_4107; *see also* CALPERS_12679.

[359] CERES89277 at CERES89277 (referring to Ceres, CalPERS, NYS, and BNP Paribas as "collaborators"); *see also* CERES57222 at CERES57223.

[360] *See* CERES62869 at CERES62988.

[361] CERES57222 at CERES57223.

[362] ENGINENO1-118HJC-PROD-54 at ENGINENO1-118HJC-PROD-55.

[363] CERES1260 at CERES1263; *see also* CERES117847 at CERES117848.

[364] CALPERS_13365 at CALPERS_13665.

The climate cartel also worked with the Minnesota state public pension, MSBI, to support the ExxonMobil board "refreshment" campaign. A member of Climate Action 100+ since2019,[365] the MSBI participated in the "engagement with Exxon by CalSTRS and . . . Climate Action 100+,"[366] and "played a key role in electing . . . new directors beyond directly voting in favor of the dissident directors."[367] The MSBI saw the climate cartel's campaign as focused on "the need for the company's business strategy to evolve in response to climate change and society's transition toward a lower-carbon economy."[368] During the climate cartel's 2020 vote- no campaign, the "[M]SBI . . . voted against the entire board as part of this engagement,"[369] and in 2021, the MSBI was the deciding vote that secured the takeover of the ExxonMobil board.

This was because "the 3.5 million shares held by the [M]SBI amounted to about 5% of the difference between the 3rd dissident director winning a seat and the closest management nominated candidate who did not win a seat."[370]

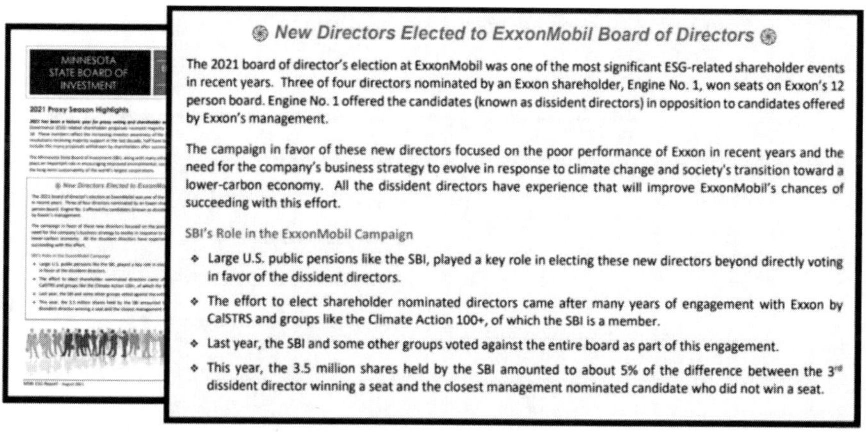
MINNESOTA STATE BOARD OF INVESTMENT

2021 Proxy Season Highlights

New Directors Elected to ExxonMobil Board of Directors

The 2021 board of director's election at ExxonMobil was one of the most significant ESG-related shareholder events in recent years. Three of four directors nominated by an Exxon shareholder, Engine No. 1, won seats on Exxon's 12 person board. Engine No. 1 offered the candidates (known as dissident directors) in opposition to candidates offered by Exxon's management.

The campaign in favor of these new directors focused on the poor performance of Exxon in recent years and the need for the company's business strategy to evolve in response to climate change and society's transition toward a lower-carbon economy. All the dissident directors have experience that will improve ExxonMobil's chances of succeeding with this effort.

SBI's Role in the ExxonMobil Campaign

- Large U.S. public pensions like the SBI, played a key role in electing these new directors beyond directly voting in favor of the dissident directors.
- The effort to elect shareholder nominated directors came after many years of engagement with Exxon by CalSTRS and groups like the Climate Action 100+, of which the SBI is a member.
- Last year, the SBI and some other groups voted against the entire board as part of this engagement.
- This year, the 3.5 million shares held by the SBI amounted to about 5% of the difference between the 3rd dissident director winning a seat and the closest management nominated candidate who did not win a seat.

The MSBI played a "key role" in the ExxonMobil campaign, providing the deciding vote for the climate cartel's third director.[371]

[365] MINN. STATE BD. OF INV., ESG STEWARDSHIP REPORT 13 (2021), https://msbi.us/sites/default/files/2022-01/MSBI%20ESG%20Stewardship%20Report%20FY2021.pdf.
[366] ENVIRONMENTAL, SOCIAL, GOVERNANCE REPORT, *supra* note 24, at 1.
[367] *Id.*
[368] *Id.*
[369] *Id.*
[370] *Id.*
[371] *Id.*

5. The Climate Cartel Engaged the "Big 3" Asset Managers to Secure a "Critical Mass" of Votes

While European investment firms and "blue-state" public pensions provided credibility and influence to the climate cartel's board "refreshment" campaign, crucial to its success was the support of the "Big 3" asset managers. BlackRock, State Street Global Advisors, and Vanguard together control over $23.8 trillion in assets and combined are the largest shareholder in 88% of all companies in the S&P 500.[372] In 2021, the "Big 3" owned 20.5% of ExxonMobil shares.[373] They also cast about a quarter of all votes at S&P 500 companies.[374] Therefore, "[i]n elections with margins within 25%, the Big Three acting together will often have the power to determine the outcome."[375] The climate cartel believed that "[t]he 'big three' have the clout to change outcomes" of shareholder votes,[376] so "[i]n their own way, they hold the fate of humanity in their hands[;] . . . all they need to do is check the 'FOR' box instead of 'AGAINST.'"[377] As a result, it sought to "[r]ecruit a critical mass to actively vote in support of climate resolutions, including the major passive asset managers BlackRock . . . , Vanguard and State Street."[378]

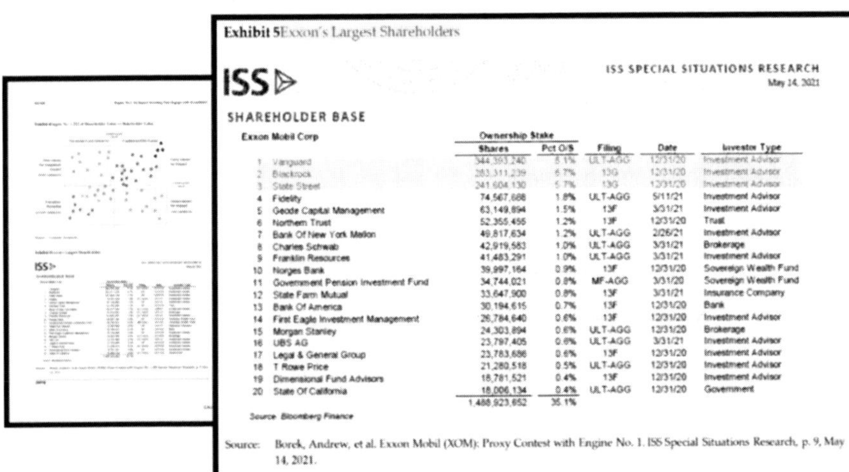

Exhibit 5 Exxon's Largest Shareholders

ISS SPECIAL SITUATIONS RESEARCH
May 14, 2021

SHAREHOLDER BASE

Exxon Mobil Corp

		Ownership Stake				
		Shares	Pct O/S	Filing	Date	Investor Type
1	Vanguard	344,393,240	8.1%	ULT-AGG	12/31/20	Investment Advisor
2	Blackrock	283,311,239	6.7%	13G	12/31/20	Investment Advisor
3	State Street	241,604,130	5.7%	13G	12/31/20	Investment Advisor
4	Fidelity	74,567,688	1.8%	ULT-AGG	5/11/21	Investment Advisor
5	Geode Capital Management	63,149,894	1.5%	13F	3/31/21	Investment Advisor
6	Northern Trust	52,355,455	1.2%	13F	12/31/20	Trust
7	Bank Of New York Mellon	49,817,634	1.2%	ULT-AGG	2/26/21	Investment Advisor
8	Charles Schwab	42,919,583	1.0%	ULT-AGG	3/31/21	Brokerage
9	Franklin Resources	41,483,291	1.0%	ULT-AGG	3/31/21	Investment Advisor
10	Norges Bank	39,997,164	0.9%	13F	12/31/20	Sovereign Wealth Fund
11	Government Pension Investment Fund	34,744,021	0.8%	MF-AGG	3/31/20	Sovereign Wealth Fund
12	State Farm Mutual	33,647,900	0.8%	13F	3/31/21	Insurance Company
13	Bank Of America	30,194,615	0.7%	13F	12/31/20	Bank
14	First Eagle Investment Management	26,784,640	0.6%	13F	12/31/20	Investment Advisor
15	Morgan Stanley	24,303,894	0.6%	ULT-AGG	12/31/20	Brokerage
16	UBS AG	23,797,405	0.6%	ULT-AGG	3/31/21	Investment Advisor
17	Legal & General Group	23,783,686	0.6%	13F	12/31/20	Investment Advisor
18	T Rowe Price	21,280,518	0.5%	ULT-AGG	12/31/20	Investment Advisor
19	Dimensional Fund Advisors	18,781,521	0.4%	13F	12/31/20	Investment Advisor
20	State Of California	18,006,134	0.4%	ULT-AGG	12/31/20	Government
		1,488,923,652	35.1%			

Source: Bloomberg Finance

Source: Borek, Andrew, et al. Exxon Mobil (XOM): Proxy Contest with Engine No. 1. ISS Special Situations Research, p. 9, May 14, 2021.

---

372 Fichtner et al., *supra* note 74, at 313.
373 CALPERS_4388 at CALPERS_4392.
374 BEBCHUK & HIRST, *supra* note 75, at 9.
375 Caleb N. Griffin, *Margins: Estimating the Influence of the Big Three on Shareholder Proposals*, 73 SMU L. REV. 409, 420 (2020).
376 CERES1260 at CERES1262.
377 CERES13432 at CERES13433.
378 CERES60818 at CERES60819.

The "Big 3"—Vanguard, BlackRock, and State Street Global Advisors—were, by far, ExxonMobil's largest shareholders.[379]

i. The "Big 3" Joined NZAM Months Before the ExxonMobil Board "Refreshment"

In 2021, just months before the ExxonMobil board "refreshment" vote, BlackRock, State Street Global Advisors, and Vanguard joined GFANZ's "net-zero" asset managers alliance, NZAM.[380] In a 2021 letter to investors, BlackRock committed to engaging "companies to disclose a business plan aligned with the goal of limiting global warming well below 2°C, consistent with achieving net zero global greenhouse gas emissions by 2050."[381] BlackRock joined the GFANZ Principals Group, the alliance's governing body, as a result of its membership in NZAM.[382]

After joining GFANZ, State Street Global Advisors President and CEO Cyrus Taraporevala similarly declared that State Street Global Advisors was "especially keen to leverage [its] position as one of the world's largest asset managers to raise awareness of the systemic risks associated with climate change."[383] In its initial "net-zero" commitment, State Street Global Advisors warned the companies it invests in that it "expect[s] all of client assets" in its "net-zero" committed portfolio and "invested in carbon-intensive industries to be (i) achieving net zero or (ii) aligned to net zero" by 2040.[384] State Street Global Advisors believes "ESG/sustainability factors should be considered alongside traditional, material investment factors when making investment decisions."[385]

---

379 CALPERS_4388 at CALPERS_4405.

380 See Signatory Disclosure: BlackRock, supra note 71; see also Signatory Disclosure: State Street Global Advisors, supra note 72; Signatory Disclosure: Vanguard, NET ZERO ASSET MANAGERS INITIATIVE (Dec. 4, 2022), https://web.archive.org/web/20221204011812/https://www.netzeroassetmanagers.org/signatories/vanguard/.

381 Letter from BlackRock Inc. Global Executive Committee to BlackRock Clients (2021), https://www.blackrock. com/corporate/investor-relations/2021-blackrock-client-letter.

382 *See* GFANZ2454 at GFANZ2469.

383 The Net Zero Asset Managers Initiative Grows to 87 Investors Managing $37 Trillion, with the World's Three Largest Asset Managers Now Committing to Net Zero Goal, NET ZERO ASSET MANAGERS INITIATIVE (Apr. 20, 2021), https://www.netzeroassetma nagers. org/the-net-zero-asset-managers-initiative-grows-to-87-investors-managing-37-trillion-with-the-worlds-three-largest-asset-managers-now-committing-to-net-zero-goal/.

384 Signatory Disclosure: State Street Global Advisors, supra note 72.

385 Invest in ESG ETFs, STATE ST. GLOB. ADVISORS, https://www.ssga.com/nl/en_gb/institutional/ic/capabilities/esg (last visited Dec. 6, 2024).

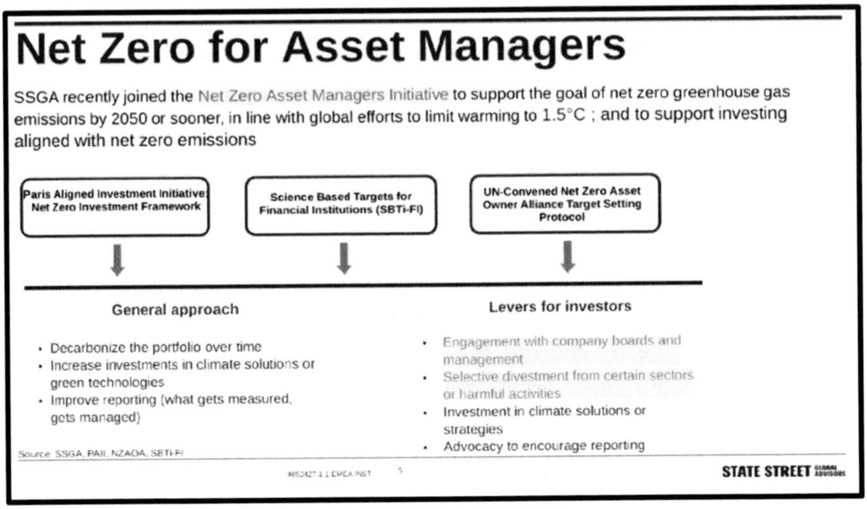

NZAM expected its "Big 3" members to pursue "net zero," including through engagement and selective divestment.[386]

Vanguard, likewise, recognized after it joined NZAM that it would have to pressure companies to reduce GHG-emitting production to reach its own "net-zero" commitments. Because the vast majority of Vanguard's assets are in fixed index funds, "divestment[] is not an option," but "engagement is a key lever available to meaningfully move index funds towards net zero through encouraging companies to transition to a low carbon economy. Furthermore, substantial shifts in the global economy are required for market based indexes to achieve net zero emissions by 2050 or sooner."[387] Accordingly, Vanguard expected that its membership in NZAM would require it to "more explicitly communicate [its] escalation policies and, with that, prepare for [its] voting record to meaningfully shift to less management support."[388] When Vanguard joined NZAM, "it committed to clear escalation policy to support the [net-zero] transition."[389]

ii. The Climate Cartel Pushed BlackRock and State Street Global Advisors to Join Climate Action 100+

While the "Big 3" joined NZAM, they each initially refused to join Climate Action 100+. Vanguard communicated to the Climate Action 100+ Steering

---

[386] SSGA-HJC.106608 at SSGA-HJC.106612.
[387] VAN_HJC_30030 at VAN_HJC_30032.
[388] VAN_HJC_31168 at VAN_HJC_31168.
[389] *Id.*

Committee "concerns about acting in concert and about being attacked in the media if [it] did not support Climate Action 100+ positions."[390] In addition, Vanguard identified "flagged" proposals by the initiative as "an example of . . . [an] activity that made [it] stay away from CA100+."[391] Likewise, State Street Global Advisors initially had "concerns" about joining CA100+, including "collusion," being "required to or . . . being pressured to vote in a certain way," and the "perception of engaging or voting as a block."[392]

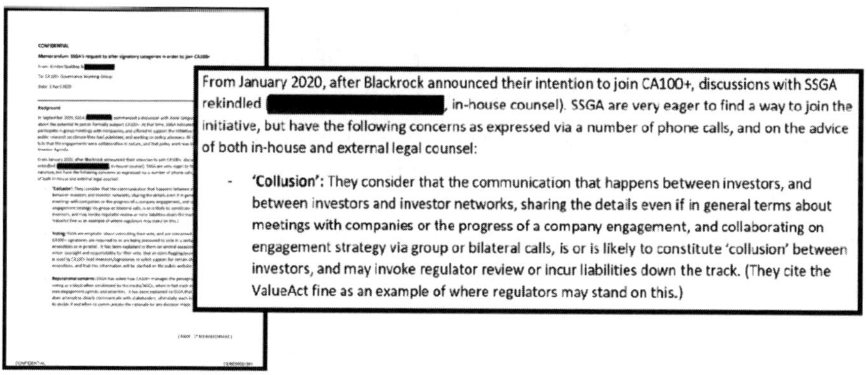

From January 2020, after Blackrock announced their intention to join CA100+, discussions with SSGA rekindled [redacted], in-house counsel). SSGA are very eager to find a way to join the initiative, but have the following concerns as expressed via a number of phone calls, and on the advice of both in-house and external legal counsel:

- **'Collusion':** They consider that the communication that happens between investors, and between investors and investor networks, sharing the details even if in general terms about meetings with companies or the progress of a company engagement, and collaborating on engagement strategy via group or bilateral calls, is or is likely to constitute 'collusion' between investors, and may invoke regulator review or incur liabilities down the track. (They cite the ValueAct fine as an example of where regulators may stand on this.)

State Street Global Advisors initially hesitated to join Climate Action 100+ because of "collusion."[393]

Similarly, BlackRock "didn't initially join CA100+ (in December 2017)," in part, "on the basis that . . . collaborative engagement was considered a core component of CA100+ membership but engaging alongside other investors may trigger regulatory issues for BlackRock."[394] Additionally, BlackRock viewed Climate Action 100+'s prior campaigns to vote against the ExxonMobil board as "extremely irresponsible."[395] It was concerned that "if [it] [were] a part of CA100+ [it] w[ould] be called out if [it] d[id]n't vote with [its] peers, regardless of [its] independent assessment of the merits of a particular proposal or vote no campaign."[396]

---

[390] CERES35007 at CERES35009.
[391] VAN_HJC_31264 at VAN_HJC_31264.
[392] CERES1561 at CERES1561 (emphasis omitted).
[393] *Id.*
[394] BLK-HJC-100207 at BLK-HJC-100207.
[395] BLK-HJC-119259 at BLK-HJC-119259.
[396] BLK-HJC-99648 at BLK-HJC-99648.

In November 2019, BlackRock and Ceres held a closed-door meeting to discuss BlackRock's participation in Climate Action 100+.[397] After Ceres pushed BlackRock to improve its voting record on ESG-related shareholder proposals, BlackRock communicated its "frustration" with Ceres, stating that it "do[es] the work and others take the credit."[398] More specifically, BlackRock said it "is 'leagues ahead of' PIMCO,'" another large institutional investor that supported 87% of ESG shareholder resolutions in 2019,[399] "and others that get the public credit fore [sic] being ESG leaders."[400]

Nevertheless, BlackRock would not join CA100+.[401] It expressed concern with what it called "a CA100+ problem," where "an [asset owner] client of [BlackRock] asked [it] to engage for [the asset owner] on CA100+ asks, contrary to some other [BlackRock] clients' views and interests" and expressed to Ceres that elevating the views of Climate Action 100+ asset owners above its other clients "would be a conflict of interest."[402] BlackRock concluded succinctly: "We don't do collective action/engagements. Too risky."[403]

In response, the climate cartel resolved "to sort of go to war with" BlackRock to pressure it to join Climate Action 100+.[404] Ceres believed that its "relationships with BlackRock . . . and State Street [made] it hard for [Ceres] [to] publicly pressure them forcefully enough to move them."[405] Instead, Climate Action 100+ recognized that its "asset owner partners have considerable leverage; they represent these large asset managers' most valuable clients,"[406] so it "convened large asset owners to align around using their influence as clients" to pressure BlackRock to join CA100+.[407]

In January 2020, two months after it met with Ceres, BlackRock joined Climate Action 100+.[408] According to Ceres, "BlackRock was influenced to join CA100+ after [Japan's Government Pension Investment Fund]," a

---

[397] CERES69955 at CERES69956.
[398] *Id*
[399] Jackie Cook, ESG Proxy Resolutions Find More Support in 2019, MORNINGSTAR (Feb. 28, 2020), https://www. morningstar.com/sustainable-investing/esg-proxy-resolutions-find-more-support-2019.
[400] CERES69955 at CERES69955.
[401] *See id.* at CERES69956.
[402] *Id.*
[403] *Id.*
[404] CERES13432 at CERES13432.
[405] *Id.*
[406] CERES50191 at CERES50195.
[407] CERES12698 at CERES12698.
[408] CERES14474 at CERES14476.

Climate Action 100+ member and the world's largest pension fund worth $1.7 trillion,[409] "withdrew $50B from BlackRock, and when Scottish Widows," a U.K.-based financial institution that contracts BlackRock to manage assets worth €30 billion,[410] "insisted on putting CA100+ into [its] asset management contract with BlackRock."[411] Further, Scottish Widows assumed "a formal role in overseeing BlackRock's participation in Climate Action 100+."[412]

Likewise, in "January 2020, after Blackrock announced [its] intention to join CA100+, discussions with [State Street Global Advisors] rekindled."[413] Similarly, Ceres convened asset owners to communicate to State Street Global Advisors, "[i]f you don't join in, you are suspect—and if you are not transparent in how you are engaging focus companies on climate, then your credibility is in question."[414] Later that year, State Street Global Advisors joined Climate Action 100+ as well.[415] In its announcement, State Street Global Advisors declared,

> [T]oday, it is clear we need to work not only side-by-side on these issues, but hand-in-hand. In joining Climate Action 100+, we look forward to sharing with our peers what we've learned in our engagements with more than 600 companies across multiple industries and markets on climate-related issues since 2014. We also are excited about this opportunity to work closely with other asset managers and asset owners to scale our impact on climate change risks.[416]

---

409 *Id.* at CERES14474.

410 David Thorpe, *BlackRock Wins £30 Billion of Scottish Widows Assets*, FT ADVISER (Oct. 12, 2018), https://www.ftadviser.com/investments/2018/10/12/blackrock-wins-30bn-of-scottish-widows-assets/.

411 CERES63234 at CERES63234.

412 CERES37770 at CERES37791.

413 CERES1561 at CERES1561

414 CERES50191 at CERES50195.

415 Cyrus Taraporevala, *Why We're Joining Climate Action 100+*, LINKEDIN (Nov. 30, 2020), https://www.linkedin.com/pulse/why-were-joining-climate-action-100-cyrus-taraporevala/?trackingId=1uioXQF%2BRVe46JvMa%2Fs7 Kw%3D%3D.

416 *Id.*

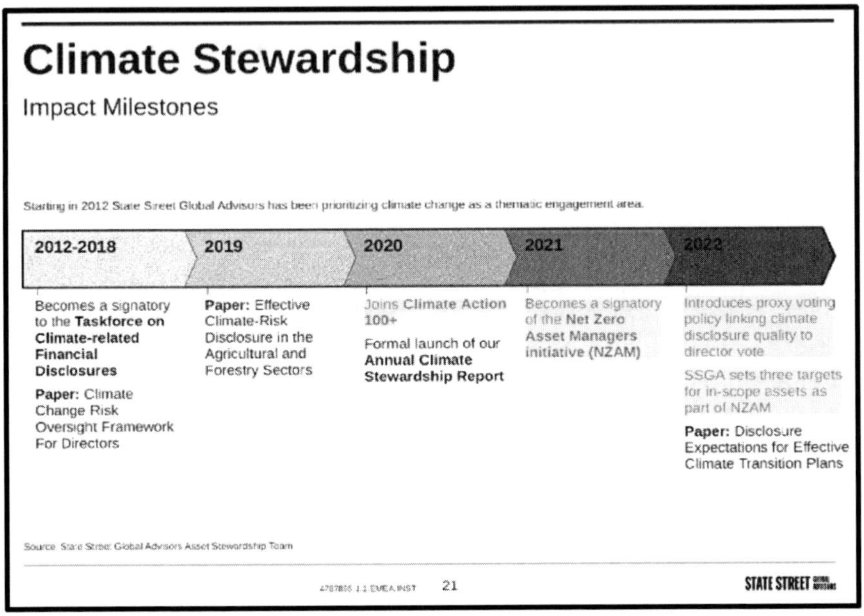

By early 2021, State Street Global Advisors had joined Climate Action 100+ and NZAM.[417]

iii. The Climate Cartel Pressured the "Big 3" to Vote in Lockstep to "Refresh" the ExxonMobil Board

With the "Big 3" in NZAM and BlackRock and State Street Global Advisors in Climate Action 100+, the climate cartel prepared to escalate its engagement against ExxonMobil. Upon joining the initiative, BlackRock discussed with Ceres that because of its "large asset size and resultant percentage holdings," BlackRock "may face constraints under US regulations."[418] Specifically, it stated that "forming a concert group . . . is precluded in US listed companies."[419] However, BlackRock offered that it could "engage in parallel" with the Climate Action 100+ engagement groups,[420] while "report[ing] [its] progress into a shared portal or survey."[421] BlackRock emphasized that the

[417] SSGA-HJC.219333 at SSGA-HJC.219356.
[418] CERES40303 at CERES40304.
[419] *Id.*
[420] *Id.*
[421] CERES64411 at CERES64413.

"notion of not in the same room is key."[422] It later agreed to "engage in parallel" several U.S. companies for Climate Action 100+, including ExxonMobil.[423]

However, BlackRock did not initially support the climate cartel's pressure campaign at ExxonMobil. In March 2020, when Ceres suggested a "possible Board refresh strategy" at ExxonMobil, BlackRock stated that it "was not drawn to commit but might."[424] Privately, the climate cartel considered "a mechanism to kick out BlackRock if [it] vote[d] wrong."[425] Ceres expressed that "[l]egally, [BlackRock] [would] have to vote on [its] own, CA100+ [couldn't] require a vote, but [it] c[ould] highlight in advance and afterwards how they voted."[426]

In advance of its 2020 campaign to "vote no" against the ExxonMobil board, Edward Mason of the Church Commissioners, a Climate Action 100+ ExxonMobil engagement group lead investor, publicly described "Exxon's business strategy as 'a challenge of the most fundamental order to the purpose of CA100+.' [Mason] said that he expect[ed] investors participating in CA100+—including its 'newest members'—to 'consider their voting options very carefully.'"[427] Internally, BlackRock understood Mason's warning "to

---

[422] CERES40303 at CERES40304. "[M]erely parallel conduct that could just as well be independent action," without "something more," is not itself unlawful. *Bell Atlantic Corp. v. Twombly*, 550 U.S. 544, 557, 560 (2007). However, parallel conduct "that stems from" an agreement—such as the climate cartel engaging in parallel to execute its agreement to reduce disfavored output reduction—may violate Section 1 of the Sherman Act. *Id.* at 553; *see, e.g., supra* Section I.B; CLIMATE CONTROL: EXPOSING THE DECARBONIZATION COLLUSION IN ENVIRONMENTAL, SOCIAL, AND GOVERNANCE (ESG) INVESTING, *supra* note 4, at 2–4; HOW GOVERNOR TIM WALZ'S STATE PUBLIC PENSION FUND COLLUDES WITH THE CLIMATE CARTEL TO RAISE ENERGY PRICES FOR AMERICAN CONSUMERS, *supra* note 84, at 8–10; Compl. ¶¶ 113–51, *Texas v. BlackRock*, No. 6:24-cv-00437 (Nov. 27, 2024). Likewise, a "hub- and-spoke" conspiracy violates Section 1 of the Sherman Act. *United States v. Huff*, 609 F.3d 1240, 1243–44 (11th Cir. 2010). "A hub-and-spoke conspiracy occurs where a central core of conspirators recruits separate groups of co- conspirators to carry out the various functions of the illegal enterprise. The core conspirators move from spoke to spoke, directing the functions of the conspiracy. Where the various spokes are aware of each other and of their common aim there is a single conspiracy." *Id.* (cleaned up). Accordingly, investors who collude or coordinate through a climate coalition intermediary in pursuit of their net-zero agreement may violate antitrust law, even when they are not in the "same room." *See id.*

[423] *See* CERES40145 at CERES40149; CERES64411 at CERES64413; *see also* CERES40300 at CERES40301.

[424] CERES40303 at CERES40304.

[425] CERES23915 at CERES23915.

[426] CERES24367 at CERES24379.

[427] BLK-HJC-100517 at BLK-HJC-100519.

mean that there w[ould] be repercussions for the newest members of CA100+," including BlackRock, "if [they] d[id]n't toe the line and vote consistent with the NYS/Church Commissioners' campaign."[428]

In the months leading up to the ExxonMobil board "refreshment," BlackRock, State Street Global Advisors, and Vanguard met with Ceres staff and the ExxonMobil engagement group's lead investors,[429] with BlackRock speaking to Ceres staff "daily."[430] In the end, BlackRock voted for three of the climate cartel's slate of directors; State Street and Vanguard both voted for two.[431] None of the "Big 3" asset managers voted against any board candidate on the climate cartel's slate.[432] On the day of the board "refreshment" vote, BlackRock emailed Anne Simpson of lead investor CalPERS and then-chair of the Climate Action 100+ Steering Committee, stating, "Thanks for your communications in the run up to the Exxon meeting. I know part of our vote at Exxon is no secret"[433] Simpson responded, "[A] new day at Exxon . . Appreciate all the good work BlackRock is doing. It makes a difference."[434]

6. The Climate Cartel "Flagged" the Vote to Signal Climate Cartel Support

In the middle of the board "refreshment" campaign, as it privately pressured the "Big 3" for support, the climate cartel critically "flagged" the vote to signal for broad investor signatory support. The climate cartel believes that "flagging" shareholder votes "[s]trengthen[s] [its] ability to win key votes"[435] by putting shareholder voting campaigns "firmly on the agenda of investors."[436] Shareholder vote "flagging" also aids the climate cartel with monitoring the voting records of its investor signatories and identifying "defectors" from the cartel's strategic goals.

After a shareholder vote is "flagged," the climate cartel "will track vote results of all flagged and alerted shareholder resolutions [and] specifically track[] the voting of CA100+signatories."[437]

---

428 *Id.* at BLK-HJC-100517.

429 *See* CALPERS_3163 at CALPERS_3163; *see also* CERES57210 at CERES57210; CERES62869 at CERES62959; SSGA-HJC.41084; VAN_HJC_91738.

430 CERES62869 at CERES62959.

431 CALPERS_4388 at CALPERS_4401.

432 CERES15811.

433 BLK-HJC-674 at BLK-HJC-675.

434 *Id.*

435 CERES10442 at CERES10447.

436 Transcribed Interview of Andrew Logan, *supra* note 11, at 85:12–87:3.

437 CERES10442 at CERES10448.

The climate cartel uses shareholder vote "flagging" to efficiently coordinate investor signatory support. Ceres recommends that Climate Action 100+ engagement "co-leads discuss and make a unified decision about flagging a resolution" and do so "as early as possible to build a longer runway for build-the-vote efforts."[438] Once "flagged," the climate cartel campaigns to secure board support for the shareholder vote. According to Ceres,

> Flagging a vote (e.g. . . . director vote) elevates the vote to the proxy season page of the Climate Action 100+ website, with the message that investors should take the vote into consideration for the current proxy season. Ceres supports flagged votes by coordinating build-the-vote efforts, including setting up one-on-one calls with the largest asset managers, sharing key climate-related votes on CA100+ webinars for a proxy advisor and investor audience, and including flagged votes in various communications strategies. Recent Ceres research shows higher votes on CA100+ flagged resolutions amongst both CA100+ signatories and investors broadly.[439]

Historically, climate cartel members have expressed legal concerns with the Climate Action 100+ "flagging" process. As recently as March 2022, lead investors of the Climate Action 100+ ExxonMobil engagement group told Ceres,

> I hate to dig up all of the legal discussions we've had in the past about the flagging process, but I'm still not comfortable with it. First, my firm doesn't pre-declare votes, so the 'public declaration' is a problem. Second, it sounds like something that should be filed with the SEC as an exempt solicitation. I'm also not comfortable being the "gate keeper" who gets to decide which proposals get a bump and which ones don't.[440]

In April 2021, the month before the ExxonMobil board "refreshment," the Climate Action 100+ Steering Committee discussed the prospect of flagging director votes.[441] Ceres staff warned that with "director votes . . . we are entering the realm of control of the company and we must be aware that the size of the initiative might draw the attention of regulators due to our potential

---

438 CALPERS_28645 at CALPERS_28647.
439 *Id.*
440 *Id.* at CALPERS_28646.
441 CERES35007 at CERES35009–11.

for influencing votes,"[442] but nevertheless concluded that Climate Action 100+ is "in a position to educate signatories; flagging votes allows [it] to tell investors which issues are a priority for the initiative."[443]

In February 2021, after conversations with "Charlie [Penner] from Engine 1," Ceres staff communicated internally that it would be "critical . . . for the [ExxonMobil] director vote to be flagged as part of the CA100+ process [F]lagging the vote would do a lot to help raise the profile of the whole effort to promote change at Exxon."[444] Ceres staff believed, "Conversely, not flagging the vote would look like [it was] giving the green light to Blackrock et al to not be supportive of the slate."[445]

Ultimately, Climate Action 100+ flagged the "board refreshment at Exxon, proposed by Engine No. 1."[446] Alongside the Climate Action 100+ "flag," it announced that the vote was "supported by CalPERS and CalSTRS, which both filed letters with the SEC to allow them to share views with other shareholders, as well as leading investors [Equity Ownership Services] at Federated Hermes, New York City Comptroller's Office, New York State Common Retirement Fund, [Legal & General Investment Management] and Aviva Investors."[447] Soon after that, the climate cartel used the Climate Action 100+ "flag" status to "buil[d] momentum" for the ExxonMobil board refreshment campaign[448] and put "investor signatories . . . under significant pressure to vote affirmatively for [votes] . . . flagged by the initiative."[449]

---

[442] *Id.* at CERES35009.
[443] *Id.*
[444] CERES17169 at CERES17171.
[445] *Id.*
[446] *2024 Proxy Season & Flagged Shareholder Votes*, *supra* note 121.
[447] *Id.*
[448] CERES4013 at CERES4015.
[449] In Stunning Vote, Shareholders Elect Two New Directors Put Forth by Shareholders at ExxonMobil, Seeking Climate Expertise and Action, supra note 32.

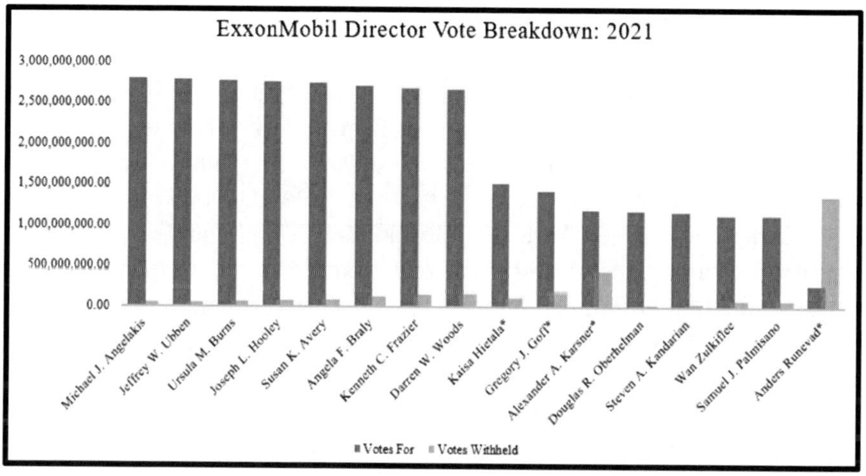

*After being "flagged," three of the four Engine No. 1-proposed director candidates secured majority support and seats on ExxonMobil's board (*Engine No. 1-proposed candidates).*[450]

After the climate cartel successfully completed its board "refreshment" at ExxonMobil, Ceres concluded that the "[f]lagging process was key to moving the Exxon vote."[451] Ceres found that the "flagging of [the] director vote" was a "critical strategic move on [the] part of CA100+" because it communicated to investor signatories that they are "being scrutinized on how [they] vote."[452] To illustrate "how powerful the flagging process is," Ceres recounted that it "heard pushback" from BlackRock, which was "not eager for [Climate Action 100+] to flag votes like this."[453] Yet, BlackRock voted for three of the climate cartel's four ExxonMobil board candidates.[454] Ceres concluded that the flagging process was the "engine behind Engine 1."[455]

7. The Climate Cartel Collaborated with the Proxy Advisor Duopoly to Broaden Its Influence

In advance of the 2021 ExxonMobil board "refreshment" campaign, a top "[p]riorit[y]" for the climate cartel was to "[a]lign [p]roxy [a]dvisors" with its

---

[450] See ExxonMobil Corporation, Current Report (Form 8-K) (June 2, 2021).
[451] CERES1307 at CERES1311.
[452] CERES9645 at CERES9645.
[453] *Id.*
[454] CALPERS_4388 at CALPERS_4401.
[455] CERES9645 at CERES9645.

goals.[456] The climate cartel recognized that the proxy advisor duopoly of ISS and Glass Lewis would significantly strengthen its influence because "[m]ost institutional investors rel[y] on professional proxy advisory firms to decide how to vote their shares, as the investment firms did not have the personnel to evaluate proxy statements from the thousands of companies in which they invested."[457] Within the proxy advisor market, ISS and Glass Lewis dominate with a combined market share of approximately 97%[458] and contracts with investors managing a combined $50.4 trillion in assets.[459] As such, the proxy advisor duopoly's voting recommendations can swing votes anywhere from 10% to 30%.[460] Consequently, if the climate cartel "could persuade those two firms to support its candidates . . . they would likely prevail."[461]

During the board "refreshment" campaign, the climate cartel leveraged the proxy advisory duopoly by aligning its voting recommendations with the Climate Action 100+ Net Zero Company Benchmark. It first "engaged with ISS and Glass Lewis on the CA100+ Net Zero Benchmark . . . framework to ensure the analysts can utilize the company assessments when making recommendations about . . . company directors that are failing to ensure that shareholder requests via CA100+ are being met."[462] As a result of its engagement, "in early 2021, both proxy advisors updated their guidance and/or policies to better align with CA100+ goals."[463]

The climate cartel also engaged ISS and Glass Lewis to formally recommend that their client bases vote in favor of its campaign. The year before, in 2020, Glass Lewis recommended 100% of shareholder resolutions flagged by CA100+, while ISS recommended in favor of all but two.[464] The following year, the climate cartel continued to "engage both ISS and Glass Lewis on the resolutions and votes flagged by CA100+."[465] On May 11, 2021, Anne Simpson of lead investor CalPERS and then-chair of the Climate Action 100+ Steering Committee, informed Courteney Keatinge, Head of ESG at

---

456 CERES20116 at CERES20117.
457 CALPERS_4388 at CALPERS_4392.
458 Larcker, *supra* note 93.
459 Shu, *supra* note 94, at 6.
460 Larcker, *supra* note 93.
461 CALPERS_4388 at CALPERS_4392.
462 CERES57272 at CERES57276.
463 *Id.*; *see, e.g.*, ISS-HJC-241950 at ISS-HJC-241960 (scheduling a meeting with Edward Mason to discuss "how development of [ISS's] climate policy could be better tailored to meet the . . . needs of . . . climate-committed investors . . . in advance of ISS's planned "review of [its] current climate policy").
464 CERES20116 at CERES20128.
465 CERES57272 at CERES57276; *see also* CERES14602 at CERES14602; CALPERS_34029.

Glass Lewis, that the shareholder votes at ExxonMobil "will be . . . iconic . . . so Glass Lewis' take on this will be vitally important."[466] Subsequently, both ISS and Glass Lewis endorsed three of the climate cartel's director nominees.[467]

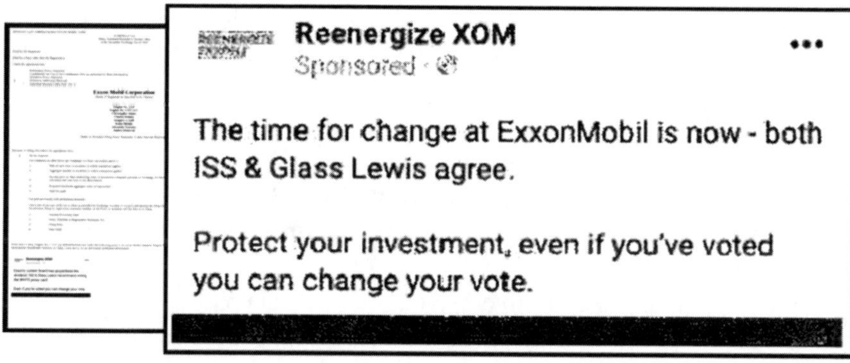

Engine No. 1 used the proxy advisor duopoly's influential endorsement to build support.[468]

In addition, Glass Lewis worked with the climate cartel to build investor support for the board "refreshment" campaign. In March 2021, Glass Lewis convened a "Climate Webinar" and allowed Ms. Simpson and Ceres staff to "[p]resent the benchmark" and "[d]iscuss philosophy on voting against directors" to its investor clients.[469] Before the webinar, Glass Lewis emailed Ms. Simpson and Ceres staff to "let [Glass Lewis] know if there are any questions [they] d[id] not want to be asked/topics [they] d[id] not wish to discuss."[470]

Glass Lewis also collaborated with the climate cartel to "develop[] and launch[] in advance of the 2021 Proxy Season a CA100+ Alert Mechanism."[471] To further influence the investment market to support the climate cartel's efforts, Glass Lewis's "Alert Mechanism" "informs its client base of CA100+ flagged shareholder resolutions. This mechanism, which was developed following extensive engagement between CA100+ and Glass Lewis, helps ensure that CA100+ flagged resolutions rise to the top of the

---

466 CALPERS_13337 at CALPERS_13337.
467 CALPERS_4388 at CALPERS_4401.
468 ENGINENO1-118HJC-PROD-313 at ENGINENO1-118HJC-PROD-313.
469 CALPERS12784 at CALPERS_12788.
470 Id.
471 CERES57272 at CERES57276.

voting queue for all investors crucially bringing added attention to a wider audience of investors."[472] According to Glass Lewis, it utilizes the "Climate 100 Flag and alerting mechanism" to notify its 1,300 institutional investor clients of Climate Action 100+ priority shareholder votes.[473] Notably, Glass Lewis asks Climate Action 100+ to notify it about "which proposals [it is] flagging about 30 days prior to the [shareholder] meeting" so that it does not miss considering "flagged" shareholder proposals "when [it is] performing [its] analysis and making recommendations."[474]

F. Commit: The Climate Cartel's Successful "Refresh" of ExxonMobil's Board Secured "Net-zero" Climate Commitments

From the beginning, the ultimate "goal of the campaign" was to force ExxonMobil to make "net-zero" commitments or at least "get[] the company to set Scope 1 and 2 targets for its emissions . . . [and] make progress against the benchmark that Climate Action 100+ ha[d] set up to measure company performance."[475] By installing new board members at ExxonMobil with "strong competence on climate issues," the climate cartel sought to "advance [its] climate agenda."[476] Almost immediately after the board "refreshment" vote, Ceres staff noted that it had "calls set up with [the] new Exxon board members," which gave it "more access" to the company.[477]

However, even before it secured seats on ExxonMobil's board of directors, the climate cartel's campaign secured numerous climate commitments. On December 14, 2020—one week after Engine No. 1 sent its letter to the ExxonMobil board announcing the "refreshment" campaign—ExxonMobil committed to a "2025 greenhouse gas emission reduction plan: intensity of upstream emissions to drop by 15–20%; methane intensity by 40–50%; flaring intensity by 35–45%."[478] On December 24, 2020, ExxonMobil emailed CalPERS, which had filed a Scope 3 emissions disclosure proposal, stating that "it will begin providing scope 3 (indirect emissions that include

---

472 Id.

473 GL2161 at GL2164.

474 GL4683 at GL4683.

475 Transcribed Interview of Andrew Logan, supra note 11, at 62:11, 103:8–105:13.

476 CERES46032 at CERES46039.

477 CERES62869 at CERES62955.

478 *ExxonMobil Announces Emission Reduction Plans; Expects to Meet 2020 Goals*, ExxonMobil (Dec. 14, 2020), https://corporate.exxonmobil.com/news/news-releases/2020/1214_exxonmobil-announces-2025-emissions- reductions_expects-to-meet-2020-plan.

the consumption and use of the company's products) on an annual basis" beginning in January 2021 and requested that CalPERS therefore "withdraw [its] shareholder proposal this year."[479] In response, Engine No. 1 stated, "[N]othing in ExxonMobil's stated plans better positions it for long-term success in a world seeking to reduce total greenhouse gas emissions" and urged investors to still elect its slate of "new directors."[480]

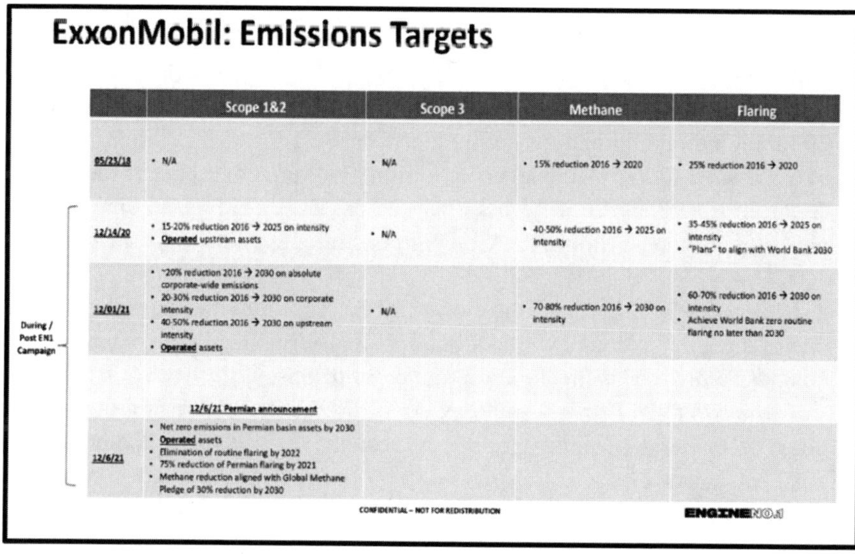

ExxonMobil: Emissions Targets

	Scope 1&2	Scope 3	Methane	Flaring
05/23/18	• N/A	• N/A	• 15% reduction 2016 → 2020	• 25% reduction 2016 → 2020
12/14/20	• 15-20% reduction 2016 → 2025 on intensity • Operated upstream assets	• N/A	• 40-50% reduction 2016 → 2025 on intensity	• 35-45% reduction 2016 → 2025 on intensity • "Plans" to align with World Bank 2030
12/01/21	• ~20% reduction 2016 → 2030 on absolute corporate-wide emissions • 20-30% reduction 2016 → 2030 on corporate intensity • 40-50% reduction 2016 → 2030 on upstream intensity • Operated assets	• N/A	• 70-80% reduction 2016 → 2030 on intensity	• 60-70% reduction 2016 → 2030 on intensity • Achieve World Bank zero routine flaring no later than 2030
	12/6/21 Permian announcement			
12/6/21	• Net zero emissions in Permian basin assets by 2030 • Operated assets • Elimination of routine flaring by 2022 • 75% reduction of Permian flaring by 2021 • Methane reduction aligned with Global Methane Pledge of 30% reduction by 2030			

During / Post EN1 Campaign

CONFIDENTIAL – NOT FOR REDISTRIBUTION

ENGINE NO.1

During the board "refreshment" campaign, ExxonMobil made a series of "net-zero" commitments for the first time.[481]

Less than a year after the climate cartel successfully installed three directors on ExxonMobil's board, the company announced "its ambition to achieve net zero greenhouse gas emissions for operated assets [*i.e.*, Scope 1 and 2] by 2050," including "net-zero plans for Permian Basin operations."[482] In May 2022, Engine No. 1 boasted,

---

[479] CALPERS_2882 at CALPERS_2882, CALPERS_2883.

[480] *Engine No. 1 Comments on ExxonMobil's New Emissions Targets*, REENERGIZE EXXON (Dec. 14, 2020), https:// reenergizexom.com/materials/engine-no-1-comments-on-exxonmobils-new-emissions-targets.

[481] ENGINEN01-118HJC-PROD-12640 at ENGINEN01-118HJC-PROD-12640.

[482] *ExxonMobil Announces Ambition for Net Zero Greenhouse Gas Emissions by 2050*, EXXONMOBIL (Jan. 18, 2022), https://corporate.exxonmobil.com/news/news-releases/2022/0118_exxonmobil-announces-ambition-for-net-zero-greenhouse-gas-emissions-by-2050. The Permian Basin is the most productive oil shale reserve in the U.S., accounting for forty-three percent of U.S. oil production. *See* Editorial Board, *Biden's Raid on the*

Since the election of Engine No. 1's candidates to the Board, Exxon has taken a multitude of actions to reduce its emissions footprint and has begun to lay the foundations for a viable low-carbon business strategy:

November 2021: Committed to investing $15 billion over the next six years to advance low-carbon solutions.

December 2021: Announced that the Company had achieved 2025 Scope 1 and 2 greenhouse gas (GHG) emissions reduction targets nearly four years early.

December 2021: Announced new 2030 Scope 1 and 2 GHG emissions reduction targets.

December 2021: Announced net-zero GHG emissions in Permian by 2030, including eliminating flaring in the basin.

January 2022: Announced ambition for net-zero Scope 1 and 2 GHG emissions by 2050 across operated assets, including an annually published report outlining the Company's strategic plans to achieve net zero.

January 2022: Added the Low Carbon Solutions business unit as one of three units around which the Company is organized. The other two business units are Upstream and Product Solutions.

March 2022: Brought in an external hire in Dan Ammann, former head of General Motors' Cruise, to lead the Low Carbon Solutions business unit.[483]

Ceres expressed that ExxonMobil's new "net-zero" commitments "represent[ed] a pretty significant turnaround in the company's approach."[484] For "many years[,] [ExxonMobil] had this very strong position that it simply didn't believe in the idea of setting targets"—"if [it] d[id]n't set targets for [its] production, [it] [was] not going to set targets on emissions."[485] ExxonMobil's newfound net-zero commitments suggest "the new board members' influence is starting to be felt."[486]

Now that ExxonMobil has "some climate competent board members," Anne Simpson stated following the election of the climate cartel's three directors, the company should "take the Climate Action 100+ benchmark assessment and set targets for each of the . . . elements, which includes aligning

---

Permian Basin, WALL ST. J. (June 29, 2022), https://www.wsj.com/articles/the-epas-de-facto-fracking-curb-permian-basin-environmental-protection-agency-ozone-11656109324?.

483 *ExxonMobil: One Year Later*, *supra* note 40 (emphasis added).

484 CALPERS50277 at CALPERS50277.

485 Transcribed Interview of Andrew Logan, *supra* note 11, at 103:15–18.

486 CALPERS50277 at CALPERS50277.

[capital expenditures] with Paris" and "time bound emissions reductions across the whole life cycle of emissions, from cradle to grave."[487] Ms. Simpson concluded, "[T]he job . . . [has] only just begun."[488]

III. The Climate Cartel Plans to Escalate Its "Net-zero" Agenda Across the U.S. Economy

After its successful ExxonMobil board "refreshment" campaign in 2021, the climate cartel not only continued its campaign against the company but also leveraged its success to pressure more U.S. companies to adopt "net-zero" commitments.[489] Ceres considers it "obvious that companies don't like to have activist campaigns targeting them. And so [Ceres] [thought] [that] if a campaign were successful at one company, it could cause other companies to take notice."[490] As a result, following the 2021 campaign, Ceres shaped its "ambitions and strategies . . . to reflect and take advantage of [t]he Exxon effect."[491] Now that "three climate activists" have joined ExxonMobil's board following "extensive CA100+ engagement," Ceres boasted in a 2021 funding progress report, "[A]ll focus companies facing major climate risk are on notice that they cannot ignore investors without subjecting their board members to possible replacement. Simply put, investors are no longer requesting, but effectively requiring companies to address the risks and opportunities of the energy transition."[492]

---

[487] CALPERS_4585 at CALPERS_4587.

[488] *Id.*; *see also* CERES92232.

[489] Most recently, in 2024, ExxonMobil was forced to sue climate cartel members Arjuna Capital and Follow This after they filed a shareholder resolution calling for ExxonMobil to "accelerat[e] the pace of emission reductions . . . across Scope 1, 2, and 3" after the Biden-Harris Administration's SEC refused to remove it from consideration by shareholders and despite the company explaining to the activists in meetings that "Scope 3 is demand for [its] products." Complaint ¶¶ 8, 66, 105, *ExxonMobil Corp. v. Arjuna Capital, LLC*, No. 4:24-cv-00069-P (N.D. Tex. 2024), ECF No. 1; ARJUNA012822. After the two activist investors withdrew the shareholder resolution, the United States District Court for the Northern District of Texas dismissed Exxon's claim as moot. *ExxonMobil Corp. v. Arjuna Capital, LLC*, No. 4:24-cv-00069-P (N.D. Tex. 2024).

[490] Transcribed Interview of Andrew Logan, *supra* note 11, at 84:17–19.

[491] CERES91503 at CERES91508.

[492] CERES29333 at CERES29338; *see also* CERES110550.

A. The Climate Cartel Leverages the "Exxon Effect" to Pressure Other "Focus Companies"

At the heart of the climate cartel's efforts to leverage the "Exxon Effect" was its "partnership" with Engine No. 1.[493] Following its success with ExxonMobil, Engine No. 1 sought out new opportunities to force "structural change"[494] at other U.S. companies and, along with other climate cartel members, "use the victory at Exxon as a way to push for broader change in the [Oil & Gas] sector."[495] As Ceres recognized, "in the wake of the vote, Engine 1 had a certain prominence in the investment world and certainly had the attention of other oil and gas companies [I]t allowed them to engage companies at a level that they wouldn't have been able to before for an investor of their size."[496]

1. The Climate Cartel Continues to Collude to Secure "Net-zero" Commitments from U.S. Energy Companies

In fall 2021, Engine No. 1 and the climate cartel began engaging several U.S. energy companies—including Chevron Corporation, ConocoPhillips Company, Pioneer Corporation, Devon Energy, and Occidental Petroleum Corporation[497]—"to define a set of 203[0] goals for oil companies."[498] According to Ceres, it "had a large role in shaping the list of asks. They are all consistent with what is in the CA100+ benchmark."[499] By December 2021, Ceres reported that

> Engine #1 [was] now doing confidential direct negotiations with 5 companies leveraging their success with Exxon, to get 5 companies to agree to goals that align with this framework. Once those 5 companies agree, Ceres will take the lead on mobilizing investors to spur a larger number of companies across the industry as a whole, to adopt the same

---

493 Transcribed Interview of Andrew Logan, *supra* note 11, at 114:6–115:18.

494 Brower & Aliaj, *supra* note 312.

495 CERES112405 at CERES112405.

496 Transcribed Interview of Andrew Logan, *supra* note 11, at 116:23–117:2.

497 *See* CERES111348 at CERES111349; *see also* ENGINENO1-118HJC-PROD-21416 at ENGINENO1-118HJC-PROD-21418–19; ENGINENO1-118HJC-PROD-21412 at ENGINENO1-118HJC-PROD-21414–16.

498 CERES85006 at CERES85009; *see also* CERES112405 at CERES112405; CERES112655 at CERES112656.

499 CERES111552 at CERES111552.

> goals. A key part of our role will be to move big investors to sign onto this effort.[500]

In January 2022, Engine No. 1 and Ceres met with representatives from the five companies to negotiate their joining the Oil and Gas Methane Partnership (OGMP) 2.0.[501] As "a partnership between the oil and gas industry and the United Nations," the OGMP 2.0 is a framework commitment for energy companies to "measure and manage their methane emissions."[502] As a result of the climate cartel's efforts, all five energy companies joined OGMP.[503] In September 2022, Ceres recounted the extent of the climate cartel's success:

> [F]ollowing extensive engagement by Ceres, our partners at Engine No. 1, and others, ConocoPhillips, Devon, and Pioneer announced that they will join the [Oil and Gas Methane Partnership] (OGMP).
>
> . . . OGMP membership requires that companies shift from estimating their methane emissions to directly measuring these emissions—forcing companies to confront and address the true extent of their emissions across oil fields. The commitment also requires that companies reach near-zero methane emissions by 2025, requiring immediate, near-term action to dramatically cut their emissions by capping wells, ending flaring, and addressing leakage from pipelines and other distribution methods. The robust nature of these commitments required CEO- and board-level buy-in from each company prior to its OGMP commitment; Ceres, Engine No. 1, and our partners had multiple conversations with these companies' senior leadership to get the commitments over the finish line. Indeed, as this process approached its conclusion and companies were wavering, Ceres mobilized some of [its] largest investors to make clear to the companies just how important this commitment was to them. [Ceres was then] working with [its] investors to build on the Engine1 [*sic*] commitments and make OGMP something that all companies in the sector are expected to commit to.[504]

---

[500] *Id.*
[501] Transcribed Interview of Andrew Logan, *supra* note 11, at 107:7–110:25.
[502] *Id.* at 108:23–114:23.
[503] *Id.* at 114:9–120:3.
[504] CERES59762 at CERES59764–65.

2. The Climate Cartel Has Hijacked the Proxy Advisor Duopoly and Expanded Its "Net-zero" Campaign "Beyond CA100+"

In addition to the oil and gas sector, the climate cartel is leveraging "[t]he Exxon effect" to secure "net-zero" climate commitments throughout the entire U.S. economy. Following the ExxonMobil board "refreshment," Ceres declared, "[Its] efforts to compel companies, through direct engagement and investor pressure have helped to catalyze change through [its] global campaigns like Climate Action 100+, and [it is] achieving results beyond [its] goals."[505] Ceres boasted that "[i]n CA100+ [it] . . . created a new model for organizing investor pressure on companies," which "has been a game changer."[506]

This "new model" involved the climate cartel integrating its goals into the proxy advisor duopoly's voting recommendations. In 2022, ISS changed its proxy voting guidelines,[507] announcing that for companies "on the current Climate Action 100+ Focus Group list," it will recommend that investors "generally vote against or withhold from the incumbent chair of the responsible committee (or other directors on a case-by-case basis) in cases where ISS determines that the company is not taking the minimum steps needed to understand, assess, and mitigate risks related to climate change to the company and the larger economy."[508] Additionally, until 2024—after it received a subpoena from the Committee relating to its oversight of U.S. antitrust law[509]—Glass Lewis's proxy voting guidelines stated that it would consider recommending votes against boards of directors at "companies identified by groups including Climate Action 100+" that fail to provide sufficient "climate-related disclosures."[510]

---

505 CERES91503 at CERES91503.

506 CERES84991 at CERES84991.

507 *See* CERES382 at CERES392.

508 *United States Proxy Voting Guidelines: Benchmark Policy Recommendations*, INST. S'HOLDER SERVS. 17 (2024), https://www.issgovernance.com/file/policy/active/americas/US-Voting-Guidelines.pdf.

509 Letter from Rep. Jim Jordan, Chairman, Comm. on the Judiciary, to Nichol Garzon-Mitchell (Dec. 20, 2023).

510 *2023 Policy Guidelines*, GLASS LEWIS (2023), https://www.glasslewis.com/wp-content/uploads/2022/11/US-Voting-Guidelines-2023-GL.pdf.

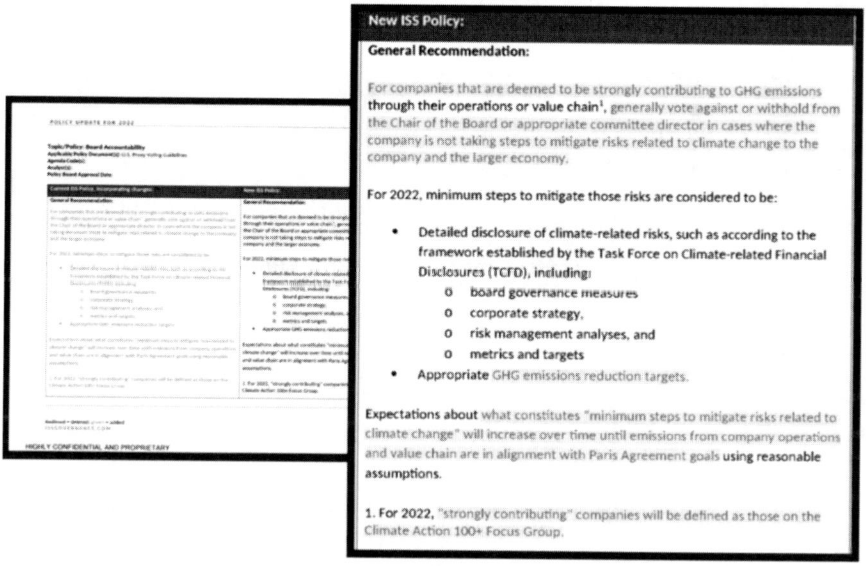

New ISS Policy:

General Recommendation:

For companies that are deemed to be strongly contributing to GHG emissions **through their operations or value chain**[1], generally vote against or withhold from the Chair of the Board or appropriate committee director in cases where the company is not taking steps to mitigate risks related to climate change to the company and the larger economy.

For 2022, minimum steps to mitigate those risks are considered to be:

- **Detailed disclosure of climate-related risks, such as according to the framework established by the Task Force on Climate-related Financial Disclosures (TCFD), including:**
  - **board governance measures**
  - **corporate strategy,**
  - **risk management analyses, and**
  - **metrics and targets**
- **Appropriate** GHG emissions reduction targets.

Expectations about what constitutes "minimum steps to mitigate risks related to climate change" will increase over time until emissions from company operations and value chain are in alignment with Paris Agreement goals **using reasonable assumptions.**

1. For 2022, "strongly contributing" companies will be defined as those on the Climate Action 100+ Focus Group.

ISS will recommend voting against board members of companies "strongly contributing to GHG emissions," defined as the "Climate Action 100+ Focus Group."[511]

In June 2021, almost immediately following the ExxonMobil board "refreshment," Ceres staff remarked that "[o]nce the proxy advisors are using [the Climate Action 100+ Net Zero Company Benchmark], it will extend far beyond CA100+."[512] Today, ISS's benchmark reports rely on data and analytics "from both the CA100+ benchmark and Carbon Tracker" for U.S. oil and gas companies, such as "ExxonMobil . . . Chevron [], ConocoPhillips [], Phillips 66 [], Occidental [], and Valero []."[513]In addition, both ISS and Glass Lewis proxy recommendations warn their investor clients if Climate Action 100+ has targeted a company on its "focus list."[514]

---

[511] ISS-HJC-6949 at ISS-HJC-6949.
[512] CERES62869 at CERES62955.
[513] ISS-HJC-47144 at ISS-HJC-47145.
[514] *See, e.g.*, GL11764 at GL11778; ISS-HJC-40907 at ISS-HJC-40919.

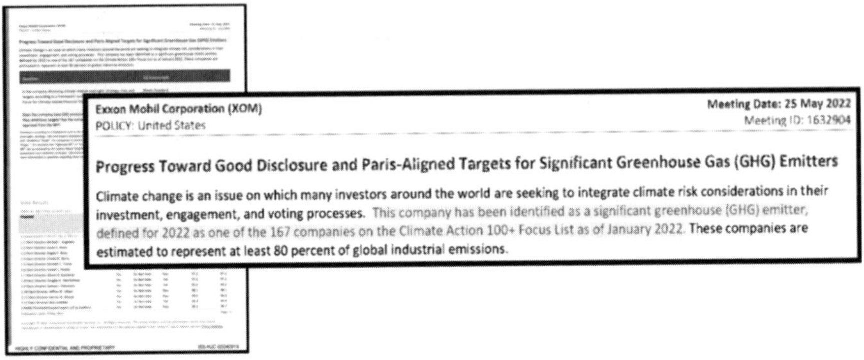

Exxon Mobil Corporation (XOM)
POLICY: United States

Meeting Date: 25 May 2022
Meeting ID: 1632904

Progress Toward Good Disclosure and Paris-Aligned Targets for Significant Greenhouse Gas (GHG) Emitters

Climate change is an issue on which many investors around the world are seeking to integrate climate risk considerations in their investment, engagement, and voting processes. This company has been identified as a significant greenhouse (GHG) emitter, defined for 2022 as one of the 167 companies on the Climate Action 100+ Focus List as of January 2022. These companies are estimated to represent at least 80 percent of global industrial emissions.

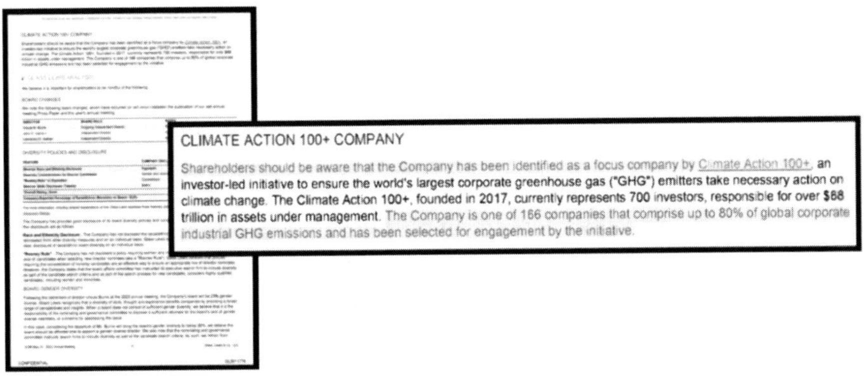

CLIMATE ACTION 100+ COMPANY

Shareholders should be aware that the Company has been identified as a focus company by Climate Action 100+, an investor-led initiative to ensure the world's largest corporate greenhouse gas ("GHG") emitters take necessary action on climate change. The Climate Action 100+, founded in 2017, currently represents 700 investors, responsible for over $68 trillion in assets under management. The Company is one of 166 companies that comprise up to 80% of global corporate industrial GHG emissions and has been selected for engagement by the initiative.

The proxy advisor duopoly, using almost identical language, warns investors about companies on the Climate Action 100+ "focus list."[515]

Furthermore, the climate cartel has broadened its climate crusade beyond the Climate Action 100+ "focus list." Through the Climate Action 100+ "focus list," the climate cartel targets 170 of the world's largest companies with $10.3 trillion in market capitalization in sectors ranging from aviation to oil and gas to agriculture.[516] After its success at ExxonMobil, however, Ceres felt

> poised to use and adapt that model to a much wider set of companies, beyond the CA100+ [focus] list. Here's the transformation: The Ceres proposed program takes a group of investors who have been acting individually with individual companies and turns them into effective

---

[515] *Compare* ISS-HJC-40907 at ISS-HJC-40919, *with* GL11764 at GL11778.

[516] *Companies*, *supra* note 126.

cohorts committed to a focus list of companies and thereby transforming sectors.[517]

Ceres believed that it could expand its work through Climate Action 100+ because "[o]nly recently d[id] [it] have rapidly growing pools of investors to recruit from," including "Ceres['s] rapidly growing network, CA100[+] signatories, NZAM commitments, and more."[518] In April 2022, Climate Action 100+ funder CIFF agreed to grant Ceres $4 million to launch its "Beyond CA100+" program, which Climate Action 100+ would use to "turn the process of investors doing corporate engagement work from an individual activity . . . into a collective activity."[519]

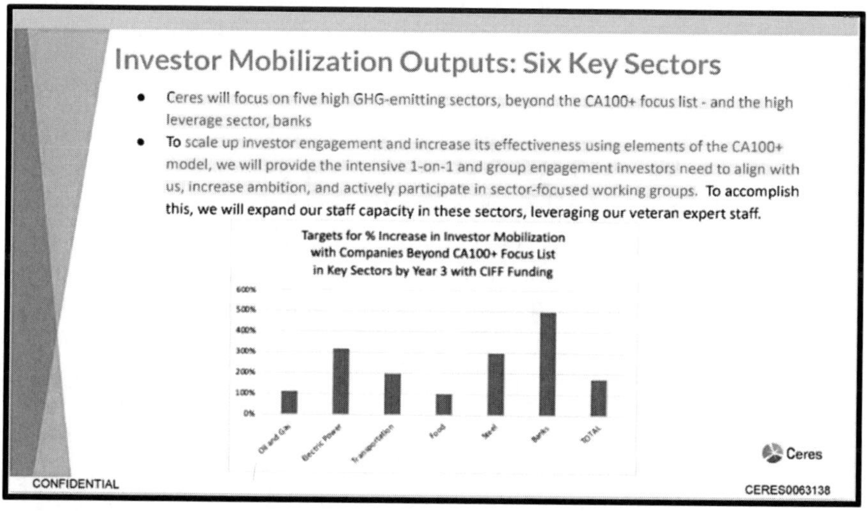

Using the "CA100+ model," Ceres has expanded its "net-zero" pressure campaigns beyond Climate Action 100+ "focus list" companies.[520]

The climate cartel's "Beyond CA100+" project organizes investor engagements against many sectors of the U.S. economy, including oil and gas, transportation, food, steel, and electric power.[521] It also targets consumers by putting "investor pressure on the users" of "transport, utilities, [and]

---

[517] CERES84991 at CERES84991 (emphasis omitted).
[518] *Id.* at CERES84992.
[519] *Id.*
[520] CERES63134 at CERES63138.
[521] CERES63134 at CERES63138–39; *see generally* CERES115490.

manufacturing like steel and cement."[522] The climate cartel reasons that for "Exxon [to] kick[] it[]s oil habit," its "customers need to switch" from oil to other energy alternatives.[523] Accordingly, the "Beyond CA100+" project targets banks that finance GHG- emitting assets, electric & gas utilities that rely on GHG-emitting power sources, and steel produced using GHG-emitting infrastructure.[524] To pressure these sectors to make "net-zero" commitments, "Ceres has developed specific guidance for investors on key board governance campaigns and is now poised to promote investor action to vote against specific board members or run an alternate board slate."[525]

By targeting a wide array of sectors, the climate cartel aims for a U.S. economy-wide transformation to "net zero." For example, the climate cartel plans to escalate engagements against existing Climate Action 100+ "focus companies" in the U.S. automotive industry by pressuring companies up and down their supply chain. According to Ceres,

> The major vehicle manufacturers (Daimler, Paccar, VW, Volvo, Ford, GM, etc.) are already on the Climate Action 100+ focus company list and the CA100+ investor network partners are staffed for these engagements. Yet there is still a key impact opportunity to engage directly with vehicle manufacturers' major suppliers who are not on the focus list, such as Meritor, Magna, Eaton, and Dana, Bosch, and Cummins, as they shift to electrification from internal combustion. . . . Ford and GM have robust CA100+ engagement teams, though GM is tough to move. Toyota is different and could use more pressure in that CA100+ engagement. *Toyota needs an Exxon-type engagement*.[526]

"Put more simply," Ceres explained, the climate cartel is "aiming to influence a critical mass of critical companies [O]nce this number of companies has committed to action, that action becomes the norm to which all companies are held."[527]

---

[522] CALPERS_4585 at CALPERS_4585–86.
[523] *Id.* at CALPERS_4585.
[524] *See* CERES70576 at CERES70579–88.
[525] CERES84991 at CERES84996.
[526] *Id.* at CERES85001 (emphasis added).
[527] *Id.* at CERES85003.

3. With the "Exxon Effect," the Climate Cartel Has Secured More Votes and More "Net-zero" Commitments

The climate cartel's engagements have been increasingly destructive since the ExxonMobil board "refreshment." According to Ceres, its "global partnerships have helped to catalyze more aggressive commitments from companies and [its] new initiatives like Net Zero Asset Managers . . . have grown during their short tenure resulting in new commitments from key asset managers, asset owners, and banks."[528] Ceres credits this increasing success to "the unprecedented Exxon factor, where shareholders (led by Ceres board members at NY State Common, CalSTRS, and CalPERS) voted to replace 3 corporate members at Exxon—a shockwave heard around the globe."[529] With the potential threat of similar board "refreshments" at other U.S. companies, the climate cartel believes that its "[s]hareholder resolutions now have sharper teeth."[530]

In particular, since the 2021 ExxonMobil board "refreshment," Climate Action 100+- flagged votes have received "a high level of attention from the market including proxy advisors such as Glass Lewis and ISS."[531] According to a Climate Action 100+ survey, of the shareholder resolutions flagged in the year after the "refreshment" campaign, "72% either received majority support . . . or achieved above 30% in support."[532] Also that year, the shareholder resolutions filed by the climate cartel were increasingly more aggressive: "[o]f the 75 submitted proposals related to GHG reduction strategies or targets, at least 55 specifically request inclusion of Scope 3 emissions."[533]

---

[528] CERES91503 at CERES91503.

[529] *Id.*

[530] CERES92232 at CERES92235 (emphasis omitted).

[531] CERES62503 at CERES62506.

[532] CERES62685 at CERES62693 (emphasis omitted). Ceres notes that according to "Glass Lewis, 20% or more support has been considered the threshold by which company boards should demonstrate some level of responsiveness to address the concerns of shareholders." Id.

[533] Brigid Rosati et al., A Look Back at the 2022 Proxy Season, HARV. L. SCH. F. CORP. GOVERNANCE (Oct. 23, 2022), https://corpgov.law.harvard.edu/2022/10/23/a-look-back-at-the-2022-proxy-season/.

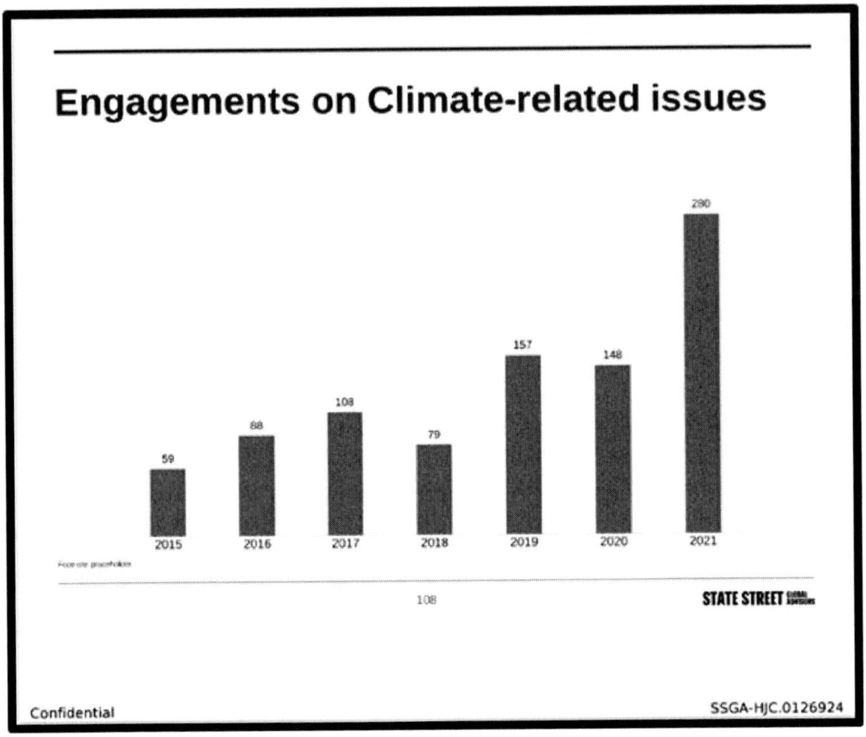

In 2021, its first year as a member of both NZAM and Climate Action 100+, State Street Global Advisors increased its climate-related engagements.[534]

In fact, since 2021, "[t]he implication of the flagged vote which is likely to garner majority support may be enough to drive company action" and secure "net-zero" commitments.[535] While voting support for Climate Action 100+ flagged resolutions and climate- related resolutions generally declined in 2022 and 2023, the cartel still noted that "[t]he threat of flagging the resolutions proved successful in pushing companies to make commitments ahead of [annual general meetings] in return for a withdrawal."[536] The year after the ExxonMobil board "refreshment," the cartel highlighted that "more than 100 climate resolutions were withdrawn as agreements were reached before the vote, a 50% increase from 2021," and Climate Action 100+ is responsible for

[534] SSGA-HJC.126804 at SSGA-HJC.126924.
[535] CERES62503 at CERES62506.
[536] CERES62708 at CERES62709.

at least 27 of th[ose] withdrawn resolutions for agreements."[537] Significantly, in the words of one cartel member, "[t]his is nearly double from the 2021 proxy season in which 15 resolutions were withdrawn for agreements."[538] In the wake of the ExxonMobil board "refreshment," the climate cartel bragged that "[t]he headwinds" to its pressure campaigns "are dying as is the fossil fuel industry."[539]

When Climate Action 100+ was formed in 2017, "only five focus companies had set net zero commitments."[540] Moreover, before the ExxonMobil board vote in 2021, only three climate-related shareholder resolutions had received majority support at oil and gas companies.[541] Today, after five years of the climate cartel's "net-zero" pressure campaigns, Climate Action 100+ boasted that 77% of its "focus companies" have committed to net zero for at least Scope 1 and Scope 2 emissions, 90% have committed to disclosing their emissions, 59% have committed to disclosing how they implement GHG-emission reductions, and 93% now have a board-level committee dedicated to climate change.[542] According to a member of the Climate Action 100+ Steering Committee,

> [O]ne of the initiative's strengths is that it has emboldened investors to ask and expect more of companies. Investors are more willing to vocalize their demands. The development of the benchmark and sharing of information has supported engagements and built confidence. We have facilitated a true collaborative model that has spread ambition.[543]

If companies resist its "net-zero" agenda in the future, the climate cartel remains committed to "refresh" their board members. Ceres continues to believe that board "refreshment" campaigns are "the only compulsory mechanism[s] that [passive investors] have" to secure "net- zero" commitments.[544] Following the 2021 ExxonMobil board "refreshment" vote,

---

[537] CERES62685 at CERES62693 (emphasis omitted).
[538] *Id.*
[539] CERES96350 at CERES96350.
[540] CERES22224 at CERES22225.
[541] CERES13003 at CERES13015.
[542] *Climate Action 100+ Net Zero Company Benchmark 2.0 2023 Results*, CLIMATE ACTION 100+ 7 (2023), https:// www.climateaction100.org/wp-content/uploads/2023/10/2023-Key-Findings.pdf; *Progress Update 2023*, CLIMATE ACTION 100+ 4 (2023), https:// www.climateaction100.org/wp-content/uploads/2024/01/Climate-Action-100-Progress-Update-2023.pdf.
[543] CERES66494 at CERES66498.
[544] Transcribed Interview of Andrew Logan, *supra* note 11, at 52:16–20.

CalSTRS warned, "While the ExxonMobil board election is the first of a large U.S. company to focus on the global energy transition, it will not be the last."[545] While it may not "necessarily be an Engine#1 in every case,"[546] referring to the hedge fund's takedown of the ExxonMobil board, Ceres staff believes that several of the climate cartel's engagements are in "need [of] something more transformational," with "Berkshire Hathaway and Toyota bubbl[ing] up from [its] lists" as possible focus company candidates for a future board "refreshment."[547] As it escalates and expands its crusade, the climate cartel will continue to ask, "Who is the next Exxon?"[548]

B. The Climate Cartel Demands That U.S. Companies Adopt "Transition Plans" to Shrink Production

The most recent and, perhaps, the final chapter in the climate cartel's "net-zero" crusade is to pressure U.S. companies to implement "transition plans" to eliminate GHG emissions from their business strategies entirely. According to GFANZ Co-Chair Mark Carney, "A transition plan is—as the English would say, it is what it says on the tin it's a company outlining what its current emissions are, what it intends to do, what its strategy is in order to reduce those emissions."[549] In contrast to the climate cartel's calls for climate "disclosures" or "targets," implementing "transition plans" requires U.S. companies to specify how it plans to "phase out" emitting assets "before the end of their technically useful life."[550] Critically, for U.S. oil and gas companies, net-zero "transition plans" would "ultimately require the phaseout of fossil fuels."[551] According to climate cartel member, As You Sow, its strategy is "to go to every public company[] to get a climate transition plan that's aligned with the Climate Action 100+ benchmarks."[552]

---

545 In Stunning Vote, Shareholders Elect Two New Directors Put Forth by Shareholders at ExxonMobil, Seeking Climate Expertise and Action, supra note 32.
546 CERES62869 at CERES62956.
547 Id. at CERES62940.
548 Id.
549 Transcribed Interview of Mark Carney, supra note 47, at 17:18–18:2.
550 *Id.* at 98:3–100:21, 110:7–111:7.
551 Deposition of Andrew Behar, *supra* note 328, at 25:13–27:11.
552 TRILLIUM_1759 at TRILLIUM_1771.

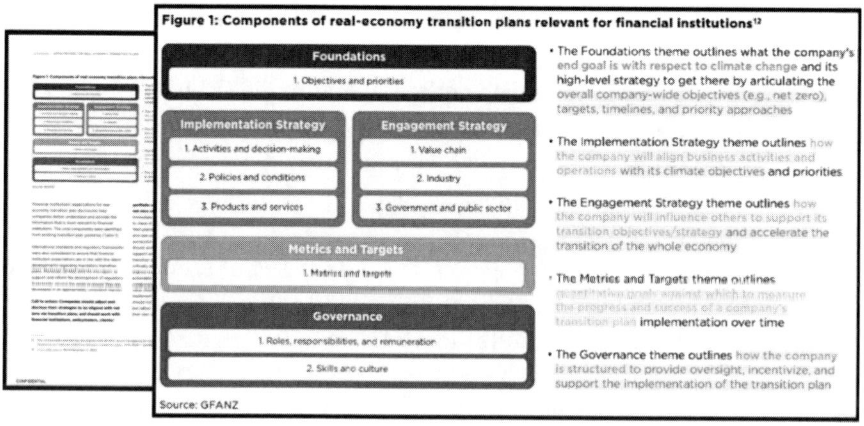

GFANZ expects companies to implement detailed "transition plans" to shift their business activities to "net zero."[553]

1. Climate Action 100+'s "Phase 2" Requires U.S. Companies to Implement "Transition Plans" Despite Fiduciary Duty

On June 8, 2023, Climate Action 100+ announced its "Phase 2."[554] Because it believed "the need for urgent action on climate change by 2030 is clear . . . Climate Action 100+ has enhanced the three original goals to ask companies to not only disclose but to *implement* robust transition plans."[555] Ceres expects that Climate Action 100+'s "Phase 2" will include campaigns for "[s]cope 3 targets," which "implies moving away from fossil fuels," "[t]actic[s] . . . to increase engagement with boards to put more pressure on management," and a " focus[] on executive compensation to ensure targets get actually achieved."[556] The climate cartel's engagements will be "about *action* at this point, not just words/commitments/disclosure."[557] Because "[c]ompanies will not achieve zero emissions without transition plans for getting there,"[558] Climate Action 100+ investors will increasingly ask focus companies to adopt net-zero transition plans consistent with the CA100+ Net-Zero Company

---

553 GFANZ462 at GFANZ466.

554 *Climate Action 100+ Announces Its Second Phase*, CLIMATE ACTION 100+ (June 8, 2023), https://www.climate action100.org/news/climate-action-100-announces-its-second-phase/.

555 *Climate Action 100+ Phase 2: Summary of Changes*, CLIMATE ACTION 100+ 6 (2023), https://www.climateaction100.org/wp-content/uploads/2023/06/CA100-Phase-2-Sum mary-of-Changes.pdf (emphasis added).

556 CERES59121 at CERES59159.

557 *Id.* at CERES59160.

558 CERES61506 at CERES61508.

Benchmark's "stronger focus on emissions reductions" and "alignment with 1.5°C pathways."[559]

Before this "Phase 2" announcement, several of the Climate Action 100+ investor signatories expressed concerns about engaging companies to implement "transition plans" aligned with the Paris Agreement's 1.5°C goal. In late 2022, the Climate Action 100+ Steering Committee noted that if the initiative adopts "a clear goal of 1.5C" for its investor signatories' engagements, "some large US [asset managers] [would] not be[] able to commit to that from their legal perspectives."[560] In fact, "[t]wo signatories . . . explicitly stated that they w[ould] leave if the 1.5C/net zero references are too strong."[561] Additionally, the Steering Committee noted that Climate Action 100+-affiliated "lawyers [did] not think 1.5C is feasible and they d[id] not believe it aligns with the fiduciary duty (if CA100+ tries to tie fiduciary duty to 1.5C it would be legally challenged in the US)."[562] Ceres itself recognizes that engaging U.S. oil and gas companies to "implement transition plans" is a "fruitless exercise" because "they don't think of their business plan in terms of there being a transition."[563] Instead, climate cartel members like As You Sow have vaguely suggested that a U.S. oil company transitioning to "net zero" should, "rather than putting all of their [capital expenditure] into searching for more oil . . . invest some of it into other things like geothermal."[564] The Climate Action 100+ Steering Committee saw its "choice" as "whether CA100+ wants to keep [the concerned, large asset managers] in or not (i.e. 1.5C with a smaller coalition, or water it down and keep the bigger [asset managers])."[565]

Ultimately, Climate Action 100+ announced that in its "Phase 2," investor signatories must engage U.S. companies "to limit warming to 1.5°C" by "implement[ing] transition plans to deliver on robust targets."[566] Ceres now maintains that "[i]f an investor signatory refuses to participate in phase two . . . it [cannot] remain [a] [Climate Action 100+] investor signatory."[567]

---

[559] *Climate Action 100+ Phase 2: Summary of Changes*, *supra* note 555, at 15, 16.
[560] CERES73347 at CERES73369.
[561] *Id.* at CERES73348.
[562] *Id.* at CERES73370.
[563] Transcribed Interview of Andrew Logan, *supra* note 11, at 16:22–17:3.
[564] Deposition of Andrew Behar, *supra* note 328, at 75:4–76:3.
[565] CERES73347 at CERES73369.
[566] *Climate Action 100+ Phase 2: Summary of Changes*, *supra* note 555, at 7 (emphasis omitted).
[567] Transcribed Interview of Andrew Logan, *supra* note 11, at 141:8–142:11.

2. Climate Action 100+ Continues to Pursue Its "Phase 2" Agenda Even After Mass Withdrawals Following the Committee's Efforts

In the year after Climate Action 100+'s "Phase 2" announcement, dozens of investor signatories, including BlackRock, Inc. and State Street Global Advisors, left the initiative.[568] In its February 2024 withdrawal letter to the Climate Action 100+ Steering Committee, BlackRock explained that it "owes contractual and fiduciary duties to [its] clients and is subject to various antitrust and competition laws across various jurisdictions. Such obligations extend to [its] investment and stewardship activity."[569] Two months prior, the Committee subpoenaed BlackRock and State Street Global Advisors as part of its oversight of the adequacy and enforcement of U.S. antitrust laws.

On June 11, 2024, the Committee released an interim staff report detailing "evidence that a 'climate cartel' of left-wing environmental activists and major financial institutions has colluded to force American companies to 'decarbonize' and reach 'net zero.'"[570] A month later, on July 30, 2024, the Committee sent letters to Climate Action 100+'s U.S.-based investor signatories requesting they "preserve documents and provide information" about their participation in the initiative and efforts to impose ESG-related goals on U.S. companies.[571] Following the Committee's interim report and letters, at least 39 Climate Action 100+ investor signatories have withdrawn.[572] In total, since the Committee began its investigation in December 2022, at least 70 investor signatories have left Climate Action

---

[568] *See* Transcribed Interview of Andrew Logan, *supra* note 11, at 141:8–142:11. Simon Jessop, *Invesco Joins List of US Asset Managers to Exit CA100+ Climate Group*, REUTERS (Mar. 1, 2024), https://www.reuters.com/sustainability/invesco-joins-list-us-asset-managers-exit-ca100-climate-group-2024- 03-01/; *see also* Letter from Sean D. Reyes, Utah Attorney General, et al. to Climate Action 100+ Members 2 (Apr. 3, 2024).

[569] Letter from BlackRock to the Climate Action 100+ Steering Committee (Feb. 2, 2024) 1, https://www.blackrock.com/corporate/literature/publication/2024-our-participation-in-climate-action-100.pdf.

[570] *See* Climate Control: Exposing the Decarbonization Collusion in Environmental, Social, and GOVERNANCE (ESG) INVESTING, *supra* note 65, at i.

[571] See Press Release, H. COMM. ON THE JUDICIARY, Jordan and Massie Demand Information from Over 130 Companies Surrounding Their Involvement with Woke ESG Cartel Climate Action 100+, https://judiciary.house. gov/media/press-releases/jordan-and-massie-demand-information-over-130-companies-surrounding-their (July 30, 2024).

[572] Compare Investor Signatories, CLIMATE ACTION 100+ (June 3, 2024), https://web.archive.org/web/20240603171 029/https://www.climateaction100.org/whos-involved/investors/, with Investor Signatories, CLIMATE ACTION 100+, https://www.climateaction100.org/whos-involved/investors/ (last visited Dec. 6, 2024); see also Letters from former Climate Action 100+ investor signatories to Comm. (on file with the Comm.).

100+.[573] Notably, on December 1, 2024, U.S.-based asset manager Franklin Templeton, whose Global Head of Sustainability Anne Simpson helped found Climate Action 100+ and served as Chair of its Steering Committee during the ExxonMobil board "refreshment," left the initiative as well after receiving the Committee's letter.[574]

Nevertheless, the climate cartel remains committed to its radical "net-zero" agenda. As You Sow has previously described efforts to oppose the climate cartel's ESG agenda as "an orchestrated, expanding effort from the alt-right to derail ESG investing."[575] It maintains,

> *We can—we must—fight back.* We cannot cede ESG investing and corporate accountability, especially on climate and justice, to the alt- right. . . . This is an all-hands-on-deck moment. The scale and stridency of the right is absolute proof we're making a difference. *We have got to protect that progress.* We have got to protect and expand shareholders' ability to hold corporations accountable. *We cannot allow the right to steal ESG . . . the way they've stolen CRT* [Critical Race Theory].[576]

"[T]o stymy the right's attempts to block [it]," As You Sow has called for members of the climate cartel to "[e]xpand [its] capacity to file resolutions" and "conduct 'inside-outside' campaigns pressuring both corporations and asset managers to offer climate-safe investments, escalating as needed to litigation."[577]

In response to the "recent departures," the Climate Action 100+ Steering Committee stated that "[w]hile [it is] disappointed to see them go, hundreds of investor signatories remain committed Climate Action 100+ has been consistent in its fundamental purpose of ensuring the world's largest corporate greenhouse gas emitters take necessary action on climate change. *The initiative has always been action-orientated and about more than*

---

573 *Compare Investor Signatories*, CLIMATE ACTION 100+ (Nov. 14, 2022), https://web.archive.org/web/2022111418 4301/https://www.climateaction100.org/whos-involved/investors/, *with Investor Signatories*, CLIMATE ACTION 100+, https://www.climateaction100.org/whos-involved/investors/ (last visited Dec. 6, 2024); *see also* Letters from former Climate Action 100+ investor signatories to Comm. (on file with the Comm.).

574 *US Asset Management Giant Joins Climate Action 100+ Exodus*, RESPONSIBLE INV. (Dec. 6, 2024), https://www. responsible-investor.com/us-asset-management-giant-joins-climate-action-100-exodus/?utm_source=newsletter-daily&utm_medium=email&utm_campaign =ri-daily-bronze&utm_content=06-12-2024.

575 ARJUNA7490 at ARJUNA7492.

576 *Id.* at ARJUNA7493.

577 *Id.* (emphasis omitted).

disclosure."[578] Even without its most prominent investor signatories, Climate Action 100+ is willing to continue to pursue its agenda: "Remember we have clout—we don't necessarily need BlackRock to sign on to CA100+ to negotiate deals and get results."[579]

3. GFANZ Members—Including BlackRock and State Street Global Advisors— Demand "Transition Plans" to Be on the "Right Side of Climate History"

While not formally within Climate Action 100+, the "Big 3" and other large U.S.-based asset managers remain committed to impose the climate cartel's "net-zero" goals. BlackRock and State Street Global Advisors maintain participation in the climate cartel through membership in GFANZ, where BlackRock holds a leadership role in its Principals Group,[580] and asset manager's alliance, NZAM.[581] While Vanguard formally left GFANZ and NZAM in December 2022[582] and publicly maintains that it "does not use investment stewardship activities to pursue public policy objectives on environmental and social matters,"[583] Vanguard privately "called [GFANZ Vice-Chair and former SEC Chair Mary Schapiro] about a half an hour before they withdrew [from GFANZ and NZAM] to say they were withdrawing, not that they were walking away from their commitments."[584] In addition to the "Big 3" asset managers, other large U.S.- based investors continue to participate in the climate cartel as investor signatories of GFANZ and NZAM, including Fidelity International, J.P. Morgan Asset Management, Capital Group, Invesco, Franklin Templeton Investments, T. Rowe Price Group, Inc., Federated Hermes Limited, and AllianceBernstein Limited.[585]

---

[578] *Climate Action 100+ Reaction to Recent Departures*, CLIMATE ACTION 100+ (Feb. 26, 2024), https://www.climateaction100.org/news/climate-action-100-reaction-to-recent-depar tures/.

[579] CERES77099 at CERES77102.

[580] *About Us*, GFANZ, *supra* note 99.

[581] *Signatory Disclosure: BlackRock*, *supra* note 71.

[582] Ross Kerber & Tommy Reggiori Wilkes, *Vanguard's Climate Group Exit Shows Retail Investors Trail on ESG* (Jan. 12, 2023), https://www.reuters.com/business/sustainable-business/vanguards-climate-group-exit-shows-retail- investors-trail-esg-2023-01-12/.

[583] *Investment Stewardship: 2023 Annual Report*, VANGUARD 9 (2023), https://corporate. vanguard.com/content/dam/corp/advocate/investment-stewardship/pdf/ policies-and-reports/investment_stewardship_2023_annual_report. pdf.

[584] Transcribed Interview of Mary Schapiro, Vice Chair, GFANZ (Feb. 14, 2024) at 38:9–39:8 (emphasis added).

[585] *See Signatories*, NET ZERO ASSET MANAGERS INITIATIVE, https://www.netzeroasset managers.org/signatories/ (last visited Dec. 6, 2024).

Similar to Climate Action 100+, GFANZ and NZAM investor signatories, such as the "Big 3," engage U.S. companies to adopt "a net-zero transition plan . . . consistent with achieving net zero by 2050, at the latest, in line with global efforts to limit warming to 1.5 degrees C."[586] GFANZ warns that "companies that do not have credible transition plans may face higher costs and/or restricted access to financial products and services (e.g., higher costs of capital)."[587] As a result, U.S. companies "must think critically about how to revise their strategy to be aligned with net zero and then disclose it through actionable transition plans GFANZ urges both companies and financial institutions to be ambitious when developing transition plans."[588] GFANZ expects U.S. companies to adopt net-zero "transition plans" with "the breadth, specificity, [and] the ability to action that plan," so that investor signatories can "look at it and say, 'This is a good plan, I want to finance it,' or make judgments on the basis of those plans."[589]

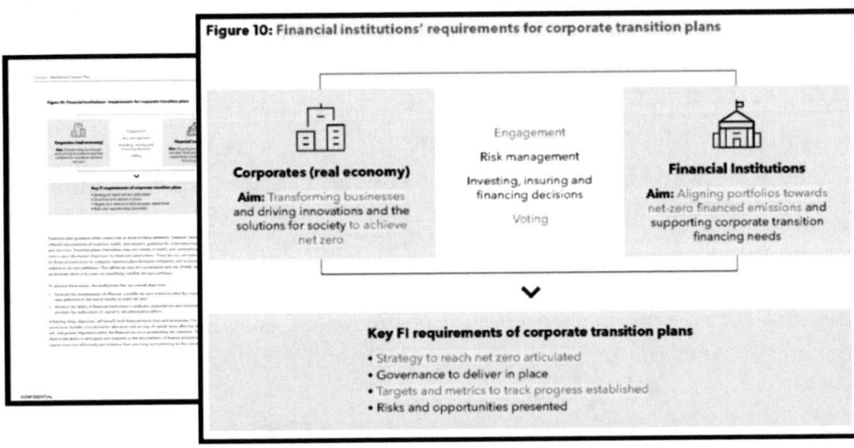

GFANZ members use engagement and voting to transform businesses to achieve "net zero."[590]

Every year, as a GFANZ and NZAM investor signatory, BlackRock conducts "approximately 2,500 engagements" and "vote[s] at approximately 16,000 shareholder meetings" to "integrat[e] environmental and social issues[] within an investment context"and "hold directors accountable for their action

586 GFANZ462 at GFANZ480.
587 *Id.* at GFANZ465.
588 *Id.* at GFANZ466–67.
589 Transcribed Interview of Mark Carney, *supra* note 47, at 110:21–111:7.
590 GFANZ10786 at GFANZ10841.

or inaction."[591] Last year, BlackRock conducted1,402 climate-related engagements.[592] BlackRock maintains "climate risk" as "one of its five key priorities for engagement."[593]

Likewise, to impose GFANZ and NZAM's net-zero "transition plan" agenda, State Street Global Advisors continues "climate investing . . . to foster change and provide momentum to the transition to net zero The goal is to assist those companies who have the will and a planned net zero pathway, while penalizing those who don't."[594] As part of its NZAM "campaign," State Street Global Advisors engages U.S. companies to adopt net-zero "transition plans" with "[i]ntended [o]utcomes" including "holding directors accountable" and an "increase proportion of financed emissions engaged in line with [its] NZAM target."[595] Last year, State Street Global Advisors conducted 162 engagements surrounding "climate-related topics," and engaged with 85 companies to reinforce their climate transition plans, including companies "within the Energy, Utilities, and Materials sectors."[596] Because of its status as a "signator[y] of [NZAM]," State Street Global Advisors believes that, somehow, "assessing corporate Climate transition plans has become part of [its] fiduciary duty."[597]

---

591 *BlackRock Investment Stewardship*, BLACKROCK 3, 19 (2020), https://www.blackrock.com/corporate/literature/publication/blk-profile-of-blackrock-investment-stewardship-team-work.pdf.

592 *Investment Stewardship Annual Report: January 1–December 31, 2023*, BLACKROCK 12, 67, 111 (2023), https:// www.blackrock.com/corporate/literature/publication/annual-steward ship-report-2023.pdf.

593 BLK-HJC-100193 at BLK-HJC-100193.

594 SSGA-HJC.126804 at SSGA-HJC.126940.

595 SSGA-HJC.427583 at SSGA-HJC.427594.

596 *Environmental Stewardship Highlights*, STATE ST. GLOB. ADVISORS 2, 4 (2024), https://www.ssga.com/library- content/assets/pdf/global/asset-stewardship/environmental-stewardship-highlights-2024.pdf.

597 SSGA-HJC.126804 at SSGA-HJC.126921.

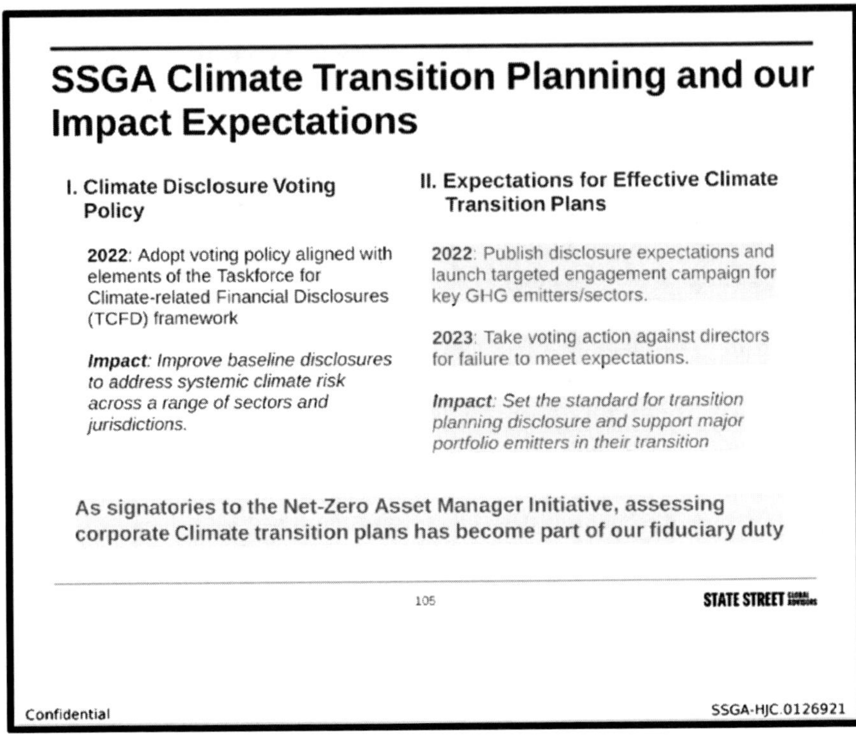

NZAM-member State Street Global Advisors votes against directors based on "Climate Transition Plans."[598]

GFANZ is clear: "[t]o be on the right side of climate history, a company would have a transition pathway to decarbonize [by] working to remove [its] emissions. Or, if it's more effective to work with [its] suppliers[,] . . . adjust [its] product so that Scope 3 emissions are being reduced."[599] In other words, U.S. companies should adopt and implement a plan that would ensure "high emitting assets . . . [are] retired before the end of their productive life."[600] GFANZ believes its investor signatories should "push every . . . sector to commit to scope 3 . . . even if it means making the s[&]p500 the s[&]p490!!"[601] If companies refuse to comply, like ExxonMobil in 2021, asset managers are

598 *Id.*
599 Transcribed Interview of Mark Carney, supra note 47, at 105:2–108:3.
600 Id. at 98:3–100:21.
601 GFANZ22894 at GFANZ22894.

to "vote against a company's slate of directors if there is no net zero transition plan in place."[602]

Conclusion

The Committee's ongoing investigation of agreements among financial institutions to impose radical ESG-related goals on U.S. companies has uncovered substantial evidence of collusion and anticompetitive behavior. In 2021, the climate cartel successfully colluded to remove and replace board members at America's largest energy company to force it to implement the climate cartel's "net-zero" agenda. Unfortunately, the pressure campaign against ExxonMobil is not an isolated incident. Through coordinated shareholder pressure campaigns at U.S. companies, the climate cartel seeks to use the trillions of dollars it manages to impose its agenda on the U.S. economy and drain it of affordable energy.

Most concerningly, not only has the Biden-Harris Administration failed to enforce U.S. antitrust law in light of clear collusion, but it has also aided, recruited, and emboldened the climate cartel to escalate its "net-zero" ambitions. Likewise, "blue-state" public pensions actively collude with the world's largest financial institutions to impose through market power the same climate policy goals left-wing policymakers in Washington, D.C. have failed to enact for decades. Despite this collusion, at least 70 investor signatories have withdrawn from Climate Action 100+ following the Committee's oversight efforts.[603]

Nevertheless, through both Climate Action 100+ and GFANZ's alliances, the climate cartel remains resolved to continue its climate crusade, pressuring U.S. companies to stop producing the affordable energy Americans need. The Committee will continue to fulfill its duty and examine the sufficiency of federal law to "[p]rotect[] trade and commerce against unlawful restraints and monopolies" such as the climate cartel's anticompetitive collusion.[604]

---

602 *Id.*

603 *Compare Investor Signatories*, CLIMATE ACTION 100+ (Nov. 14, 2022), https://web.archive.org/web/20221114184301/https://www.climateaction100.org/whos-involved/investors/, *with Investor Signatories*; *see also* Letters from former Climate Action 100+ investor signatories to Comm. (on file with the Comm.).

604 Rules of the House of Representatives R. X(1)(l)(16) (2023).

Chapter 2

How Governor Tim Walz's State Public Pension Fund Colludes with the Climate Cartel to Raise Energy Costs for American Consumers*

U.S. House of Representatives

Executive Summary

U.S. antitrust law forbids collusive agreements designed to limit the production of disfavored goods and services.[1] It does so because collusion to constrain supply inevitably harms American consumers by raising prices and reducing choice.[2] In recent years, however, a growing number of environmental activists and institutional investors have colluded to shrink affordable, carbon-based energy production to "net zero" in pursuit of radical left-wing environmental, social, and governance (ESG)-related goals.[3] As the Committee has previously detailed, these activists use a constellation of coalitions and alliances to create a climate cartel that pressures U.S. companies to "decarbonize" by eliminating affordable energy products that millions of Americans need and use.[4]

---

* This is an edited, reformatted and augmented version of Interim Staff Report of the Committee on the Judiciary, U.S. House of Representatives, dated Otober 24, 2024.

[1] See 15 U.S.C. § 1; see also Fashion Originators' Guild v. FTC, 312 U.S. 457, 467 (1941).

[2] See FTC v. Sup. Ct. Trial Laws. Ass'n, 493 U.S. 411, 423 (1990).

[3] *See* H. COMM. ON THE JUDICIARY, 118TH CONGR., CLIMATE CONTROL: EXPOSING THE DECARBONIZATION COLLUSION IN ENVIRONMENTAL, SOCIAL, AND GOVERNANCE (ESG) INVESTING 32–41 (June 11, 2024).

[4] *See id.* at 1–4.

In: The Climate Cartel
Editor: Gabriel A. Darrick
ISBN: 979-8-90134-148-3

At the forefront of the climate cartel are blue-state public pension funds.[5] These funds are run by Democrat-controlled state and local governments throughout the United States and hold the retirement savings of millions of state and local public employees—including teachers, nurses, police officers, and firefighters.[6] Blue-state public pension funds use these retirement savings as leverage to impose a "net zero" climate agenda, coercing the companies in which they invest to commit to eliminate their greenhouse gas emissions by 2050.[7] By colluding with other members of the climate cartel, these blue-state pension funds increasingly operate as de facto interstate climate regulators, threatening U.S. companies to comply with "net-zero" standards beyond their state lines and across the entire U.S. economy.[8]

One of the more prominent blue-state public pensions within the climate cartel is the Minnesota State Board of Investment (MSBI), chaired by Minnesota Governor Tim Walz.[9] Under Governor Walz, the MSBI uses $140 billion in the retirement savings of Minnesota public employees to "participate in ESG coalitions and engage with corporations on ESG related issues."[10] Two of the MSBI's "ESG coalitions" are the Ceres Investor Network and the Ceres-facilitated initiative known as Climate Action 100+.[11] These climate coalitions

[5] CERES30849 at CERES30854.

[6] *See State and Local Government Pensions*, URB. INST., https://www.urban.org/policy-centers/cross-center- initiatives/state-and-local-finance-initiative/projects/state-and-local-backgrounders/state-and-local-government- pensions (last visited Oct. 22, 2024).

[7] *See* MEKETA INV. GRP., MINNESOTA STATE BOARD OF INVESTMENTS (SBI): CLIMATE CHANGE INVESTMENT ANALYSIS 13 (May 16, 2022), https://msbi.us/sites/ default/ files/2022-05/Climate%20Change%20Investment%20Analysis%20-%20Phase% 20II%20-%20Public%20Pension%20Climate%20Leaders%20Survey.pdf.

[8] The Supreme Court has held that the Commerce Clause holds an implied limit on state power that generally prohibits state governments from interfering with interstate commerce to achieve public policy goals, such as environmental regulation, without a legitimate local interest. *See Hughes v. Oklahoma*, 441 U.S. 322, 331 (1979). While the Court has recognized a limited "market participant" exception to this rule, it has prohibited states from entering the market to impose "downstream restrictions" that "restrict[] the post-purchase activity of the purchaser," like the climate cartel's "net-zero" standards. *See, e.g., South-Central Timber Dev., Inc. v. Wunnicke*, 467 U.S. 82, 93, 99 (1984).

[9] *Resolution of the Minnesota State Board of Investment Concerning Environmental, Social, and Governance Initiatives*, MINN. STATE BD. OF INV. 2 (Feb. 26, 2020), https://msbi.us/ sites/default/files/2021-02/msbi_resolution_on_esg_-_february_26_ 2020.pdf.

[10] *See Assets Under Management*, MINN. STATE BD. OF INV., https://msbi.us/assets-management (last visited Oct. 22, 2024); *see also Environmental, Social and Governance (ESG) Stewardship*, MINN. STATE BD. OF INV., https://msbi. us/ESG-stewardship (last visited Oct. 22, 2024).

[11] MINN. STATE BD. OF INV., ENVIRONMENTAL, SOCIAL, GOVERNANCE REPORT 1, 3 (Feb. 2020), https://msbi.us/sites/default/files/2021-02/esg_report_-_february_2020.pdf [hereinafter MSBI Feb. 2020 ESG Report].

form the spine of the climate cartel by "convening" hundreds of investors to launch "net-zero" pressure campaigns against U.S. companies.[12] With the support of the MSBI, Ceres and its initiatives like Climate Action 100+ strive to "create [an] army of committed engagers" to pressure U.S. companies to commit to "net zero" and reduce carbon-based energy production.[13]

In recent years, Governor Walz has used the MSBI's participation in the climate cartel as a weapon in a broader climate crusade against affordable electricity. In 2023, after extensive coordinated engagement and support from Ceres,[14] Governor Walz "signed one of America's most aggressive climate laws, mandating that 100% of . . . [Minnesota's] electricity come from carbon-free sources by 2040."[15] At the same time, the MSBI colluded behind the scenes with other climate cartel investors to escalate Governor Walz's "net-zero" climate campaign against affordable electricity and extend it across the entire U.S. economy. Since 2019, "[a]s a member of the Climate Action 100+[,] the [M]SBI [has] actively participat[ed] in engagement with Xcel Energy, Inc.,"[16] one of America's largest electric and gas utilities, with 5.9 million customers across eight states.[17] According to documents produced to the Committee, following a pressure campaign from Governor Walz's MSBI and Climate Action 100+, Xcel Energy surrendered to the climate cartel and made a series of "net-zero" climate commitments, forcing it to "retire" carbon-based energy production and raise electricity prices throughout the Midwest.

Governor Walz's embrace of the climate cartel and its collusive conduct has serious adverse consequences for American energy consumers. From nonpublic documents produced as a part of the Committee's oversight, the Committee has found:

- *The climate cartel has vowed to pressure the U.S. power sector to eliminate affordable carbon-based energy sources.* The climate cartel

---

[12] *See* H. COMM. ON THE JUDICIARY, *supra* note 3, at 1–4.

[13] CERES82598 at CERES82603.

[14] *See* CERES97694 at CERES97695–96.

[15] Joshua Antonini & Jason Hayes, *Walz's Climate Policies Could Leave the Midwest in the Dark*, WALL ST. J. (Aug. 9, 2024), https://www.wsj.com/opinion/walzs-climate-policies-could-leave-the-midwest-in-the-dark-energy- electricity-net-zero-d1014efb; *accord* H.F. 7, 93rd Leg. (Minn. 2023).

[16] MINN. STATE BD. OF INV., ENVIRONMENTAL, SOCIAL, GOVERNANCE REPORT 2 (June 2020), https://msbi.us/sites/default/files/2021-02/esg_report_-_june_2020.pdf [hereinafter MSBI June 2020 ESG Report].

[17] *See* XCEL ENERGY, 2023 INVESTOR FACT BOOK 2 (Oct. 2023), https://s202.q4cdn.com/586283047/files/docdownloads/factbook/2022-investor-fact-book-october-final.pdf; *see also* CERES59890 at CERES59903.

intends to conduct a "transformation in the global power sector,"[18] so that "[b]oth coal and gas fired [electrical] generation . . . [are] phased out to achieve global net-zero emissions by mid- century."[19] For U.S. companies that "resist stepped-up investor pressure," the climate cartel intends to escalate its "net-zero" campaigns by "hold[ing] Boards and C-Suites accountable."[20]

- *The MSBI, chaired by Governor Walz, and climate cartel investors launched a multi-year pressure campaign against Xcel Energy to force "net-zero" commitments.* Climate Action 100+ has branded Xcel Energy as a targeted "focus company" and colluded with the MSBI, as an "active[] participa[nt]" in its engagement group, to pressure "Xcel Energy, Inc. on a variety of ESG issues."[21] Since 2018, the climate cartel has repeatedly escalated its campaign, threatening to "flag" climate-related shareholder resolutions and calling for Xcel Energy to "retire" power plants early.[22]
- *Following the climate cartel's collusive efforts, Xcel Energy surrendered and made a series of "net-zero" commitments.* Following the MSBI-supported investor engagements, Xcel Energy "committed to reduce carbon emissions to zero by 2050" for its electricity and natural gas businesses,[23] forcing it to shut down power plants in Governor Walz's state of Minnesota and elsewhere "precisely at a time when those resources will be needed the most to keep electricity flowing 24/7/365."[24]
- *The MSBI and climate cartel investors pledge to escalate their "net-zero" climate campaign against the electric power sector and beyond.* Following its success pressuring Xcel Energy, the climate cartel believes it is "nearly at the tipping point needed to push the

---

[18] Inst. Inv. Grp. on Climate Change, Global Sector Strategies: Investor Interventions to Accelerate NET ZERO ELECTRIC UTILITIES 6 (Oct. 2021), https://www.climateaction100.org/wp-content/uploads/2021/10/Global-Sector-Strategy-Electric-Utilities-IIGCC-Oct-21.pdf.

[19] GFANZ13103 at GFANZ13146.

[20] CERES43806 at CERES43819.

[21] MSBI June 2020 ESG Report, *supra* note 16, at 2.

[22] *See* CERES62685 at CERES62690; *see also* CERES110913.

[23] CERES9175 at CERES9179; *see also* XCEL ENERGY, 2021 SUSTAINABILITY REPORT 6 (June 2022), https://www.xcelenergy.com/staticfiles/xe-responsive/Company/Sustainability%20Report/2021%20SR/2021-Sustainability-Report-Full.pdf.

[24] Letter from S.D. Pub. Utils. Comm'n to Ryan Long, President, Xcel Energy 1 (Jan. 4, 2024), https://s3. documentcloud.org/documents/24362424/2024-xcel-reliability-ltr.pdf.

whole sector forward to rapidly decarbonize."[25] As a result, it plans to broaden its pressure campaign to target even more U.S. companies with "large state pension funds" including "Minnesota" becoming "much more active as lead engagers."[26]

- Xcel Energy's "net-zero" commitments have forced it to raise electricity prices *across the Midwest and elsewhere.* In 2022 and 2023, Xcel Energy's "net-zero" pledges forced it to raise electricity prices in Colorado by 6.4 percent and 4.4 percent respectively to "cover the cost of retiring a handful of coal-fired power plants."[27] Likewise, Xcel Energy increased electricity costs in Minnesota by 9.6 percent due to its efforts "to lead the clean energy transition."[28] As a result of the "net-zero" commitments, the company also plans to charge Minnesotans as much as seven times more for electricity during "peak" usage periods "to avoid building a new power plant to meet peak demand."[29]

Despite substantial evidence of anticompetitive conduct, the Biden-Harris Administration has refused to enforce existing U.S. antitrust law against the climate cartel. In contrast, the Committee remains committed to protecting "trade and commerce against unlawful restraints and monopolies," like the climate cartel's "net-zero" crusade.[30] So far, the Committee has received and reviewed 278,553 documents and 2,596,401 pages of non-public information, interviewed five key individuals affiliated with the climate cartel, and issued document subpoenas to several key stakeholders in the climate cartel.[31] Since

---

[25] CERES62685 at CERES62689.

[26] CERES115490 at CERES115516.

[27] Sam Brasch, *Xcel Energy Customers Can Expect Higher Electricity Bills Starting in September*, CPR NEWS (Aug. 17, 2023), https://www.cpr.org/2023/08/17/xcel-energy-electricity-bills-rate-increase/; Mark Jaffe, *Xcel Energy to Raise Residential Electric Bills by 6.4% in April, Two More Rate Increases Loom*, COLO. SUN (Mar. 17, 2022), https://coloradosun.com/2022/03/17/xcel-rate-hike-electricity-colorado/.

[28] Andrew Hazzard, *Energy Equity Advocates Help Keep Xcel Energy's Rate Hike to a Minimum*, SAHAN J. (June 8, 2023), https://sahanjournal.com/climate-environment/xcel-rate-case-minnesota/.

[29] Kirsti Marohn, *Xcel Energy Hopes Charging More for Electricity During Peak Hours Will Encourage Customers to Shift Energy Use*, MPR NEWS (Apr. 10, 2024), https://www.mprnews.org/story/2024/04/10/xcel-energy-charging- more-electricity-peak-hours-time-of-use-rates-utilities.

[30] Rules of the House of Representatives R. X(1)(l)(16) (2023).

[31] *See* Letter from Rep. Jim Jordan, Chairman, Comm. on the Judiciary, to John Eichlin (Nov. 1, 2023); Letter from Rep. Jim Jordan, Chairman, Comm. on the Judiciary, to Matthew Miller (June 14, 2023); Letter from Rep. Jim Jordan, Chairman, Comm. on the Judiciary, to Andrew Herman (Nov. 1, 2023); Letter from Rep. Jim Jordan, Chairman, Comm. on the

the beginning of the Committee's oversight, at least 70 investors have withdrawn from Climate Action 100+, including the former lead investor of Climate Action 100+'s Xcel Energy engagement, Morgan Stanley subsidiary Calvert Research & Management.[32] In light of the continued collusion among climate cartel investors like the MSBI, the Committee's investigation remains ongoing to inform potential legislative reforms. This interim report, however, presents a case study of how one blue-state public pension fund colluded with other climate activists to raise costs for American consumers.

Governor Walz's and the Climate Cartel's "Net-zero" Crusade Against Xcel Energy

The climate cartel is an alliance of environmental activists and major financial institutions unified by a shared commitment: to impose "net-zero" greenhouse gas (GHG)- emission requirements on the U.S. economy that drain it of affordable, carbon-based energy.[33] In its ranks are hundreds of "investor signatories" with tens of trillions of dollars in assets under management in a sprawling network of climate coalitions—such as the Glasgow Financial Alliance for Net Zero (GFANZ), the Net Zero Asset Managers Initiative (NZAM), Ceres, and Climate Action 100+.[34] Using their collective influence in the investment market, the climate cartel attempts to circumvent the democratic process by forcing U.S. companies to implement climate mandates far beyond what U.S. law requires.[35] When U.S. companies refuse to surrender and comply, the climate cartel has even colluded to enforce its "net-zero" demands by voting to remove and replace their board members.[36]

Judiciary, to Veronica Renzi (Dec. 11, 2023); Letter from Rep. Jim Jordan, Chairman, Comm. on the Judiciary, to Alyssa DaCunha (Dec. 15, 2023); Letter from Rep. Jim Jordan, Chairman, Comm. on the Judiciary, to Donald Deng (Dec. 15, 2023); Letter from Rep. Jim Jordan, Chairman, Comm. on the Judiciary, to Robert Kelner (Dec. 11, 2023); Letter from Rep. Jim Jordan, Chairman, Comm. on the Judiciary, to Aaron Cutler (Dec. 20, 2023); Letter from Rep. Jim Jordan, Chairman, Comm. on the Judiciary, to Nichol Garzon-Mitchell (Dec. 20, 2023).

[32] *See* E-mail from Calvert to Comm. Staff (July 31, 2024) (on file with the Comm.).

[33] *See* H. COMM. ON THE JUDICIARY, *supra* note 3, at 24–39.

[34] *See id.* at 1–4.

[35] *See id.* at 8–15.

[36] *See id.* at 24–31.

Blue-state Public Pensions like the MSBI Collude to Impose "Net-zero" Climate Policy Goals

The climate cartel is led by a vanguard of blue-state public pension funds that use the retirement savings they manage to pressure U.S. businesses to meet climate policy objectives. According to Ceres, these Democrat-controlled public investment houses are the "[leaders] on ESG in the U.S."[37] With the retirement accounts of state and local government employees, blue- state public pension funds "unit[e] with investors around the globe to engage with the world's largest greenhouse gas emitters."[38] Through GFANZ investor alliances, Ceres, Climate Action 100+, and other climate coalitions, a growing number of blue-state public pension funds have joined the climate cartel's ranks. In fact, according to a recent survey conducted by the Minnesota State Board of Investment (MSBI), all major Democrat-controlled state and local public pensions in the United States hold membership in at least one climate coalition, and eighty-five percent are investor signatories of Climate Action 100+.[39]

The MSBI, chaired by Minnesota Governor Tim Walz, holds memberships in a variety of climate coalitions and "work[s] to integrate appropriate ESG frameworks into its processes."[40] Using $140 billion in assets under management from the pension plans of Minnesota public employees,[41] the MSBI "has a long history of engaging with corporations" on ESG-related objectives.[42] In February 2020, as Chair of the MSBI, Governor Tim Walz signed an order "recogniz[ing] the importance of addressing Environmental, Social and Governance (ESG) risk"[43] and "direct[ing] the [M]SBI's Executive Director to, among other things, report on ESG risks and review options for reducing long-term carbon risk in the [M]SBI's investment portfolio."[44] The following year, "the MSBI dedicated a senior full-time staff person to Stewardship and ESG integration. In 2023, this role was elevated to an

---

[37] CERES30849 at CERES30854.

[38] CALPERS5908 at CALPERS5911.

[39] MEKETA INV. GRP., *supra* note 7, at 13.

[40] Jill E. Schurtz, *United Nations Principles of Responsible Investment Reporting: Senior Leadership Statement*, MINN. STATE BD. OF INV. 2 (2023), https://msbi.us/sites/default/files/2024-01/SBI%20Senior%20Leadership%20Statement%20-%202023%20PRI%20reporting.pdf.

[41] *See Assets Under Management*, *supra* note 10.

[42] Resolution of the Minnesota State Board of Investment Concerning Environmental, Social, and Governance Initiatives, supra note 9, at 1.

[43] Id.

[44] MSBI June 2020 ESG Report, supra note 16, at 1.

independent division reporting directly to the Executive Director and Chief Investment Officer."[45]

Furthermore, "to conduct many of its stewardship and ESG integration activities, the MSBI maintains membership in several investor organizations," including the "Ceres Investor Network" and "Climate Action 100+."[46] In fact, "[t]he [M]SBI's engagement activities are all associated with institutional investor coalitions."[47] As a member of the Ceres Investor Network, the MSBI contributes to Ceres's "net-zero" campaign "to harness the extraordinary power of financial system leaders to accelerate the transition of the global economy to net-zero by steering massive flows of capital . . . away from investments that lock in greenhouse gas emissions."[48] Likewise, as part of Climate Action 100+, the MSBI colludes with climate cartel investors "to spur companies" on the Climate Action 100+ focus list of 170 target companies "to accelerate their emission reductions" by abandoning carbon-based energy production.[49] Climate Action 100+ organizes collusive investor engagements designed to ensure that "[a]ll companies on [its] focus list have committed to net zero or gone out of business as investors are no longer providing them with capital."[50] The MSBI reports that "[a]s a member of the Climate Action 100+, [it] supports engagements with many companies on Climate Change risk related topics."[51]

---

[45] Schurtz, *supra* note 40, at 2.
[46] *Id.*
[47] MINN. STATE BD. OF INV., ESG STEWARDSHIP REPORT 4 (2021), https://msbi.us/sites/default/files/2022-01/MSBI%20ESG%20Stewardship%20Report%20FY2021.pdf (emphasis added).
[48] CERES37663 at CERES37668.
[49] CERES72388 at CERES72388; *see generally* CERES72399 at CERES72399–413.
[50] CERES51901 at CERES51908.
[51] ESG STEWARDSHIP REPORT, *supra* note 47, at 13; *see also* CERES108016.

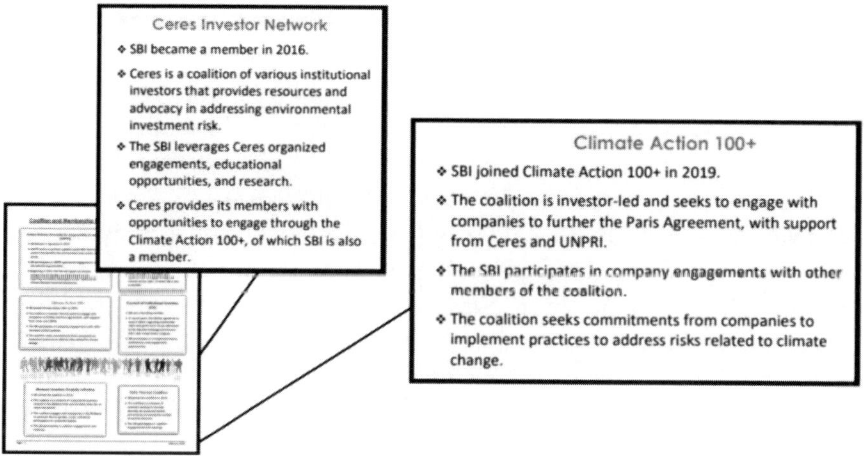

The MSBI publicly admits that it is an investor signatory of the Ceres Investor Network and Climate Action 100+.[52]

In addition to coordinating ESG engagements with the MSBI, Ceres has worked for years to further Governor Walz's radical "net-zero" climate agenda in Minnesota. In 2019, Governor Walz's first year in office, Ceres and its networks engaged the Minnesota state government to enact radical "net-zero" climate legislation.[53] Soon after that, Governor Walz pledged that Minnesota would reach "net zero by 2050 or sooner"[54] and "signed one of America's most aggressive climate laws, mandating that 100% of the state's electricity come from carbon-free sources by 2040,"[55] boasting twice afterward about the Ceres-coordinated engagement in support of the law's enactment.[56] In the years since, the MSBI has collaborated with Ceres and Climate Action 100+ to extend its "net-zero" agenda beyond Minnesota by pressuring the largest companies in the U.S. power sector to rid themselves of carbon-based energy sources.[57]

---

[52] MSBI Feb. 2020 ESG Report, supra note 11, at 3. "SBI" or State Board of Investment, as used here, refers to the Minnesota State Board of Investment (MSBI). Id. at 1.

[53] See CERES97694 at CERES97695–96.

[54] Joshua Antonini & Jason Hayes, Shorting the Great Lakes Grid: How Net Zero Plans Risk Energy RELIABILITY 38 (2024), https://www.mackinac.org/archives/2024/s2024-04.pdf.

[55] *Walz's Climate Policies Could Leave the Midwest in the Dark*, *supra* note 15; *see also* H.F. 7, 93rd Leg. (Minn. 2023).

[56] *See* CERES97694 at CERES97696.

[57] *See* ESG STEWARDSHIP REPORT, *supra* note 47, at 13.

The Climate Cartel Has Targeted the U.S. Electric Power Sector to Eliminate Affordable and Reliable Carbon-based Energy

While its “net-zero” campaign targets all corners of the U.S. economy,[58] Climate Action 100+ believes electric “power is arguably the most important sector to decarbonise over the next decade.”[59] This is because America’s vast power sector relies primarily on affordable, carbon- based energy sources, such as coal and natural gas.[60] More than sixty percent of the energy used to generate electricity in the United States comes from fossil fuels.[61] Every day, U.S. electric utilities use affordable carbon-based energy sources to generate electricity to heat and cool millions of American homes and power a rising number of American electric vehicles.[62] The U.S. power sector also provides the electrical lifeline for American industry, manufacturing, and technological innovation.[63] America’s economy is so reliant on affordable electricity that there is nearly a 90% correlation between total retail electricity sales and U.S. economic growth.[64]

In recent years, however, the U.S. power sector has struggled to keep up with historic increases in electricity demand. Electric power demand is “rising faster than at any time in the past five or more years,” leading to “clear evidence of growing resource adequacy concerns over the next 10 years.”[65] Climate Action 100+ itself recognizes that “electricity demand [is] predicted to grow over 166% globally by 2050.”[66] As a result, the average American already experiences an average of five and a half hours of electrical failures

---

[58] *See* H. COMM. ON THE JUDICIARY, *supra* note 3, at 32–40.

[59] INST. INV. GRP. ON CLIMATE CHANGE, *supra* note 18, at 6.

[60] *See id.* at 21.

[61] *Transformative Power Systems*, OFF. OF FOSSIL ENERGY & CARBON MGMT., https://www.energy.gov/fecm/ transformative-power-systems (last visited Oct. 22, 2024).

[62] *See Electricity Explained: Use of Electricity*, U.S. ENERGY INFO. ADMIN., https:// www.eia.gov/energyexplained/electricity/use-of-electricity.php (last updated Dec. 18, 2023).

[63] *See id.*

[64] *See* VIPIN ARORA & JOZEF LIESKOVSKY, ELECTRICITY USE AS AN INDICATOR OF U.S. ECONOMIC ACTIVITY 7(2014), https://www.eia.gov/workingpapers/pdf/electricity_ indicator.pdf.

[65] . AM. ELEC. RELIABILITY CORP., 2023 LONG-TERM RELIABILITY ASSESSMENT 6 (Dec. 2023), https://www.nerc.com/pa/RAPA/ra/Reliability%20Assessments%20DL /NERC_LTRA_2023.pdf.

[66] Climate Action 100+ Sets Decarbonisation Expectations for Electric Utility Companies to Achieve Net Zero Emissions Globally by 2040, CLIMATE ACTION 100+ (Oct. 20, 2021), https://www.climateaction100.org/news/climate-action-100-sets-decarbonisation-expectations-for-electric-utility-companies-to-achieve-net-zero-emissions-globally-by-2040/.

annually,[67] and large swaths of the United States currently stand at a "high" or "elevated" risk for electrical blackouts in the next four years.[68]

Despite the growing need for affordable electrical generation and the fact that fossil fuels are by far the most inexpensive way to generate electricity,[69] the climate cartel aims to carry out a "transformation in the global power sector"[70] where "[b]oth coal and gas fired [electrical] generation . . . [are] phased out to achieve global net-zero emissions by mid-century."[71] In 2021, to "inform the engagement activities of [its] signatories,"[72] Climate Action 100+ announced a set of "decarbonisation expectations for electric utility companies to achieve net zero emissions globally by 2040."[73] In its report, Climate Action 100+ called on climate cartel investors to pressure U.S. power companies to take "bold action now" by setting a "company-wide emissions target," requiring "annual emissions from electricity generation [to] reach[] net zero by 2035."[74] To achieve this "net-zero" commitment, Climate Action 100+ emphasized that U.S. power companies must "immediate[ly] halt . . . the construction of coal-fired power plants" and begin a "phase out of [existing] coal" power generation.[75] Additionally, Climate Action 100+ declared that electricity generation from natural gas must fall by 79 percent globally between 2030 and 2040, with "advanced economies" like the United States entirely "decarbonis[ing] [its] power sector[] by 2035."[76] In total, to achieve its "net-zero" ambitions, Climate Action 100+ declared that it expected global fossil-fuel-based generation to shrink by a staggering 41 percent, "from 17

---

67 *U.S. Electricity Customers Averaged Five and One-half Hours of Power Interruptions in 2022*, U.S. ENERGY INFO. ADMIN. (Jan. 25, 2024), https://www.eia.gov/todayinenergy/detail.php?id=61303.

68 N. AM. ELEC. RELIABILITY CORP., *supra* note 65, at 6–9.

69 *See* NAT. COAL COUNCIL, POWER RESET: OPTIMIZING THE EXISTING COAL FLEET TO ENSURE A RELIABLE AND RESILIENT GRID 6, 10 (Sept. 4, 2018), https://www.burnmorecoal.com/wp-content/uploads/2018/10/NCC-Power-Reset-2018.pdf.

70 INST. INV. GRP. ON CLIMATE CHANGE, *supra* note 18, at 6.

71 GFANZ13103 at GFANZ13146.

72 INST. INV. GRP. ON CLIMATE CHANGE, *supra* note 18, at 18.

73 Climate Action 100+ Sets Decarbonisation Expectations for Electric Utility Companies to Achieve Net Zero Emissions Globally by 2040, supra note 66.

74 INST. INV. GRP. ON CLIMATE CHANGE, *supra* note 18, at 12.

75 *Id.* at 6.

76 *Id.* at 23; *see also id.* at 4 (defining "[a]dvanced economies" to include "the OECD regional grouping); *see also* INT'L ENERGY AGENCY, NET ZERO BY 2050: A ROADMAP FOR THE GLOBAL ENERGY SECTOR 214 (Oct. 2021), https://iea.blob.core.windows.net/assets/deebef5d-0c34-4539-9d0c-10b13d840027/NetZeroby2050-ARoadmapfor theGlobalEnergy Sector_CORR.pdf (defining "OECD" to include the United States).

m[illion] GWh [(gigawatt hours)] to 10 m[illion] GWh by 2030, largely driven by coal."[77]

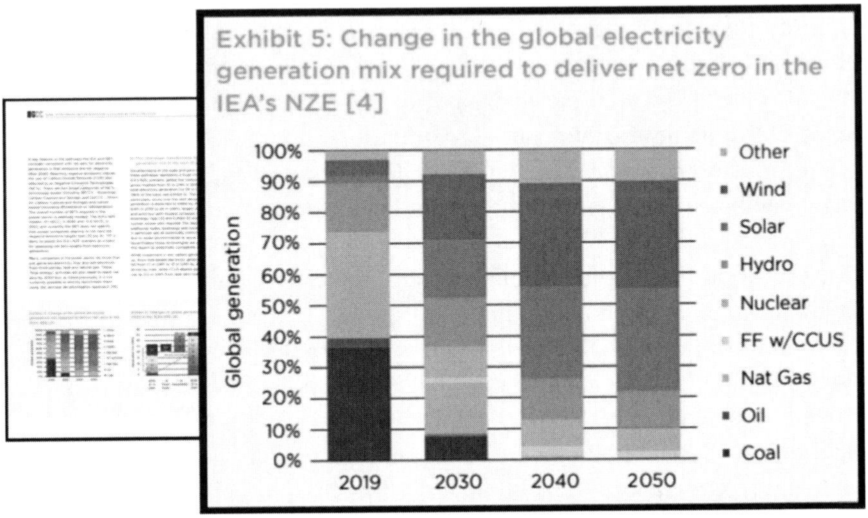

Climate Action 100+ concedes that the climate cartel's "net-zero" goal shrinks electricity generation from unabated fossil fuels from more than 60% to zero.[78]

To secure "net-zero" commitments and drain the U.S. power sector of fossil fuels, Climate Action 100+ calls for its investor signatories to pressure U.S. companies to "establish credible net zero transition plans"[79] and have a

---

[77] INST. INV. GRP. ON CLIMATE CHANGE, *supra* note 18, at 22. A gigawatt hour (GWh) is the "electrical energy unit of measure equal to" one billion watts of power "supplied to, or taken from, an electric circuit steadily for one hour." *Glossary*, U.S. ENERGY INFO. ADMIN., https://www.eia.gov/tools/glossary/index.php?id=W (last visited Oct. 22, 2024) (defining "Watthour"); *accord Glossary*, U.S. ENERGY INFO. ADMIN., https://www.eia.gov/tools/glossary/ index.php?id=G (last visited Oct. 22, 2024) (defining "Gigawatthour"). The 7 million GWh of global fossil-fuel- based generation that Climate Action 100+ aims to eliminate is equivalent to the electric power generated by 1.5 billion Photovoltaic (PV) Solar Panels or 234,931 utility-scale wind turbines. *See How Much Power Is 1 Gigawatt*, U.S. DEP'T OF ENERGY (Aug. 21, 2024), https://www.energy.gov/eere/articles/how-much-power-1-gigawatt; *see also* Zach Stein, *Gigawatt (GW)*, CARBON COLLECTIVE (last modified Oct. 1, 2024), https://www.carbon collective. co/sustainable-investing/gigawatt-gw ("To convert [gigawatt hours (GWh)] into gigawatts (GW), you would divide the GWh value by the number of hours in a year (8,760 hours).").

[78] INST. INV. GRP. ON CLIMATE CHANGE, *supra* note 18, at 22.

[79] *Id.* at 15.

"retirement date assigned to each coal or gas unit" they operate.[80] While Climate Action 100+ admits that its "net-zero" pressure campaign against the U.S. power sector could result in the "[d]isplacement of well-paid jobs" and "electricity price increases,"[81] it nevertheless directs its investor signatories to "[s]et out escalation strategies (e.g. vote on directors) for companies that do not respond to engagement and for those accentuating [net-zero] transition risks by constructing new fossil fuel generation."[82] Climate Action 100+ warns: "[a]s with other sectors, in cases where companies resist stepped-up investor pressure . . . we will work to hold Boards and C-Suites accountable."[83]

The MSBI and Climate Cartel Investors Pressured Xcel Energy to Commit to "Net Zero" and "Retire" Carbon-based Energy

As part of its "net-zero" campaign against the U.S. power sector, the MSBI and climate cartel investors have targeted Minneapolis-based Xcel Energy, one of the largest electric and gas utilities in the United States.[84] Operating in eight states—Colorado, Michigan, Minnesota, New Mexico, North Dakota, South Dakota, Texas, and Wisconsin—Xcel Energy "provides a comprehensive portfolio of energy-related products and services to 3.8 million electricity customers and 2.1 million natural gas customers."[85] For the last six years, the climate cartel has waged a "net-zero" pressure campaign against Xcel Energy using a familiar sequence of engagement tactics employed against all other companies across the U.S. economy.[86] To begin, the climate cartel labels U.S. companies as "focus companies" to "trigger" and "start . . . the [engagement] process."[87] The climate cartel then coordinates collusive investor engagements to pressure U.S. companies to disclose, reduce, and enforce "net-zero" climate commitments.[88]

In July 2018, Climate Action 100+ announced that Xcel Energy was one of thirty-one electric utility "focus companies" it planned to target through

---

[80] GFANZ13103 at GFANZ13146.
[81] INST. INV. GRP. ON CLIMATE CHANGE, *supra* note 18, at 38.
[82] *Id.* at 15.
[83] CERES43806 at CERES43819.
[84] *See Company Assessment: Xcel Energy Inc.*, CLIMATE ACTION 100+, https://www.climateaction100.org/company/ xcel-energy-inc/ (last visited Oct. 22, 2024).
[85] 2023 INVESTOR FACT BOOK, *supra* note 17, at 2.
[86] *See* H. COMM. ON THE JUDICIARY, *supra* note 3, at 18–23.
[87] CERES62869 at CERES62952.
[88] *See* H. COMM. ON THE JUDICIARY, *supra* note 3, at 18–23.

coordinated investor engagements.[89] Labeling Xcel Energy as a "focus company" allowed Climate Action 100+ to organize an "engagement group" to push it to adopt "net-zero" commitments.[90] As of 2021, the engagement group was led by Morgan Stanley subsidiary Calvert Research & Management and included at least eight investor signatories.[91] Beginning in 2019, the MSBI joined the Climate Action 100+ engagement group to "actively participat[e] in engagement with Xcel Energy, Inc. on a variety of ESG issues including[] Xcel's plans to transition to carbon free electricity generation by 2050[] [and] risks associated with the company's continued use and development of natural gas infrastructure."[92]

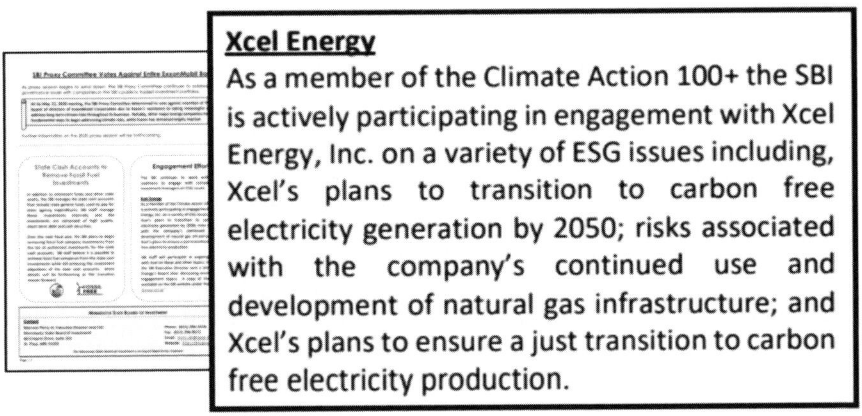

As a Climate Action 100+ investor signatory, the MSBI actively engages Xcel Energy.[93]

Almost immediately after the climate cartel branded it as a "focus company" and began coordinated investor engagement, Xcel Energy began making "net-zero" commitments. In August 2018, one month after being branded a "focus company," Xcel Energy confirmed plans for "the early closure of coal-fired units 1 and 2 at Xcel's Comanche Generating Station in Pueblo County[, Colorado]" that were "capable of producing a combined 660

---

[89] *See* GFANZ13103 at GFANZ13143.

[90] *See Engagement Process*, CLIMATE ACTION 100+, https://www.climateaction100.org/approach/engagement-process/ (last visited Oct. 22, 2024).

[91] *See* CERES382 at CERES401.

[92] MSBI June 2020 ESG Report, *supra* note 16, at 2; *see also* MSBI Feb. 2020 ESG Report, *supra* note 11, at 3.

[93] MSBI June 2020 ESG Report, *supra* note 16, at 2.

megawatts of coal- fired generation,"[94] enough electricity to power hundreds of thousands of homes annually.[95] Xcel Energy later explained that it is intent on "leading the clean energy transition," but "[a]chieving [its] vision requires retiring coal plants that [it] [has] relied upon for years and transitioning to cleaner sources of power."[96]

In December 2018, five months after Climate Action 100+ branded Xcel Energy as a "focus company," Xcel Energy "committed to reduce carbon emissions to zero by 2050."[97] Ceres boasted that Xcel Energy's commitment was "one of the most ambitious climate commitment[s] to date in the US electric power industry."[98] The announcement was "notable for coming from an investor-owned utility, rather than from a state mandate."[99] At the time, Xcel Energy "produce[d] 60 percent of its power from fossil fuels,"[100] and the company's "net-zero" commitment was even more striking given that it admitted in its announcement that reaching "net zero" would "require[] technologies that are not cost effective or commercially available today."[101]

In internal communications, Ceres privately bragged that Xcel Energy's "net-zero" commitment appeared to have been caused by the collusive investor engagements.[102] Before Xcel Energy's "net-zero" commitment, Ceres explained that it had "engag[ed] Xcel for several years, and in July 2018 placed Xcel on the Climate Action 100+ focus list. Hours before a scheduled meeting with the lead Climate Action 100+ investors . . . , Xcel made its

---

94 Julia Pyper, *Xcel to Replace 2 Colorado Coal Units with Renewables and Storage*, GREENTECH MEDIA (Aug. 29, 2018), https://www.greentechmedia.com/articles/read/xcel-retire-coal-renewable-energy-storage#gs.o3g3UMo. In 2022, Xcel Energy followed through and closed Comanche 1. It has scheduled Comanche 2 to close next year. Clarion Energy Content Directors, *Committee Calls for Xcel Energy to Replace Closing Colorado Coal Plant with Advanced Nuclear*, POWER ENG'G (Jan. 8, 2024), https://www.power-eng.com/news/committee-calls-for-xcel-energy-to-replace-closing-colorado-coal-plant-with-advanced-nuclear/#gref.

95 *See What Is a Megawatt?*, U.S. NUCLEAR REG. COMM'N 1–2 (Feb. 24, 2012), https://www.nrc.gov/docs/ML1209/ ML120960701.pdf.

96 *Transitioning out of Coal Responsibly: Working with Communities and Employees Affected by Energy Transitions*, XCEL ENERGY 1 (2022), https://www.xcelenergy.com/staticfiles/xe-responsive/Environment/ Responsible-Coal-Transition-info-sheet.pdf.

97 CERES9175 at CERES9179.

98 *Id.*

99 Jeff St. John, *Xcel Energy Fast-Forwards Minnesota Coal Plant Closures but Extends Nuclear Window*, GREENTECH MEDIA (May 20, 2019), https://www.greentechmedia.com/articles/read/xcel-energy-accelerates-coal-plant-closures-to-meet-100-clean-energy-goal.

100 CERES39113 at CERES39151.

101 *Id.*

102 See CERES9175 at CERES9179.

announcement" to achieve "net zero" by 2050.[103] Ceres declared, "[T]he equilibrium change in the US electric power industry has become unmistakable—with the 9th largest utility, [Xcel], committing to become carbon neutral by 2050 . . . [which] [was] simply not part of the conversation as little as three to five years ago."[104] The climate cartel emphasized that "under Climate Action 100+ pressure," Xcel Energy has "made [a] precedent-setting commitment[] that raise[s] the bar for [its] sector."[105]

After Xcel Energy's "net-zero" announcement in December 2018, Ceres declared that it "w[ould] now seize on Xcel's new commitment to further reinforce [its] efforts to advance climate-related policies at the state level," including in "Minnesota . . . [a] target state[] from Ceres' state policy program."[106] Ceres's state policy program works alongside its collusive investor pressure campaigns to "galvanize businesses and investors to step out and advocate for climate" policies in states across America.[107] Following Xcel Energy's "net-zero" commitment, Ceres worked with "Minnesota businesses[, which] have historically been reluctant to step out," to call for Minnesota to adopt "net-zero" policies.[108] Subsequently, in March 2019, just three months after Xcel Energy surrendered to the climate cartel, Governor Walz "unveil[ed] [his] plan for all carbon-free electricity by 2050" in Minnesota.[109] In February 2023, Governor Walz signed his "net-zero" plan into state law.[110]

---

[103] *Id.*

[104] CERES59890 at CERES59903.

[105] CERES47434 at CERES47461.

[106] CERES9175 at CERES9179.

[107] CERES97694 at CERES97695.

[108] Id.

[109] Elizabeth Dunbar & Cody Nelson, Walz Unveils Plan for All Carbon-free Electricity by 2050, MPR NEWS (Mar. 4, 2019), https://www.mprnews.org/story/2019/03/04/walz-carbon-free-electricity-2050.

[110] Governor Walz Signs Bill Moving Minnesota to 100 Percent Clean Energy by 2040, MINN. COM. DEP'T (Feb. 7, 2023), https://mn.gov/commerce/news/?id=17-563384; see also H.F. 7, 93rd Leg. (Minn. 2023).

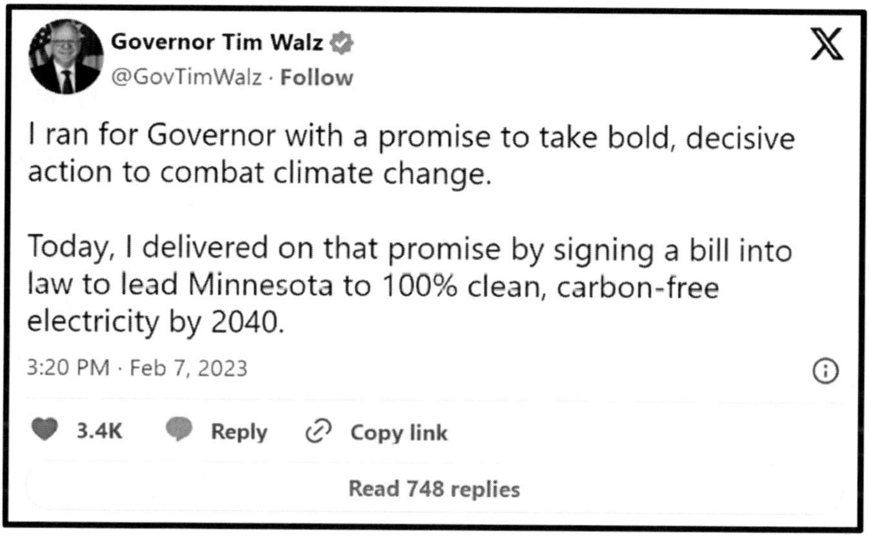

Following Xcel Energy's "net-zero" commitment, Governor Walz mandated "net-zero" electricity for Minnesota by 2040.[111]

In 2019, just one year after Xcel Energy caved to the climate cartel's collusive pressure, the MSBI signed onto Climate Action 100+ and soon joined its engagement group targeting Xcel Energy.[112] Additionally in 2019, "Xcel released a climate scenario report,"[113] and in May of that year, the company announced "plans to close its last two coal-fired power plants in Minnesota by 2030, a decade earlier than scheduled" as part of its "plan to reach 100 percent carbon-free electricity by 2050."[114] The climate cartel identified Xcel Energy's "net-zero" commitments as instrumental in the growing "Climate Action 100+ [m]omentum" where "[m]oney managers [are] the new warriors of climate change."[115]

With this momentum, the climate cartel vowed to continue its pressure campaign against Xcel Energy, explicitly targeting its natural gas business. Toward the end of 2019, Ceres noted that, at that time, "[t]he company's [net-zero] goal . . . focus[ed] on its electricity business and [had] not yet include[d]

---

[111] Governor Tim Walz (@GovTimWalz), X (Feb. 7, 2023), https://publish.twitter.com/?query=https%3A%2F%2Ftwitter.com%2FGovTimWalz%2Fstatus%2F1623054111053586440&widget=Tweet.
[112] ESG STEWARDSHIP REPORT, *supra* note 47, at 13.
[113] CERES60474 at CERES60483.
[114] St. John, *supra* note 99.
[115] *See* CERES75072 at CERES75077.

its natural gas distribution."[116] As a result, the climate cartel set as an engagement objective extending Xcel Energy's net-zero "commitment to Scope 3 emissions [*i.e.*, emissions it indirectly contributes to up and down its value chain] and natural gas distribution."[117] Additionally, the climate cartel planned to "call[] for ambitious emissions reduction targets," forcing the company to detail action steps to reach "net zero" more explicitly.[118]

Subsequently, in November 2021, Xcel Energy committed to "provid[e] net-zero gas service by 2050," with a target to "reduce greenhouse gas emissions 25% by 2030 from the supply, delivery[,] and customer use of natural gas."[119] Following the announcement, Ceres explained that "Climate Action 100+ efforts . . . [were] integral in securing significant, first-of- their-kind commitments," including Xcel Energy's pledge.[120] Specifically, the "[c]ommitment[] followed steadfast Climate Action 100+ collaborative engagement with [Xcel Energy] on GHG targets and ambition, and coalesced around the withdrawal of targeted resolutions (filed by [Climate Action 100+ member] As You Sow) partly due to pressure from the Climate Action 100+ flagging process."[121] After Xcel Energy announced its "net-zero" promise following Climate Action 100+'s engagement, the climate cartel boasted that its "new commitment ma[de] Xcel Energy one of the first North American Climate Action 100+ electric power focus companies to set a comprehensive Scope 3 GHG target."[122]

Since Xcel Energy's 2021 "net-zero" commitment for its natural gas business, the MSBI and climate cartel investors have sought to leverage their success to collusively pressure other U.S. power companies to make similar "net-zero" pledges. The climate cartel believes it is "nearly at the tipping point needed to push the whole sector forward to rapidly decarbonize."[123] According to Ceres, this "equilibrium change is," at least in part, due to "increasing

---

[116] CERES60474 at CERES60483.

[117] *Id.*

[118] CERES8188 at CERES8219.

[119] 2021 SUSTAINABILITY REPORT, *supra* note 23, at 6.

[120] CERES62685 at CERES62690.

[121] *Id.* In general, the climate cartel "flags" shareholder resolutions that call for its "focus companies" to adopt "net- zero" commitments to "[s]trengthen[] [its] ability to win key votes." CERES10442 at CERES10447. As was the case in 2021 with Xcel Energy, the climate cartel believes that "[t]he threat of flagging . . . resolutions prove[s] successful in pushing companies to make commitments ahead of [annual general meetings] in return for a withdrawal." CERES62708 at CERES62709.

[122] CERES62669 at CERES62675 (emphasis omitted).

[123] CERES62685 at CERES62689.

investor pressure."[124] Specifically, the climate cartel plans to extend its pressure campaign beyond its current Climate Action 100+ "focus list" to target even more U.S. companies.[125] Ceres believes that "[i]n order to engage the large number of companies on [its] [expanded] focus list, it is critical that [it] expand and deepen the bench of investors This has largely taken the form of mobilizing investors who are already part of the Ceres Investor Network," including "large state pension funds" such as "Minnesota to significantly increase their engagement with these focus companies and become much more active as lead engagers."[126]

The climate cartel's plan to escalate and broaden its "net-zero" pressure campaign, however, does not mean it is finished with Xcel Energy. Recently, Xcel Energy revealed that it is "[c]halleng[ing] to make significant near-term [GHG-emission reduction] target[s] and/or accelerate coal plant retirements [without] regulatory approval,"[127] and it "now [is] wary that [it] do[es]n't want to get too far ahead of [its] peers."[128] Furthermore, Ceres noted that as of July 2022, Xcel Energy "[e]ngagement [was] stalled due to company unresponsiveness," and the Climate Action 100+ engagement group's lead investors would "have to escalate if no response."[129] In the future, the climate cartel vows to pressure Xcel Energy to deepen its commitment to a "net-zero" agenda:

> [n]ow that the company has set a scope 3 target [to reduce indirect emissions from its value chain], the engagement team is focused on the topics of decarbonization strategy and capital alignment. In addition, a high priority is climate lobbying as peer companies have begun producing climate lobbying reports and Xcel will soon become a laggard.[130]

Additionally, the lead investors "are focusing engagement on greater clarity on [Xcel Energy's] coal retirement schedule, . . . reporting, and addressing emissions from natural gas plants."[131]

---

124 CERES59890 at CERES59903.
125 *See* CERES115490 at CERES115514.
126 *Id.* at CERES11516.
127 CERES382 at CERES401.
128 CERES110913.
129 CERES29861.
130 *Id.*
131 CERES110913.

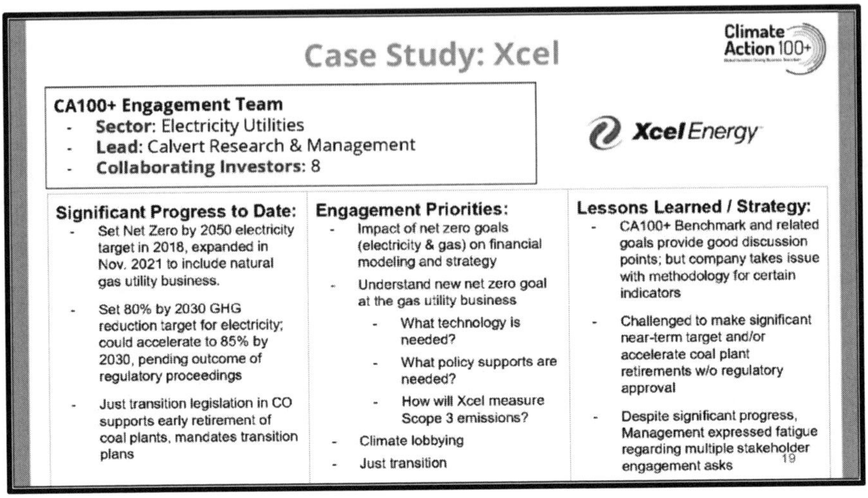

Following "net-zero" commitments, Climate Action 100+ continues to engage Xcel Energy.[132]

Since 2021, Xcel Energy has made additional fossil energy "retirements" to abide by its "net-zero" pledge. After it shut down the first two Comanche coal-fired generators in Colorado in 2018 after the climate cartel branded it a "focus company," Xcel Energy announced in 2021 plans to "retire" the third and last-remaining Comanche power generating plant "three decades earlier than expected."[133] It now plans to "retir[e] [its] remaining coal operations in Colorado" by "Jan. 1, 2031."[134]

Following these announcements, state regulators have warned Xcel Energy that the early closure of its coal-fired generators may lead to serious consequences. In January 2024, the South Dakota Public Utilities Commission urged Xcel Energy to reconsider its decision to "prematurely close the King and Sherco generating plants" that provide electricity to South Dakota residents.[135] The Commission explained to Xcel Energy that "closing these plants w[ould] take nearly three gigawatts of reliable dispatchable electricity generation off the Midcontinent Independent System Operator (MISO) grid,"

---

[132] CERES382 at CERES401.

[133] Miguel Otárola, *Pueblo's Comanche Coal Plant Is Closing Earlier than Expected. Is Its Future with Nuclear, or Renewables?*, CPR NEWS (Sept. 13, 2021), https://www.cpr.org/2021/09/13/pueblo-comanche-coal-plant-closing-early-nuclear-renewable-energy/.

[134] *Transitioning out of Coal Responsibly: Working with Communities and Employees Affected by Energy Transitions*, *supra* note 96, at 1.

[135] Letter from S.D. Pub. Utils. Comm'n to Ryan Long, President, Xcel, *supra* note 24, at 1.

an area spanning fifteen states,[136] "precisely at a time when those resources w[ould] be needed the most to keep electricity flowing 24/7/365."[137] It warned Xcel Energy that "[e]vidence is mounting that the premature closure of dispatchable generation w[ould] elevate the risk of electricity outagesThese events are likely to pose a threat to life and property."[138]

After Surrendering to the Climate Cartel, Xcel Energy's "Net-zero" Commitments Have Raised Electricity Costs

In recent years, American consumers have started to feel the cost of Xcel Energy's "net- zero" climate commitments. In 2022 and 2023, the Colorado Public Utilities Commission approved electricity rate increases of 6.4 percent and 4.4 percent, respectively, for Xcel Energy's 1.6 million Colorado customers, totaling $278 million.[139] In 2023, Xcel Energy lobbied for the rate increases, which were "need[ed] to pay for previous investments and to cover the cost of retiring a handful of coal-fired power plants."[140]

In June 2023, the Minnesota Public Utility Commission raised electricity prices for Xcel Energy's 1.3 million Minnesota customers by 9.6 percent or $306 million over the following three years.[141] However, Xcel Energy had initially asked the Commission to raise electricity costs by a staggering 21.2 percent or $677.4 million.[142] In a statement following the Commission's decision, Xcel Energy tied its plea to raise electricity rates directly to its "net-zero" commitments, announcing that the Commission's refusal to increase electricity costs to 21.2% would "limit [Xcel Energy's] ability to continue to lead the clean energy transition."[143] Overall, in 2024, the average annual Xcel Energy electricity bill for customers in Minnesota is expected to rise by $63

---

[136] Robert Walton, *South Dakota PUC Asks Xcel Energy to Reconsider Closing King, Sherco Coal Plants*, UTIL. DIVE (Jan. 17, 2024), https://www.utilitydive.com/news/south-dakota-asks-xcel-energy-reconsider-closing-king- sherco-coal-plants/704687/.

[137] Letter from S.D. Pub. Utils. Comm'n to Ryan Long, President, Xcel, *supra* note 24, at 1.

[138] *Id.*

[139] Brasch, *supra* note 27; Jaffe, *supra* note 27.

[140] Brasch, *supra* note 27.

[141] Hazzard, *supra* note 28.

[142] Kent Erdahl, *Xcel Energy Requests 21% Increase in Electricity Rates; Here's What That Could Mean*, CITIZENS UTIL. BD. (Oct. 26, 2021), https://cubminnesota.org/xcel-energy-requests-21-increase-in-electricity-rates-heres-what-that-could-mean/.

[143] Hazzard, *supra* note 28.

from 2022 levels.[144] According to Xcel Energy, "substantial and sustained investments" in alternatives to fossil fuel energy as it transitions to "net zero" are a large driver behind the rate increases.[145]

In April 2024, Xcel Energy announced a proposal to charge even higher electricity rates as a default during "peak" usage periods for its customers, "from 3 to 8 p.m. on weekdays."[146] Strikingly, under the proposal, Xcel Energy "[c]ustomers will pay seven times more per kilowatt hour for electricity during peak hours on summer weekdays than during the off-peak period."[147] According to Xcel Energy, "[w]hat's behind the thinking is really trying to drive behavior changes and usage changes, and getting customers to shift their usage to those off-peak periods where energy is more affordable and it's actually cheaper to generate and deliver."[148] As it closes down numerous power plants to reach its "net-zero" goals, Xcel Energy hopes the proposal will "allow [it] to avoid building a new power plant to meet peak demand."[149]

Conclusion

Despite the harm to American consumers, the MSBI and other climate cartel investors plan to continue pressuring U.S. companies to surrender to "net-zero" demands. Evidence uncovered by the Committee demonstrates that the climate cartel's collusive pressure campaign against Xcel Energy is but one example of a larger climate crusade to rid the U.S. economy of the affordable and accessible energy products that millions of Americans use and need.[150] The climate cartel remains intent to "step up investor engagement with the most carbon-intensive electric utilities and independent power producers to make new public commitments" that "reduc[e] investment in, and deployment of, fossil fuel-fired generation resources and related infrastructure."[151] In light of this clear evidence of collusion with economically disastrous consequences,

---

[144] *See* Emma Nelson & Walker Orenstein, *Minnesotans Take Big Hits on Non-negotiable Bills Like Electricity, Insurance*, MINN. STAR TRIB. (Jan. 3, 2024), https://www.startribune.com/minnesotan-non-negotiable-electricity-gas-insurance-trash-property-tax-services-inflation-cost-bill/600332038.

[145] *Id.*

[146] Marohn, *supra* note 29.

[147] *Id.*

[148] *Id.*

[149] *Id.*

[150] *See* H. COMM. ON THE JUDICIARY, *supra* note 3, at 32–39.

[151] CERES43806 at CERES43819.

the Biden-Harris Administration's failure to enforce existing U.S. antitrust law is striking.

Following the Committee's investigative efforts, at least 70 U.S.-based investors have withdrawn from Climate Action 100+.[152] For instance, after the release of the Committee's June 2024 interim staff report, the lead investor for Climate Action 100+'s Xcel Energy engagement, Morgan Stanley subsidiary Calvert Research & Management, suspended its involvement and confirmed to the Committee that it "is no longer a member of Climate Action 100+ and will not be participating in any of its initiatives."[153] Still, the most radical members of the climate cartel remain steadfast in their pursuit of a "net-zero" agenda. In particular, after the Committee wrote to the MSBI on July 30, 2024, requesting it to "preserve documents and provide documentation" related to its climate cartel involvement, the MSBI failed to substantively respond to any of the Committee's investigative inquiries.[154] The Committee remains committed to investigating the climate cartel's anticompetitive behavior to inform potential legislative reforms to U.S. antitrust laws.

---

[152] *Compare Investor Signatories*, CLIMATE ACTION 100+ (Nov. 14, 2022), https://web.archive.org/web/20221114184301/https://www.climateaction100.org/whos-involved/investors/, *with Investor Signatories*, CLIMATE ACTION 100+, https://www.climateaction100.org/whos-involved/investors/ (last visited Oct. 22, 2024); *see also* letters from former Climate Action 100+ investor signatories to Comm. (on file with the Comm.).

[153] E-mail from Calvert to Committee Staff, *supra* note 32.

[154] *See* Letter from Jill Schurtz, Exec. Dir. & Chief Inv. Officer, Minn. State Bd. of Inv. to Rep. Jim Jordan, Chairman, Comm. on the Judiciary, & Rep. Thomas Massie, Chairman, Subcomm. on the Admin. State, Regul. Reform, and Antitrust 1–2 (Aug. 13, 2024).

Chapter 3

Climate Control: Exposing the Decarbonization Collusion in Environmental, Social, and Governance (ESG) Investing*

U.S. House of Representatives

Executive Summary

Competition "produce[s] not only lower prices, but also better goods and services" for all Americans.[1] Collusion, on the other hand, has been described by the Supreme Court as "the supreme evil of antitrust"[2] because it "coordinate[s] reductions in output that result in higher prices for consumers."[3] Accordingly, U.S. antitrust law prohibits anticompetitive collusion,[4] and "social justifications proffered for [a] restraint of trade . . . do not make it any less unlawful."[5]

The Committee on the Judiciary is entrusted with the "[p]rotection of trade and commerce against unlawful restraints and monopolies" such as anticompetitive collusion.[6] In exercising this oversight of the adequacy and sufficiency of existing U.S. antitrust laws, the Committee has been investigating apparent collusion between left-wing activists and major

---

* This is an edited, reformatted and augmented version of Interim Staff Report of the Committee on the Judiciary, U.S. House of Representatives, dated June 11, 2024.

[1] Nat'l Soc. of Pro. Engineers v. United States, 435 U.S. 679, 695 (1978).

[2] Verizon Commc'ns Inc. v. L. Offs. of Curtis V. Trinko, LLP, 540 U.S. 398, 408 (2004).

[3] Phillip E. Areeda & Herbert Hovenkamp, Antitrust Law: An Analysis of Antitrust Principles and Their Application¶ 1478d2 (Aug. 2023).

[4] See 15 U.S.C. § 1.

[5] FTC v. Superior Ct. Trial Laws. Ass'n, 493 U.S. 411, 424 (1990).

[6] Rules of the House of Representatives R. X(1)(l)(16) (2023).

In: The Climate Cartel
Editor: Gabriel A. Darrick
ISBN: 979-8-90134-148-3

financial institutions to impose radical environmental, social, and governance (ESG) goals upon the American people. This collusion not only violates fundamental free market principles, it also threatens to raise costs and reduce choice for millions of American consumers.

The Committee has obtained evidence that a "climate cartel" of left-wing environmental activists and major financial institutions has colluded to force American companies to "decarbonize" and reach "net zero." Through their commitments to groups such as Climate Action 100+, the members of the climate cartel expressly have agreed to decarbonize the American economy by forcing corporations to disclose their carbon emissions, to reduce their carbon emissions, and to enforce (and reinforce) their disclosure and reduction commitments by handcuffing company leadership and muzzling corporate free speech and petitioning. The climate cartel imposes these radical policies by weaponizing ever-escalating pressure tactics that start with negotiations with corporate management, continue to filing and "flagging" stockholder proxy resolutions, and culminate with taking out the boards of directors at "recalcitrant companies."[7]

The climate cartel's members include:

- "convening" and "collaborating" groups like Climate Action 100+, the Net Zero Asset Managers initiative, and the Glasgow Financial Alliance for Net Zero (GFANZ);[8]
- blue state pension funds like the California Public Employees' Retirement System (CalPERS);
- radical environmental non-profit organizations like Ceres;
- stockholder engagement service providers like As You Sow;
- activist investors like Arjuna Capital, LLC (Arjuna), Trillium Asset Management, LLC, Engine No. 1 LP, and Aviva Investors Americas, LLC, which "acquire a minimal ownership stake . . . to stop climate change, not to make a financial profit";[9]
- the "Big Three" asset managers BlackRock, Inc. (BlackRock), State Street Global Advisors (State Street), and The Vanguard Group, Inc.

---

[7] Climate Action 100+, *Work Plan Prepared for CIFF* 6 (July 24, 2020), CERES66958 at CERES66964.

[8] Deposition of Andrew Behar, Chief Executive Officer, As You Sow (Mar. 28, 2024) at 12:19–20, 18:17–19, 22:7, 22, 37:20. The Committee required testimony from Mr. Behar because As You Sow has withheld responsive documentary information from the Committee.

[9] Letter from ExxonMobil employee to Follow This executive 1 (Mar. 10, 2023), ARJUNA12843 at ARJUNA12844 [hereinafter "Mar. 10, 2023, Letter"].

(Vanguard), who together own 21.9% and vote 24.9% of the shares of the Standard and Poor's (S&P) 500;[10] and

- the foreign-owned proxy advisory duopoly of Institutional Shareholder Services Inc. (ISS) and Glass, Lewis & Co. (Glass Lewis), which have a combined 90% market share and advise mutual funds controlling more than $27 trillion in assets.[11]

The Committee has received documents from each of these members of the climate cartel. In total, as part of the investigation into ESG collusion, the Committee has now received and reviewed 272,294 documents and 2,565,258 pages of non-public information. Due to their failure to produce responsive material timely and fulsomely, the Committee was forced to issue document subpoenas to GFANZ, Ceres, As You Sow, Arjuna, BlackRock, State Street, Vanguard, ISS, and Glass Lewis.[12] In addition to documentary evidence, the Committee has completed transcribed interviews or depositions of the leaders of key players within the climate cartel.

This interim report focuses primarily upon the collusive conduct of Climate Action 100+, its co-founders Ceres and CalPERS, and its radical member Arjuna. Based upon the evidence obtained by the Committee, the members of the climate cartel are colluding toward a common goal: the "decarbonization" of American industry, which necessarily reduces output and increases prices for American consumers. Thus far, the investigation has revealed how the climate cartel has escalated its attacks on American companies and is forcing companies to slash output of products and services that are critical to Americans' daily lives. The Committee has found, among other things:

---

[10] Lucian Bebchuk & Scott Hirst, *Big Three Power, and Why It Matters*, 102 B.U. L. Rev. 1547, 1552 (2022).

[11] *See* Chong Shu, *The Proxy Advisory Industry*, 154 J. Fin. Econ. 103810, 1, 29 (2024).

[12] *See* Letter from Rep. Jim Jordan, Chairman, Comm. on the Judiciary, to John Eichlin (Nov. 1, 2023); Letter from Rep. Jim Jordan, Chairman, Comm. on the Judiciary, to Matthew Miller (June 14, 2023); Letter from Rep. Jim Jordan, Chairman, Comm. on the Judiciary, to Andrew Herman (Nov. 1, 2023); Letter from Rep. Jim Jordan, Chairman, Comm. on the Judiciary, to Veronica Renzi (Dec. 11, 2023); Letter from Rep. Jim Jordan, Chairman, Comm. on the Judiciary, to Alyssa DaCunha (Dec. 15, 2023); Letter from Rep. Jim Jordan, Chairman, Comm. on the Judiciary, to Donald Deng (Dec. 15, 2023); Letter from Rep. Jim Jordan, Chairman, Comm. on the Judiciary, to Robert Kelner (Dec. 11, 2023); Letter from Rep. Jim Jordan, Chairman, Comm. on the Judiciary, to Aaron Cutler (Dec. 20, 2023); Letter from Rep. Jim Jordan, Chairman, Comm. on the Judiciary, to Nichol Garzon-Mitchell (Dec. 20, 2023).

- *The climate cartel has declared war on the American way of life.* The climate cartel is waging "a Global World War" for net zero against disfavored American companies, including those in the fossil fuel, aviation, and farming industries that allow Americans to drive, fly, and eat.[13] It has described Climate Action 100+ as "the global Navy," and compared Ceres's efforts to "the Army ground troops" and "an 'air cover' strategic and silent bombing campaign by a newly funded division of the Air Force."[14]
- *The climate cartel has agreed to force corporations to "decarbonize."* Members of groups like Climate Action 100+ expressly commit to engage "with the companies in which [they] invest" to make them reach "net zero [greenhouse gas (GHG)] emissions by 2050" by disclosing their carbon emissions, reducing their carbon emissions, and adopting enforcement mechanisms to strengthen these commitments.[15]
- *The climate cartel "[r]amp[s] up" and "[e]scalate[s]"[16] pressure against corporations on the "wrong side of climate history."[17]* The climate cartel is "willing to go to the top rung" by filing shareholder resolutions, voting against management, and "replac[ing] board members" with those of its own choosing.[18]
- *The climate cartel seeks to "keep fossil fuels in the ground," raising prices and reducing output for American consumers.[19]* To reach net zero, as ESG activists demand, "fossil fuel use has to be reduced."[20] Airplane travel must be "capp[ed] . . . at 2019 levels" and "total flights" must be reduced by 12%.[21] Food demand growth must be

---

[13] E-mail from William Gridley to Kirsten Spalding, et al. (Feb. 26, 2020), CERES27804 at CERES27806–07.

[14] *Id.*

[15] Climate Action 100+, *Climate Action 100+ Signatory Handbook* 7 (June 2023), https://www.climateaction100.org/wp-content/uploads/2023/06/Signatory-Handbook-2023-Climate-Action-100.pdf.

[16] *Work Plan Prepared for CIFF*, *supra* note 7, at CERES66983.

[17] Climate Action 100+, *2020 Progress Report* 9 (2020), GFANZ13103 at GFANZ13111.

[18] *Work Plan Prepared for CIFF*, *supra* note 7, at CERES66963–64.

[19] Ceres, *Draft Ceres Organizational Profile for the Skoll Foundation* 14 (May 1, 2019), CERES59890 at CERES59903.

[20] Transcribed Interview of Danielle Fugere, President & Chief Counsel, As You Sow (Jan. 18, 2024) at 163:4–6. The Committee required testimony from Ms. Fugere because As You Sow has withheld responsive documentary information from the Committee.

[21] Climate Action 100+, Global Sector Strategies: Investor Actions to Align the Aviation Sector with the IEA's 1.5° Decarbonisation Pathway 17, SSGA-HJC.66656 at SSGA-HJC.66673 (Mar. 2022).

"reduce[d],"[22] with beef consumption slashed to "about half of current U.S. levels."[23]

- *The climate cartel is not done attacking American consumers.* Climate Action 100+ "is about action at this point, not just words/commitments/disclosure."[24] It has"mov[ed] beyond simple disclosure requests" and is now making "more ambitious" demands to companies.[25] For the climate cartel, "the job is . . . only just begun."[26]

The Biden Administration has failed to meaningfully investigate the climate cartel's collusion—let alone bring enforcement actions against its apparent violations of longstanding U.S. antitrust law. The Committee's aggressive oversight, however, has led members of Climate Action 100+ to withdraw from the group. On February 15, 2024, BlackRock, State Street, and J.P. Morgan Asset Management—three of the world's largest asset managers—withdrew their "nearly $14 trillion of total assets" under management from Climate Action 100+,[27] leaving the group without any "of the world's five largest asset managers" as members.[28] By March 1, 2024, Pacific Investment Management Company, LLC and Invesco Ltd.—two of the "large[st] US asset managers still in Climate Action 100+"[29]—had withdrawn

---

[22] World Res. Inst., *Executive Summary (Synthesis)*, https://research.wri.org/wrr-food/execu tive-summary-synthesis.

[23] World Res. Inst., *6 Pressing Questions About Beef and Climate Change, Answered* (Mar. 7, 2022), https://www. wri.org/insights/6-pressing-questions-about-beef-and-climate-change-answered.

[24] Climate Action 100+, *Long Term Strategy Meeting 14.10.21* 40 (Oct. 14, 2021), CERES59121 at CERES59160.

[25] Climate Action 100+, *KPI Summary and Rationale* 2 (July 31, 2022), CERES62708 at CERES62709.

[26] E-mail from Anne Simpson to Robert Eccles et al. (June 5, 2021), ENGINENO1-118HJC-PROD-6866 at ENGINENO1-118HJC-PROD-6866.

[27] Simon Jessop & Ross Kerber, *JPMorgan, State Street Quit Climate Group, BlackRock Steps Back*, Reuters (Feb. 15, 2024), https://www.reuters.com/sustainability/sustainable-finance-reporting/jpmorgan-fund-arm-quits- climate-action-100-investor-group-2024-02-15/.

[28] Patrick Temple-West & Brooke Masters, *JPMorgan and State Street Quit Climate Group as BlackRock Scales Back*, Fin. Times (Feb. 15, 2024), https://www.ft.com/content/3ce06a6f-f0e3-4f70-a078-82a6c265ddc2.

[29] *Id.*

as well.[30] Dozens of other members also appear to have left Climate Action 100+ in recent months.[31]

While this interim report examines the collusive conduct of Climate Action 100+, the Committee's investigation into the broader climate cartel remains ongoing. The Committee will continue to examine the adequacy and enforcement of current antitrust laws to determine whether legislative reforms are necessary to protect competition in the American economy.

I. The Climate Cartel Consists of "Convening" Groups, Radical Activists, and Financial Institutions that Collude to Kill Carbon

Members of the climate cartel include "convening" and "collaborating" groups,[32] blue state pension funds, extremist environmental non-profits, stockholder engagement service providers, activist investors, the "Big Three" asset managers, and the foreign-owned proxy advisory duopoly. Four of its most radical offenders are Climate Action 100+, a group that expressly requires its members to work to decarbonize the companies in which they invest; its co-founders Ceres, an environmental non-profit, and the California Public Employees' Retirement System (CalPERS), a blue state pension fund; and small activist investor Arjuna Capital, LLC (Arjuna).

A. Climate Action 100+ and Similar Groups "Convene" and "Coordinate" Collusion

Climate Action 100+ "build[s] on an idea from" CalPERS[33] and was established in December 2017 by Ceres, the United Nations-backed Principles for Responsible Investment (PRI), and similar activist environmentalist

---

[30] *See* Simon Jessop, *Invesco Joins List of US Asset Managers to Exit CA100+ Climate Group*, Reuters (Mar. 1, 2024), https://www.reuters.com/sustainability/invesco-joins-list-us-asset-managers-exit-ca100-climate-group-2024-03-01/.

[31] *See* Letter from Sean D. Reyes, Utah Attorney General, et al. to Climate Action 100+ Members 2 (Apr. 3, 2024) [hereinafter "Apr. 3, 2024, Letter"].

[32] Deposition of Andrew Behar, *supra* note 8, at 12:19–20, 18:17–19, 22:7, 22, 37:20.

[33] Climate Action 100+, *Steering Committee Agenda* 28 (Sept. 15, 2022), CERES59024 at CERES59051.

groups from Europe, Asia, and Australia and New Zealand.[34] Climate Action 100+ "convene[s]" and "coordinate[s]" financial industry collusion against disfavored corporations.[35] It bills itself as the "largest-ever global investor engagement initiative on climate change,"[36] and has been described as "the global Navy" in the climate cartel's "Global World War."[37]

Hundreds of asset managers, asset owners, and stockholder engagement service providers are members of Climate Action 100+.[38] As of 2023, Climate Action 100+ had more than 700 investors with combined assets under management of close to $68 trillion.[39] Climate Action 100+ members "encompass both mainstream and vanguard investors, and the vanguard investors are leveraging influence of the mainstream investors."[40] Its members include CalPERS, As You Sow, Arjuna, Trillium Asset Management, LLC (Trillium), Engine No. 1 LP (Engine No. 1), and Aviva Investors Americas, LLC (Aviva)[41]—and, until recently, also included BlackRock, Inc. (BlackRock) and State Street Global Advisors (State Street), two of the largest asset managers in the world.[42] Climate Action 100+ currently is governed by a steering committee that continues to include members from both Ceres and CalPERS.[43]

---

[34] *See* Climate Action 100+, *About Climate Action 100+*, https://www.climateaction 100.org/about/.

[35] Deposition of Andrew Behar, *supra* note 8, at 22:19–25, 23:1–5, 39:4–6, 68:21–25, 69:1–7.

[36] *Climate Action 100+ Signatory Handbook*, *supra* note 15, at 4.

[37] E-mail from William Gridley to Kirsten Spalding, et al., *supra* note 13, at CERES27807.

[38] *See* Climate Action 100+, *Progress Update 2023* 2 (Jan. 31, 2023), https://www. Climate action100.org/wp-content/uploads/2024/01/Climate-Action-100-Progress-Update-2023.pdf.

[39] *Id.* at 2, 4. As discussed below, five large asset managers with a combined roughly $17 trillion in total assets under management withdrew from Climate Action 100+ earlier this year. *See* discussion *infra* Section I.A.4.

[40] E-mail from David Ziv-Kreger to IIGCC employee et al. (Jan. 29, 2020), CERES17869 at CERES17870.

[41] Climate Action 100+, *Investor Signatories*, https://www.climateaction100.org/whos-involved/investors/?search_ investors=aviva&investor_type=All.

[42] *See* Bebchuk & Hirst, *supra* note 10. The Vanguard Group, Inc. (Vanguard) never joined Climate Action 100+, but was a member of the Net Zero Asset Managers initiative (NZAM) until December 2022. *See* Ross Kerber & Noor Zainab Hussain, *Vanguard Quits Net Zero Climate Effort, Citing Need for Independence*, Reuters (Dec. 7, 2022), https://www. reuters.com/business/sustainable-business/vanguard-quits-net-zero-climate-alliance-2022-12-07/.

[43] *See About Climate Action 100+*, *supra* note 34.

1. Climate Action 100+ Facilitates Collusion that Reduces Output and Increases Prices for Americans

Each member of Climate Action 100+ expressly agrees to engage "with the companies in which [it] invest[s]" to ensure that they "take necessary action on climate change" by "halving [greenhouse gas (GHG)] emissions by 2030 and delivering net zero GHG emissions by 2050, in line with the goals of the Paris Agreement to pursue efforts to limit warming to 1.5°C."[44]

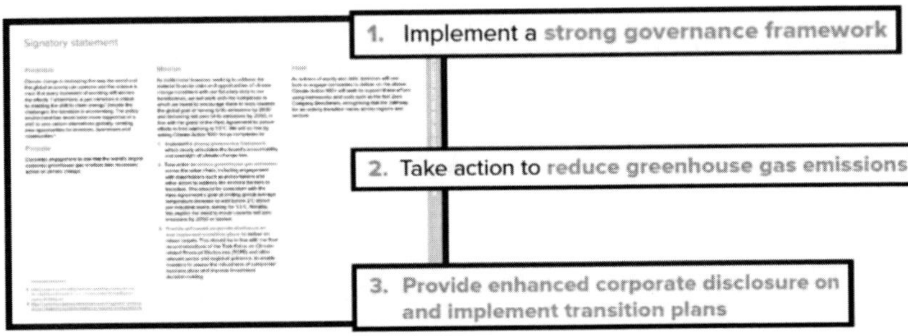

Climate Action 100+ requires its members to agree to emissions disclosure, reduction, and governance measures—i.e., to reduce, disclose, and enforce their emissions.[45]

In particular, Climate Action 100+ requires its members to push the companies in which they invest to disclose their carbon emissions, to reduce their carbon emissions, and to enforce these commitments by:

1. Implement[ing] a strong governance framework which clearly articulates the board's accountability and oversight of climate change risk.
2. Tak[ing] action to reduce greenhouse gas emissions across the value chain, including engagement with stakeholders such as policymakers and other actors to address the sectoral barriers to transition. This should be consistent with the Paris Agreement's goal of limiting

---

[44] *Climate Action 100+ Signatory Handbook*, *supra* note 15, at 7. The Paris Agreement is a United Nations-backed international treaty "to strengthen the global response to the threat of climate change" by "[h]olding the increase in the global average temperature to well below 2°C above pre-industrial levels and pursuing efforts to limit the temperature increase to 1.5°C above pre-industrial levels." Paris Agreement to the United Nations Framework Convention on Climate Change, Dec. 12, 2015, T.I.A.S. No. 16-1104, 3156 U.N.T.S. 54113.

[45] *Climate Action 100+ Signatory Handbook*, *supra* note 15, at 7.

global average temperature increase to well below 2°C above pre-industrial levels, aiming for 1.5°C. Notably, this implies the need to move towards net-zero emissions by 2050 or sooner.

3. Provid[ing] enhanced corporate disclosure on and implement[ing] transition plans to deliver on robust targets. This should be in line with the final recommendations of the Task Force on Climate-related Financial Disclosures (TCFD) and other relevant sector and regional guidance, to enable investors to assess the robustness of companies' business plans and improve investment decision-making.[46]

Thus, "Climate Action 100+ has established a common high-level agenda for company engagement to achieve clear commitments to cut emissions, improve governance and strengthen climate-related financial disclosures."[47] Its "signatories have agreed there should be a broad common engagement agenda" that "consists of seeking commitments from boards and senior management to: (1) "[p]rovide enhanced corporate disclosure"; (2) "[t]ake action to reduce greenhouse gas emissions"; and (3) "[i]mplement a strong governance framework."[48]

Other groups in the climate cartel have obtained similar commitments from their members. For example, the Glasgow Financial Alliance for Net Zero (GFANZ)-affiliated NZAM, which is comprised of more than 315 asset managers controlling $57 trillion in assets under management,[49] requires its members to "[w]ork in partnership with asset owner clients on decarbonisation goals, consistent with an ambition to reach net zero emissions by 2050 or sooner across all assets under management," by (1) "[p]ublish[ing] TCFD disclosures, including a climate action plan, annually"; (2) "[i]mplement[ing] a stewardship and engagement strategy, with a clear escalation and voting policy, that is consistent with [their] ambition for all assets under management to achieve net zero emissions by 2050 or sooner"; and (3) "[e]nsur[ing] any relevant direct and indirect policy advocacy [they] undertake is supportive of achieving global net zero emissions by 2050 or sooner."[50] Likewise, PRI,

---

[46] *Id.* (emphasis in original).

[47] Climate Action 100+, *The Three Asks*, https://www.climateaction100.org/approach/the-three-asks/[https://web.archive.org/web/20230327154741/https://www.climateaction100.org/approach/the-three-asks/].

[48] *Id.* (emphasis in original).

[49] Net Zero Asset Managers Initiative, *The Net Zero Asset Managers Initiative*, https://www.netzeroassetmanagers. org/.

[50] Net Zero Asset Managers Initiative, *Commitment*, https://www.netzeroassetmanagers.org/commitment/.

which includes 5,336 signatories controlling more than $121 trillion in assets under management,[51] requires its members to (1) "seek appropriate disclosure on ESG issues by the entities in which [they] invest," (2) "be active owners and incorporate ESG issues into [their] ownership policies and practices," and (3) "report on [their] activities and progress."[52]

These collusive decarbonization and net zero commitments necessarily require output reductions and price increases for American consumers, including in the fossil fuel, aviation, and farming industries.[53]

2. Climate Action 100+ Escalates and Flags Collusive Engagements Against Disfavored Companies

Climate Action 100+ was "designed to harness the collective influence of" its investor members in order "to spur companies" on the Climate Action 100+ focus list of 170 disfavored companies "to accelerate their emission reductions" and reach net zero.[54] "[T]he success and credibility of [Climate Action 100+] is dependent on [its] ability to show that engagement can have teeth—and that investors are willing to escalate pressure against companies that refuse to act."[55] Thus, Climate Action 100+ "[e]scalate[s] engagements with laggard focus companies" from negotiating with corporate management, to filing and supporting shareholder resolutions, to "[v]ot[ing] against" and "replac[ing] board members."[56]

---

51 Principles for Responsible Inv., *About the PRI*, https://www.unpri.org/about-us/about-the-pri.

52 Principles for Responsible Inv., *What Are the Principles for Responsible Investment?* https://www.unpri.org/ about-us/what-are-the-principles-for-responsible-investment.

53 *See* discussion *infra* Part IV.

54 Climate Action 100+, *WORK PLAN* 1 (June 23, 2020), CERES72388 at CERES72388; *see generally* Climate Action 100+, *KPIs to CIFF* (June 23, 2020), CERES72399 at CERES72399–413.

55 Memorandum from Kirsten Spalding to PMT 2 (May 6, 2020), CERES13570 at CERES13571.

56 *Work Plan Prepared for CIFF*, *supra* note 7, at CERES66963; *see* discussion *infra* section III.

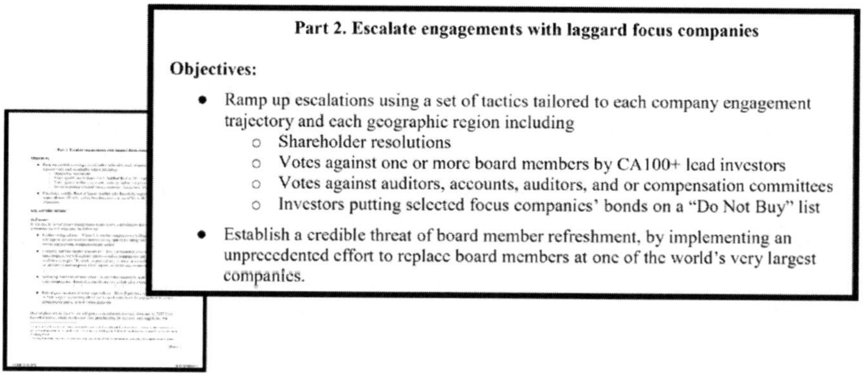

Part 2. Escalate engagements with laggard focus companies

Objectives:

- Ramp up escalations using a set of tactics tailored to each company engagement trajectory and each geographic region including
  - Shareholder resolutions
  - Votes against one or more board members by CA100+ lead investors
  - Votes against auditors, accounts, auditors, and or compensation committees
  - Investors putting selected focus companies' bonds on a "Do Not Buy" list
- Establish a credible threat of board member refreshment, by implementing an unprecedented effort to replace board members at one of the world's very largest companies.

Climate Action 100+ applies escalating "engagement" pressure to disfavored companies that it views as "laggard[s]" in caving to its radical demands.[57]

For Climate Action 100+, an especially "powerful" tool[58] is flagging "key shareholder proposals and management votes" for support by its members.[59] This flagging process "tell[s] investors which issues are a priority for the initiative"[60] and "[s]trengthen[s] [its] ability to win key votes."[61] "Votes flagged by [Climate Action 100+] have gotten a high level of attention from the market including proxy advisors such as [Glass, Lewis & Co. (Glass Lewis)] and [Institutional Shareholder Services Inc. (ISS)]."[62] Even "[t]he threat of flagging the resolutions [has] proved successful in pushing

---

[57] *Work Plan Prepared for CIFF*, *supra* note 7, at CERES66963.

[58] E-mail from Ceres employee to Morgan LaManna et al. (June 2, 2021), CERES9645 at CERES9645.

[59] Climate Action 100+, *2024 Proxy Season & Flagged Shareholder Votes*, https://www.climateaction100.org/approach/proxy-season/; *see* discussion *infra* section I.A.2. Flagging also is significant for votes on members of boards of directors. Heading into the 2021 proxy season, activist investor Engine No. 1 agreed with Ceres "how critical it would be for the [ExxonMobil] director vote to be flagged as part of the [Climate Action 100+] process." E-mail from Andrew Logan to Kirsten Spalding (Feb. 17, 2021), CERES63603 at CERES63603. Following the climate cartel's replacement of three members of the ExxonMobil board, Climate Action 100+ attributed this unprecedented success in part to having "flagged the Engine No[.] 1 slate on its website." Climate Action 100+, *Exxon Case Study* 3 (July 2021), CALPERS_4105 at CALPERS_4107.

[60] Climate Action 100+, *Steering Committee Meeting* 3 (Apr. 15, 2021), CERES35007 at CERES35009.

[61] E-mail from Cynthia McHale to Morgan LaManna et al. (Sept. 28, 2020), CERES10362 at CERES10364.

[62] Climate Action 100+, *Steering Committee Agenda* 4 (Mar. 17, 2022), CERES62503 at CERES62506.

companies to make commitments ahead of [annual general meetings] in return for a withdrawal."[63]

The objective of escalating and flagging engagements is to ensure that "[a]ll companies on the focus list have committed to net zero or gone out of business as investors are no longer providing them with capital."[64] In other words, Climate Action 100+ has taken it upon itself to "identify[] which companies will be on the right and wrong side of climate history."[65]

3. Climate Action 100+ Bullies and Threatens Asset Managers, Weaponizing Their Clients to Force Them to Join and Obey the Climate Cartel

Climate Action 100+ leverages aligned asset owners to bully asset managers to join and vote with the climate cartel.

First, the climate cartel bullies asset managers to join. In order to "[i]ncrease results on key votes," Climate Action 100+ has sought to "[m]ov[e] major asset managers—including Vanguard, State Street, Fidelity—to align with [Climate Action 100+] on voting."[66] Thus, Climate Action 100+ has discussed coordinating asset owners to "aggressively exert pressure on asset managers to align votes with [Climate Action 100+] goals."[67] This is because, as clients, "asset owners are in the best position to shift the frustrating voting behaviors of the 'big three'" asset managers, BlackRock, State Street, and Vanguard.[68]

For example, after "Blackrock and Vanguard voted against all of the US shareholder proposals backed by" Climate Action 100+ in 2019, Ceres initiated a campaign to pressure several of the world's largest asset managers, including BlackRock, State Street, and Fidelity, "to align [their] corporate engagements with Climate Action 100+" because doing so "would critically amplify [Climate Action 100+'s] pressure on recalcitrant companies."[69] As Ceres explained: "[T]here is no disputing the importance of moving [BlackRock, State Street, and Fidelity] to vote for climate proposals" because

---

63 *KPI Summary and Rationale*, *supra* note 25, at CERES62709.

64 Climate Action 100+, *Global Steering Committee—Strategy Session 1* 8 (Oct. 27, 2020), CERES51901 at CERES51908.

65 *2020 Progress Report*, *supra* note 17, at GFANZ13111.

66 *Work Plan Prepared for CIFF*, *supra* note 7, at CERES66958.

67 Climate Action 100+, *Steering Committee Meeting Minutes* 2 (Mar. 26, 2020), CERES1260 at CERES1261 (emphasis added).

68 *Id.*

69 Climate Action 100+, *Priorities for Expanded Impact* 4–5 (Nov. 25, 2019), CERES50191 at CERES50194–95.

"they would tip many important votes above50%."[70] To effect its plan, Ceres "convened large asset owners to align around using their influence as clients of big asset managers" in order to force the asset managers "to step up their climate ambition and leadership"—a situation that gave Ceres "unprecedented leverage."[71] Indeed, "BlackRock was influenced to join" Climate Action 100+[72] because the Japanese "Government Pension Investment Fund (GPIF)—at $1.7 trillion the world's largest pension fund—recently shifted $50 billion away from BlackRock,"[73] and Lloyds Banking Group subsidiary "Scottish Widows insisted on putting [Climate Action 100+] into [its] asset management contract with BlackRock."[74]

Second, like other cartels, Climate Action 100+ seeks "to detect and deter defections from [its] collusive strategies"[75] by increasing its "[s]ignatory [a]ccountability."[76] In particular, Climate Action 100+ "signatories are under scrutiny from a range of stakeholders over their voting records . . . for [Climate Action 100+] flagged votes."[77] Thus, Climate Action 100+ expects more "pressure on signatories [to] support [its] agenda with votes where possible."[78]

For example, if "BlackRock [were] not living up to its promise" to the climate cartel, then BlackRock's "asset owners [could] decide to move their money elsewhere to be managed," which "could mean billions of dollars in lost revenue to BlackRock."[79] In particular, Ceres emphasized "that BlackRock [would] be held accountable for [its] votes on shareholder resolutions"—and that if its voting "record [did] not dramatically change, Ceres [was in] a position to organize asset owner partners to call BlackRock to account."[80] Moreover, "the three other largest asset managers (Fidelity, Vanguard, State Street) [were] facing similar pressure. If they [didn't] align

---

[70] E-mail from Rob Berridge to Ceres employee (Nov. 21, 2019), CERES9649 at CERES9649.

[71] E-mail from Ceres employee to Northstar executive et al. (Feb. 20, 2020), CERES27685 at CERES27685.

[72] Climate Action 100+, *Proposal for Increasing Ambition* 1 (Mar. 26, 2020), CERES63234 at CERES63234.

[73] E-mail from David Ziv-Kreger to KR Foundation employee (Jan. 15, 2020), CERES14474 at CERES14474.

[74] *Proposal for Increasing Ambition*, *supra* note 72, at CERES63234.

[75] Margaret C. Levenstein & Valerie Y. Suslow, *What Determines Cartel Success?*, 44 J. Econ. Lit. 43, 44 (2006).

[76] Climate Action 100+, *Steering Committee Agenda* 15–16 (Dec. 17, 2020), CERES1214 at CERES1228–29.

[77] Memorandum from Cynthia McHale to CIFF 2–3 (Mar. 21, 2021), CERES23002 at CERES23003–04.

[78] *Long Term Strategy Meeting 14.10.21*, *supra* note 24, at CERES59159.

[79] E-mail from David Ziv-Kreger to KR Foundation employee *supra* note 73, at CERES14474.

[80] *Id.*

their voting with [Climate Action 100+], they too risk[ed] losing clients and revenue."[81]

4. Climate Action 100+ Signatories Withdraw from the Group Following the Launch of the Committee's Oversight Investigation

Members of Climate Action 100+ have withdrawn from the group following the launch of the Committee's investigation into their anticompetitive collusion. On February 15, 2024, BlackRock, State Street, and J.P. Morgan Asset Management (JPAM)—three of the world's largest asset managers—withdrew their "nearly $14 trillion of total assets" under management from Climate Action 100+,[82] leaving the group without any "of the world's five largest asset managers" as members.[83] BlackRock specifically withdrew because Climate Action 100+'s strategy "conflicted with US laws requiring money managers to act solely in clients' long-term economic interest."[84] State Street similarly explained that it left Climate Action 100+ because the group's "requirements for signatories [were] not consistent with [State Street's] independent approach to proxy voting and portfolio company engagement."[85] JPAM, which recently emphasized that it "does not work in concert with other investors on investment matters and makes its own independent decisions concerning investee companies," bluntly stated that it "determined that it will no longer participate in Climate Action 100+ engagements."[86]

[81] *Id*
[82] Jessop & Kerber, *supra* note 27.
[83] Temple-West & Masters, *supra* note 28.
[84] *Id.*
[85] *Id.*
[86] *Id.*

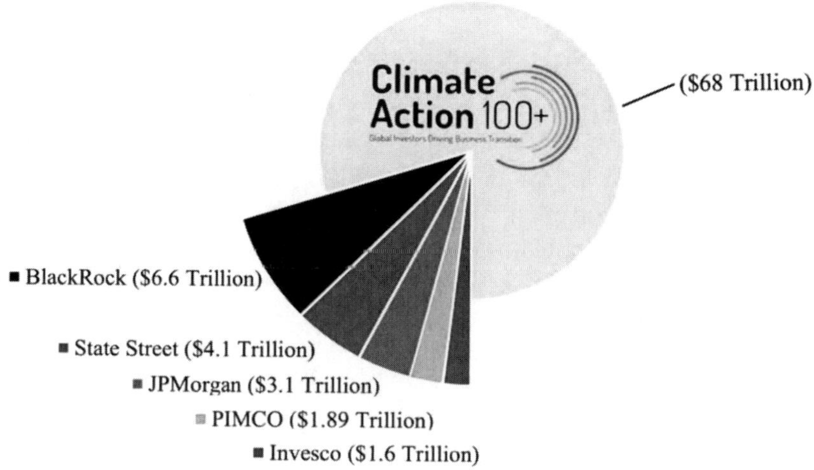

The Committee's investigation has led a large slice of pie—$17 trillion worth of assets under management—to depart Climate Action 100+ in recent months.[87]

Soon after those three asset managers left the group, two of the "large[st] US asset managers still in Climate Action 100+"[88] also withdrew from the group.[89] Specifically, the next day, on February 16, 2024, Pacific Investment Management Company, LLC (PIMCO), an asset manager with $1.89 trillion in assets under management,[90] left Climate Action 100+, emphasizing that "PIMCO operates its own portfolio-relevant engagement activities with issuers on sustainability."[91] Two weeks later, on March 1, 2024, Invesco Ltd. (Invesco), an asset manager with over $1.6 trillion in assets under management,[92] withdrew from Climate Action 100+, indicating that Invesco

---

[87] *See* Jessop & Kerber, *supra* note 27; PIMCO, *Our Firm*, https://www.pimco.com/en-us/our-firm/; *Bond Manager PIMCO Withdraws from Climate Action 100+ Investor Coalition*, Reuters (Feb. 16, 2024), https://www.reuters.com/markets/us/bond-manager-pimco-withdraws-climate-action-100-investor-coalition-2024-02-16/.

[88] Temple-West & Masters, *supra* note 28.

[89] Jessop & Kerber, *supra* note 27.

[90] PIMCO, *supra* note 87.

[91] *Bond Manager PIMCO Withdraws from Climate Action 100+ Investor Coalition*, *supra* note 87.

[92] Invesco, *Invesco Ltd. Announces April 30, 2024 Assets Under Management* (May 9, 2024), https://invesco2021tf.q4web.com/news/news-details/2024/Invesco-Ltd.-Announces-April-30-2024-Assets-Under-Management/default. aspx.

believed that its "clients' interests in this area are better served through [its] existing investor-led and client-centric issuer engagement approach."[93]

Dozens of other members also appear to have left Climate Action 100+ in recent months.[94] Despite the recent defections of a number of its members, including its largest asset managers, Climate Action 100+ remains a formidable force and a continuing threat to the welfare of American consumers. As Climate Action 100+ recently boasted: "hundreds of investor signatories remain committed to ensuring 170 of the largest greenhouse gas emitters reduce emissions, improve governance, and strengthen climate-related financial disclosures."[95]

B. Ceres and Other Radical Activists Set the ESG Agenda and Make Increasingly Extreme Demands

Ceres was established in 1989 by Joan Bavaria,[96] the former president of activist investor Trillium and the "'founding mother' of ESG investing."[97] It is a left-wing environmental non- profit that describes itself as "working to accelerate the transition to a cleaner, more just, and sustainable economy" by "inspir[ing] the world's most influential investors and companies with the greatest impact on our economy to urgently act,"[98] and has compared itself to both "the Army ground troops" and "a newly funded division of the Air Force" conducting an "'air cover' strategic and silent bombing campaign" in the climate cartel's "Global World War."[99] Like Climate Action 100+, Ceres "convenes" and "coordinates" financial industry collusion against disfavored corporations.[100] Ceres's Investor Network includes more than 220 investors controlling combined assets under management of $44 trillion.[101] Its members

---

[93] *See* Jessop, *supra* note 30.

[94] *See* Apr. 3, 2024, Letter, *supra* note 31, at 2.

[95] Climate Action 100+, *Climate Action 100+ Reaction to Recent Departures* (Feb. 26, 2024), https://www.climate action100.org/news/climate-action-100-reaction-to-recent-departures/.

[96] Ceres, *About Us*, https://www.ceres.org/about.

[97] Trillium, *40 Years of Investing for a Better World* 3 (2022), https://www.trillium invest.com/documents/40-year- brochure.

[98] *About Us*, *supra* note 96.

[99] E-mail from William Gridley to Kirsten Spalding, et al., *supra* note 13, at CERES27807.

[100] Deposition of Andrew Behar, *supra* note 8, at 18:17–18, 22:7, 38:21–24, 39:4–6, 68:21–23, 69:1–8.

[101] Ceres, *Home*, https://www.ceres.org/.

include CalPERS, As You Sow, Arjuna, Trillium, Engine No. 1, Aviva, BlackRock, and State Street.[102]

Ceres co-founded and continues to help lead Climate Action 100+.[103] In addition, Ceres also co-founded NZAM and the Paris Aligned Asset Owners, both of which coordinate investors to pressure companies to decarbonize and reach net zero.[104]

1. Ceres Coordinates Collusive Engagements Against Disfavored Companies

Ceres believes that the world economy is "highly responsive" to the interests of "[l]arge institutional investors [with] . . . vast global assets" that "have the ability to drive far reaching impact"—including "among the thousands of public and private companies they own."[105] Thus, Ceres "lead[s] a coordinated push to harness the extraordinary power of financial system leaders to accelerate the transition of the global economy to net-zero by steering massive flows of capital . . . away from investments that lock in greenhouse gas emissions."[106] In other words, Ceres "leverag[es] the financial sector to . . . mov[e] all actors in the financial system . . . to commit to, pursue, and promote a just, global transition to net-zero emissions."[107]

---

[102] Ceres, *Ceres Investor Network*, https://www.ceres.org/networks/investor.

[103] *See* discussion *supra* Section I.A.

[104] *See* The Investor Agenda, *Confidential Update for the Children's Investment Fund Foundation (CIFF)* 8 (Oct. 2021), CERES66630 at CERES66637; Paris Aligned Asset Owners, *Governance*, https://www.parisalignedasset owners.org/governance/.

[105] Ceres, The Ceres Net Zero Finance Initiative: Harnessing the Power of Investors, Banks, and Insurers to Accelerate Climate Mitigation 5 (July 2, 2021), CERES2871 at CERES2875.

[106] Ceres, *Net-Zero Finance Campaign: Updated 5-Year Plan* 6 (Mar. 2020), CERES37663 at CERES37668.

[107] *Id.*

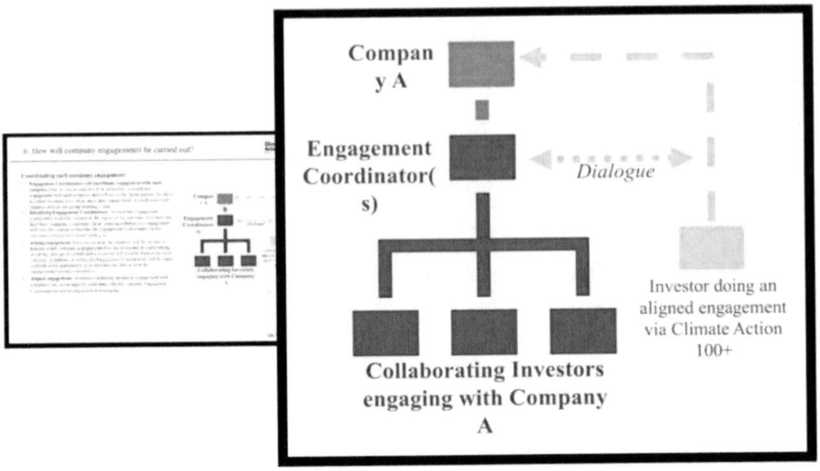

Climate Action 100+ also visually illustrates the pressure that it places on companies.[108]

To bully companies to reduce fossil fuel consumption and production, Ceres "recruit[s], educate[s], and mobilize[s] investors along the engagement continuum"[109] and "[u]s[es] 'harder- nosed' tools to increase pressure on financial actors, such as benchmarking performance . . . and shareholder engagement."[110] These efforts include "[d]evelop[ing] specific plans for engaging each of the major asset managers (e.g., BlackRock, Vanguard, Fidelity, State Street) and asset owners" to reduce emissions throughout their portfolios.[111] Ceres does so by supporting "shareholder resolutions to adopt net-zero goals" at companies "that are not working with Ceres and those that are moving too slow or are less willing to act."[112] When Ceres does not get the results that it has demanded, it may escalate to coordinating "investor campaigns to replace directors."[113]

Significantly, Ceres's engagements may be even more extreme than those coordinated through Climate Action 100+. "[W]hen [Climate Action 100+] engagement do[es]n't move fast enough, that triggers bringing in a parallel group of more ambitious investors . . . to escalate" in "good cop, bad cop"

---

[108] Climate Action 100+, Investor Briefing Pack: Overview of the Climate Action 100+ and How to Join 13 (Oct. 18, 2017), CALPERS_48039 at CALPERS_48051.

[109] Child.'s Inv. Fund Found., Ceres Long Form Grant Agreement 2 (Mar. 2022), CERES85238 at CERES85239.

[110] Net-Zero Finance Campaign: Updated 5-Year Plan, supra note 106, at CERES37671.

[111] *Id.* at CERES37675–76.

[112] *Id.* at CERES37676, CERES37678.

[113] *Id.*

engagements.[114] There, Ceres may "[e]ngage behind the scenes with more activist NGOs" and "benefit[s] from having a 'left flank' of groups creating pressure on the actors in the financial system."[115]

Ceres's objective is to make "access to finance dependent on the transition to net-zero" by "fundamental[ly] rewrit[ing] . . . the rules for capital formation."[116] Specifically, Ceres aims to "[t]ighten[] the availability" of project "financing and coverage from investors, banks, and insurers" in order to "bend the curve faster towards a 1.5°C. [sic] future."[117] Succinctly stated: Ceres "is focused on where the money is—and on redirecting it."[118]

2. Ceres Coordinates Collusion through the Ceres Investor Portal—But Has Refused to Produce its Contents in Response to the Committee's Subpoena

Ceres maintains a password-protected web platform known as the Ceres Investor Portal that is used by the climate cartel for "[e]ngagement coordination, tracking, and support" as well as "[m]onitor[ing] upcoming votes."[119] The Ceres Investor Portal "[c]ontains [a] full database of all engagements (proposals, dialogues, letters) that [Ceres] ha[s],"[120] including engagements orchestrated through Climate Action 100+.[121] Of particular significance, the Ceres Investor Portal has served as "the primary means of communication" for shareholder engagements,[122] housing a "[m]essaging function," "[n]otes from meetings," "[a]nalysis from Ceres . . . and lead investors on companies," and "[c]ollaborating investor lists."[123]

---

[114] Ceres, *Prep for CIFF Call Focused on 5 Sectors* 3 (Dec. 14, 2021), CERES85006 at CERES85008; *see* E-mail from AIGCC employee to Asset Management One employee (Jul. 15, 2020), CALPERS_9765 at CALPERS_9765.

[115] *Net-Zero Finance Campaign: Updated 5-Year Plan*, *supra* note 106, at CERES37673, CERES37678.

[116] *Id.* at CERES37668, CERES37670.

[117] *Id.* at CERES37668.

[118] *Id.* at CERES37669.

[119] Ceres, *Ceres Investor Portal* 10 (May 2018), CERES15943 at CERES15952.

[120] *Id.* at CERES15963.

[121] E-mail from Morgan LaManna to PRI employee (Nov. 19, 2018), CERES75900 at CERES75900.

[122] E-mail from Church of Commissioners for England employee to Exxon Climate Action 100+ Supporting Investors (June 12, 2018), CALPERS_4417 at CALPERS_4418.

[123] Climate Action 100+, *Ceres North America Engagement Working Group Webinar* 18 (Feb. 5, 2019), CERES75072 at CERES75090.

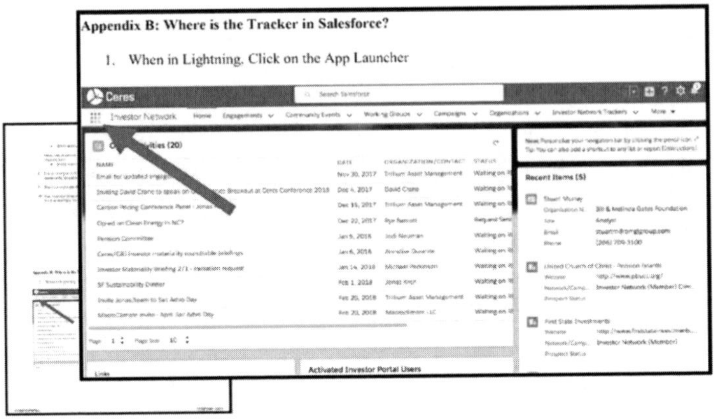

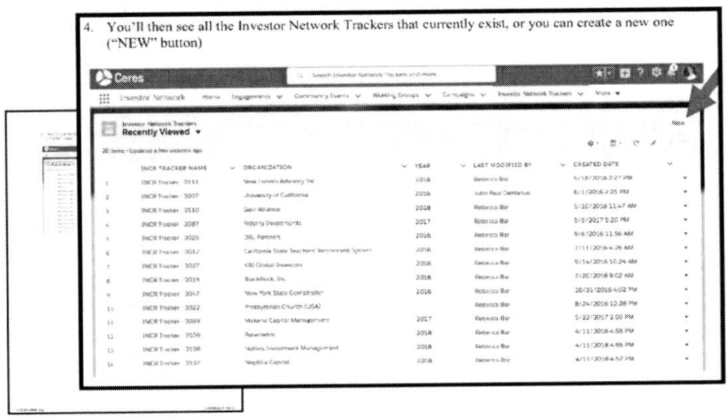

Ceres produced these screenshots of the Ceres Investor Portal to the Committee on July 7, 2023—yet Ceres's counsel claimed not to be familiar with the Ceres Investor Portal on a call with Committee staff nearly four months later on October 24, 2023.[124]

Despite the centrality of the Ceres Investor Portal to the climate cartel's operations and possible antitrust violations, and its obvious responsiveness to the categories of information demanded by the Committee's subpoena,[125] Ceres has refused to provide the Committee with meaningful access to these materials. To date, despite the Committee's repeated engagement,[126] Ceres has

---

[124] Memorandum from Ceres employee to Relationship Managers 3, 5 (May 22, 2018), CERES11369 at CERES11371, CERES11373.

[125] *See* Subpoena at 1 (June 14, 2023).

[126] *See* Letter from Rep. Jim Jordan, Chairman, Comm. on the Judiciary, to Mindy Lubber (Dec. 31, 2022) [hereinafter "Dec. 31, 2022, Letter"]; *see also* Letter from Rep. Jim Jordan,

not produced the Ceres Investor Portal to the Committee "in a form . . . in which it is ordinarily maintained or in a reasonably usable form."[127] Nor has Ceres provided the Committee with access to the Ceres Investor Portal itself, despite the Committee's repeated requests that it do so.[128] Instead, Ceres has produced just three documents, consisting of spreadsheets that were exported from data stored in searchable format on the Ceres Investor Portal[129]—even though the Ceres Investor Portal "[c]ontains [a] full database of all engagements"[130] and has served as "the primary means of communication" for shareholder engagements.[131] The format of this limited amount of material that Ceres did produce was degraded such that it was not reasonably usable in the Committee's investigation.

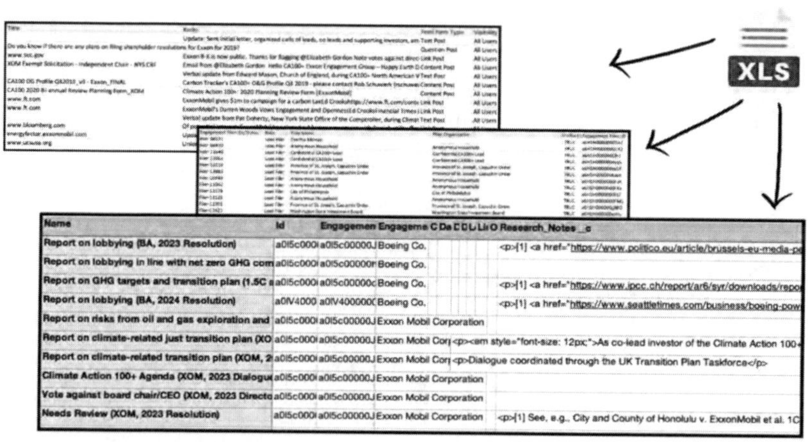

Ceres belatedly produced three spreadsheets of data exported from the Ceres Investor Portal on March 22, 2024. They are virtually unreadable.[132]

Chairman, Comm. on the Judiciary, to Mindy Lubber (May 5, 2023) [hereinafter "May 5, 2023, Letter"].

[127] Fed. R. Civ. P. 34(b)(2)(E)(ii).

[128] *See* Dec. 31, 2022, Letter, *supra* note 126; *see also* May 5, 2023, Letter, *supra* note 126.

[129] *See* Letter from Matthew Miller to Rep. Jim Jordan, Chairman, Comm. on the Judiciary 1 (Mar. 22, 2024).

[130] *Ceres Investor Portal*, *supra* note 119, at CERES15963.

[131] -mail from Church of Commissioners for England employee to Exxon Climate Action 100+ Supporting Investors, *supra* note 122, at CALPERS_4417.

[132] Ceres, Exxon Boeing Walmart Spreadsheet, CERES82584; Ceres, Exxon Boeing Walmart Bulk Query Result Spreadsheet, CERES82585; Ceres, Exxon Investor Network Groups Spreadsheet, CERES82586.

As the Committee continues its investigation, it will continue to press for Ceres's full compliance with the Committee's subpoena. All options remain on the table to ensure that the Committee receives the information that it needs.

C. California Public Employees' Retirement System (CalPERS) and Other Asset Owners Use Retirees's Money to Advance Their Left-Wing Agenda

CalPERS, the largest public pension fund in the United States, "serves more than 2 million members"[133] and controls more than $485 billion in assets.[134] It claims to be "united with investors around the globe to engage with the world's largest greenhouse gas emitters to do more to step up actions on climate change."[135] Specifically, "CalPERS is committed to achieving portfolio emissions in line with the 1.5-degree Celsius target" agreed to by Climate Action 100+ because CalPERS claims that "[c]limate change poses one of the top three risks to" its portfolio.[136]

1. CalPERS Helped Found and Helps Lead Climate Action 100+

Upon "evaluat[ing] [its] public assets' carbon footprint," CalPERS "discovered emissions were heavily concentrated" with "only 80" of the more than ten thousand companies in its portfolio "responsible for 50% of the GHG emissions."[137] Thus, CalPERS determined that "[t]he future emissions (emission trajectory) created by these companies is critical to whether the global economy meets the Paris Agreement."[138] As a result, CalPERS worked with Ceres, PRI, and similar activist environmentalist groups to launch Climate Action 100+ to focus on engaging "[t]he world's top, publicly-traded, systemically-important carbon emitters" and other "[c]ompanies with significant opportunity to drive the transition to a low-carbon economy."[139]

---

133 CalPERS, *CalPERS Story*, https://www.calpers.ca.gov/page/about/organization/calpers-story.

134 CalPERS, *Public Employees' Retirement Fund (PERF) Monthly Update* (Apr. 30, 2024), https://www.calpers. ca.gov/docs/perf-monthly-update.pdf.

135 Climate Action 100+, *Speaker Prep Memorandum with Remarks* 4 (Dec. 6, 2017), CALPERS_5908 at CALPERS_5911.

136 CalPERS, *Sustainable Investment and the Path to Net Zero* 3, 27 (Jan. 5, 2022), CALPERS_1861 at CALPERS_1863, CALPERS_1887.

137 CalPERS, *Climate Change*, https://www.calpers.ca.gov/page/investments/sustainable-investments-program/ climate-change.

138 *Id.*

139 *Id.*

CalPERS held the inaugural chair of Climate Action 100+[140] and "continues to have a significant leadership role serving as a member of the Climate Action 100+ Steering Committee."[141] In addition, CalPERS is a board member of Ceres, a founding signatory of PRI, and a member and former steering committee leader of the GFANZ-affiliated Net-Zero Asset Owner Alliance (NZAOA).[142]

2. CalPERS Aggressively Engages and Tries to Take Control of ExxonMobil

CalPERS has "assumed the lead role for 22 of the companies identified for engagement" by Climate Action 100+—"the largest number engaged by a single asset owner in the initiative."[143] "Through collaborative engagement [CalPERS] will ask these companies to curb emissions, strengthen climate-related financial disclosures, and improve governance on climate change."[144] CalPERS "generally support[s] greenhouse gas emission proposals" as well as "proposals seeking greater disclosure of a company's environmental practices."[145]

In particular, CalPERS doggedly has pursued ExxonMobil, the United States' largest oil and gas company.[146] CalPERS has served as a lead investor for Climate Action 100+'s ExxonMobil engagement.[147] As illustrated in the CalPERS "Case Study" graphic below, CalPERS escalated its engagement with ExxonMobil from filing shareholder proposals, to voting against ExxonMobil directors, to supporting Climate Action 100+'s efforts to replace the incumbent board with directors of the climate cartel's choosing:

---

140 CalPERS, CalPERS' Investment Strategy on Climate Change: First Report in Response to the Taskforce on Climate-Related Financial Disclosure 17 (June 2020), CALPERS_100 at CALPERS_118.

141 CalPERS, CalPERS United Nations Net Zero Asset Owner Alliance Partnership, https://www.calpers.ca. gov/page/investments/sustainable-investments-program/climate-change/united-nations-net-zero-asset-owner- alliance-partnership.

142 CalPERS, 2016–21 Sustainable Investment Strategic Plan: Five Year Progress Report 4, CALPERS_72 at CALPERS_75.

143 CalPERS' Investment Strategy on Climate Change: First Report in Response to the Taskforce on Climate-Related Financial Disclosure, supra note 140, at CALPERS_118.

144 Speaker Prep Memorandum with Remarks, supra note 135, at CALPERS_5911.

145 CalPERS, CalPERS Proxy Voting Guidelines 9 (May 2022), CALPERS_182 at CALPERS_192.

146 Companies Market Cap, Largest Oil and Gas Companies by Market Cap, https://companies marketcap.com/oil-gas/largest-oil-and-gas-companies-by-market-cap/.

147 *Exxon Case Study*, *supra* note 59, at CALPERS_4105–10.

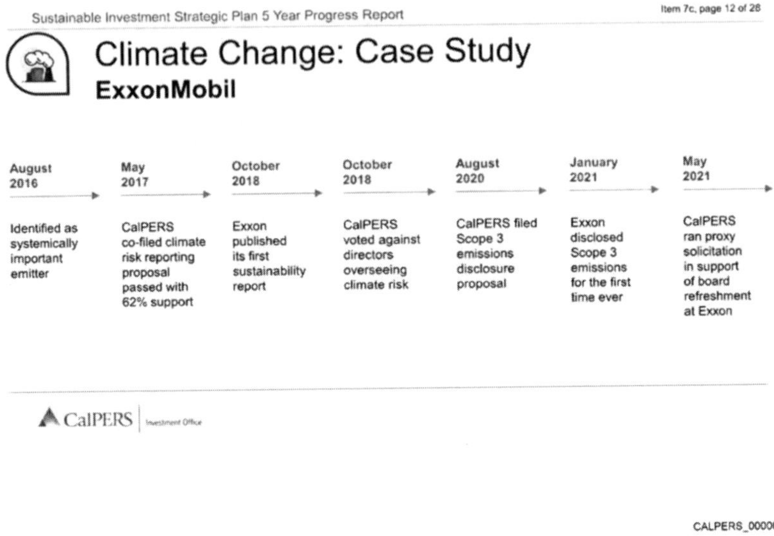

CalPERS presented the escalation of its engagement with ExxonMobil as a "case study" in its sustainable investment strategic plan five-year progress report.[148]

Although the ExxonMobil board replacement campaign was driven by "pipsqueak" activist investor Engine No. 1, which had "roughly $50 million in company shares against ExxonMobil's "market capitalization of nearly $247 billion,"[149] CalPERS played a pivotal role in the effort. Specifically, CalPERS "publicly supported" the campaign, its proxy solicitation was "flag[ged] as a key vote,"[150] and CalPERS met with Vanguard to solicit its vote for the board replacement.[151] Climate Action 100+'s then-Steering Committee Chair and CalPERS's then- Managing Investment Director, Board Governance & Sustainability Anne Simpson said that "there ought to be consequences of Exxon's decision to seek removal of [an emissions reduction] resolution" at the Securities and Exchange Commission (SEC) and that

---

[148] *2016–21 Sustainable Investment Strategic Plan: Five Year Progress Report*, *supra* note 142, at CALPERS_83

[149] E-mail from Gasthalter employee to Charlie Penner et al. (May 26, 2021), ENGINENO1-118HJC-PROD-14550 at ENGINENO1-118HJC-PROD-14555.

[150] *Id.* at CALPERS_4107.

[151] *See* E-mail from Anne Simpson to Vanguard employee (May 17, 2021), CALPERS_3163 at CALPERS_3163.

"Exxon's board members should have hell to pay."[152] Ceres concurred that "[t]he need for escalation at Exxon seems to have arrived," and stood "poised to amplify and support the next investor-led action as usual."[153]

That effort to "refresh" the board at ExxonMobil was a tremendous success for the climate cartel, resulting in the replacement of three of the company's directors with "climate activists . . . backed publicly by three of the largest pension funds in the U.S. and Climate Action 100+ signatories—CalPERS, [the California State Teachers Retirement System (CalSTRS)], and the New York State Common Retirement Fund."[154] Nevertheless, Ms. Simpson proclaimed afterward that the climate cartel's "job is . . . only just begun."[155] Indeed, on May 29, 2024, "CalPERS voted against all sitting members of ExxonMobil's board of directors, including Chief Executive Officer Darren Woods, at the company's annual general meeting" because ExxonMobil dared to challenge a radical "shareholder resolution . . . involv[ing] ExxonMobil's efforts to address climate change."[156]

D. Arjuna Capital and Other Activist Investors Hold Small Stakes but Make Draconian Demands of Corporations

Arjuna was founded in 2013 by former Trillium Senior Vice President & Chief Strategist Farnum Brown and is an activist asset manager with around $458 million in assets under management.[157] In Arjuna's view, the United States is "facing a second civil war . . . led by a pro-white, pro-Christian agenda."[158] Arjuna believes that this war "will be fought by the investors who have a voice in how corporate America responds."[159] Although relatively small, Arjuna

---

[152] Climate Action 100+, *Steering Committee Subset Meeting Minutes* 3 (Feb. 26, 2019), CERES24135 at CERES24137.

[153] E-mail from Cynthia McHale to Anne Simpson (Apr. 2, 2019), CALPERS_26293 at CALPERS_26293; E-mail from Morgan LaManna to Anne Simpson et al. (Apr. 2, 2019), CALPERS_26293 at CALPERS_26294.

[154] Ceres, *Narrative Report to Yajilarra Trust* 5 (July 30, 2021), CERES29333 at CERES29337.

[155] E-mail from Anne Simpson to Robert Eccles et al., *supra* note 26, at ENGINENO1-118HJC-PROD-6866.

[156] CalPERS, *CalPERS Votes Against ExxonMobil Directors for Anti-Shareholder Lawsuit* (May 29, 2024), https:// www.calpers.ca.gov/page/newsroom/calpers-news/2024/calpers-votes-against-exxonmobil-directors-for-anti- shareholder-lawsuit. ExxonMobil's lawsuit is discussed below. *See* discussion *infra* Section I.D.1.

[157] Arjuna Capital, LLC, Uniform Application for Investment Adviser Registration and Report by Exempt Reporting Advisers (Form ADV) (Mar. 28, 2024).

[158] Arjuna Capital, *Shareholder Engagement* 1 (Jan. 2021), ARJUNA5177 at ARJUNA5177.

[159] *Id.* at 5178.

sees itself as "the gadfly that shines a light on [a] company's serious flaws before all of its shareholders."[160] It is a member of both Climate Action 100+ and NZAM.[161]

Arjuna believes that "active engagement is essential" in a "world of widening inequality, fragile democracies, and increasing climate risk."[162] The importance that Arjuna places on engagement is reflected in the figure below from an internal Arjuna strategy presentation.

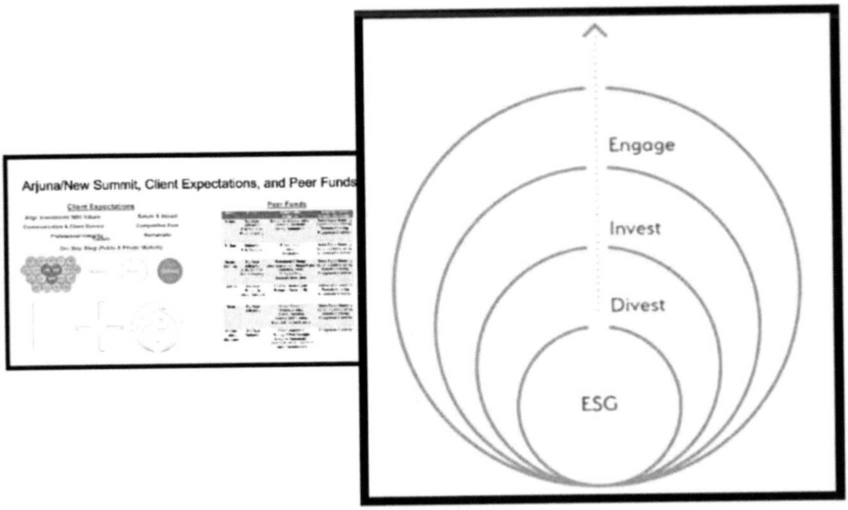

Arjuna's take on ESG investing includes divesting from disfavored companies, investing in favored companies, and engaging companies to change them from the inside.[163]

Arjuna makes investments in companies that it believes it "can influence for the better, often in spite of, but sometimes because of their serious flaws,"[164] and also will "use clients' legacy holdings to engage oil and gas

160 E-mail from Farnum Brown to Arjuna All (May 20, 2021), ARJUNA15901 at ARJUNA15902.

161 Climate Action 100+, *Investor Signatories*, https://www.climateaction100.org/whos-involved/investors/page/2/; NZAM, *Arjuna Capital*, https://www.netzeroassetmanagers.org/signatories/arjuna-capital-2/.

162 Arjuna Capital, 2023 Impact 2 (2023), https://static1.squarespace.com/static/5bc65db67d0c9102cca54b74/t/65cbe54d712c615ec481f661/1707861327081/Arjuna+Capital+-+2023+Impact+Report.pdf.

163 Arjuna Capital, *Arjuna Strategy*, ARJUNA6227 at ARJUNA6234.

164 E-mail from Farnum Brown to Arjuna All, *supra* note 160, at ARJUNA15902.

companies."[165] Further, Arjuna "press[es] companies in [its] clients' investment portfolios to also commit to net zero" because Arjuna's own "net zero goals are only as good as the goals of the underlying companies in [its] portfolios."[166]

In particular, Arjuna aggressively engages and seeks to destroy fossil fuel companies.

Under well-established principles of corporate law, "directors have a fiduciary duty to act in the best interests of the corporation's stockholders."[167] This duty means that corporations must try to maximize shareholder value by "mak[ing] as much money as possible while conforming to the basic rules of the society."[168] Arjuna, however, believes that oil companies only may seek to "'maximize returns' *within* a 1.5-degree global-temperature-rise threshold, but not beyond it."[169] Thus, Arjuna has "exercised the share ownership of a few clients with Exxon and Chevron stock to press for change" that would fundamentally alter—if not entirely destroy—those companies.[170]

In 2021, Arjuna filed a radical shareholder proposal to convert Chevron, the United States' second-largest oil company,[171] into a "public benefit corporation" that can "make decisions that promote the interests of *stakeholders*, such as employees and communities, without having to justify those decisions as also advancing *shareholders'* interest in receiving profits."[172] Arjuna acknowledged that, "[a]s a conventional corporation, directors may fear they will breach their fiduciary duties if they make decisions that might undercut the individual company's financial returns,"[173] and that Chevron's opposition to reducing "emissions . . . arising from customers' use of its products" appeared to "be tied directly to [Chevron's] commitment to capturing higher returns as a conventional corporation."[174] In

---

165 Arjuna Capital, *Draft Shareholder Piece* 2 (Oct. 19, 2022), ARJUNA19398 at ARJUNA19399.

166 *Id.* at ARJUNA19398.

167 *Unocal Corp. v. Mesa Petroleum Co.*, 493 A.2d 946, 955 (Del. 1985).

168 Milton Friedman, *A Friedman Doctrine—The Social Responsibility of Business Is to Increase Its Profits*, N.Y. Times (Sept. 13, 1970), https://www.nytimes.com/1970/09/13/archives/a-friedman-doctrine-the-social-responsibility-of-business-is-to.html.

169 Shareholder Engagement (July 2021), https://static1.squarespace.com/static/5bc65db67d0c9102cca54b74/t/61127a9168dc6b1eef94a55e/1628600977692/Arjuna+Shareholder+Engagement+-+3Q.2021+-+Climate+Tipping+Point.pdf (emphasis added).

170 *Id.*

171 Largest Oil and Gas Companies by Market Cap, supra note 146.

172 Arjuna Capital, Shareholder Rebuttal to Chevron Corp. 2 (Apr. 2021), ARJUNA13397 at ARJUNA13398 (emphasis added).

173 Id. at ARJUNA13399.

174 Id. at ARJUNA13400–01.

contrast, Arjuna's proposed transformation could lead Chevron "to take the steps that are necessary to constrain average global warming to 1.5 °C (*such as reducing its fossil-fuel production*), even if the steps cannot be justified by the board as necessarily optimizing its long-term profits."[175] Chevron's stockholders overwhelmingly rejected Arjuna's proposal by a vote of 97% to 3%.[176]

Apparently undeterred, for the 2024 proxy season, Arjuna filed a shareholder proposal that would require ExxonMobil to "further accelerat[e] the pace of [its] emission reductions."[177] Arjuna did so even though ExxonMobil had made clear to Arjuna that doing so would require it to reduce "demand for [its] products,"[178] and even though ExxonMobil shareholders "roundly rejected . . . similar proposals" in both 2022 and 2023.[179]

ExxonMobil filed suit to challenge Arjuna's resolution, explaining that it

> seeks to replace ExxonMobil management's substantial expertise and well-considered business judgment with [Arjuna's] preferred approach for reducing GHG emissions at an accelerated pace in artificial isolation. In doing so, the [resolution] seeks to directly interfere with management's business judgment and micromanage ExxonMobil's core business—the energy and petrochemical products and services that ExxonMobil offers [T]he [resolution] seeks to usurp the role of management and the board to impose [Arjuna's] personal policy preferences through a shareholder proposal process that was not designed or intended for such use.[180]

In response, Arjuna withdrew its proposal.[181] Nevertheless, on May 22, 2024, the court denied Arjuna's motion to dismiss, allowing ExxonMobil's lawsuit to move forward.[182] The court explained that Arjuna "follow[s] a 'Trojan Horse' model, aggregating enough shares to vote in various corporations and submitting proposals designed to combat climate change and reduce Big Oil's greenhouse gas emissions," and that ExxonMobil's "position

---

175 *Id.* at ARJUNA13401 (emphasis added).

176 Ceres, *Become a Benefit Corporation (CVX, 2021 Resolution)* (2021), https://engagements.ceres.org/ceres engagementdetailpage?recID=a0l1H00000BsplqQAB.

177 Compl. ¶¶ 8, 66, 105, *Exxon Mobil Corp. v. Arjuna Cap. LLC*, (No. 24-69) (N.D. Tex. Jan. 21, 2024).

178 Arjuna Capital, *ExxonMobil Pre-Engagement Call with Co-Filers Notes* 1 (Feb. 7, 2023), ARJUNA12822 at ARJUNA12822.

179 *Exxon Mobil Corp. v. Arjuna Cap. LLC*, No. 24-69, 2024 WL 2331803, at *1 (N.D. Tex. May 22, 2024).

180 Compl., *supra* note 177, ¶¶ 73–74.

181 *See Exxon Mobil Corp.*, 2024 WL 2331803, at *2.

182 *See id.* at *14.

is a rational response to entities categorically opposed to Big Oil. Exxon is big. And Exxon is Oil. And another court has already found [Arjuna] has leadership"—specifically, its Managing Partner and Chief Investment Officer Natasha Lamb—"that's 'manifestly biased' against Exxon."[183]

II. The Climate Cartel Makes Increasingly Extreme Demands to Corporations, from Disclosure to Reduction to Enforcement of Carbon Commitments

Rather than divest from disfavored companies, the climate cartel seeks to change their very nature through "engagement." In the view of the climate cartel, "divestment doesn't actually help with decarbonization" because "[i]t just moves assets around from one company to another."[184] Further, "once investors sell out they are no longer able to apply pressure to company boards."[185] After all, an investor "can't engage with EXXON if they don't hold it."[186]

Moreover, because an index fund like those managed by the "Big Three" asset managers, BlackRock, State Street, and Vanguard, "can't just divest from the companies in its index," "the main lever of influence for a passive fund is stewardship and engagement."[187] As Vanguard has explained:

> The majority of our assets under management are tracking market based indexes. For products which track these indexes, changing portfolio construction (tilting or divestment) is not an option; engagement is a key lever available to meaningfully move index funds towards net zero through encouraging companies to transition to a low carbon economy.

---

[183] *Id.* at *5.

[184] Transcribed Interview of Mary Schapiro, Vice Chair, GFANZ (Feb. 14, 2024) at 156:19–157:8; Transcribed Interview of Mark Carney, Co-Chair, GFANZ (Apr. 17, 2024) at 73:12–74:15, 94:22–95:15, 99:3–7. The Committee required testimony from Ms. Schapiro and Mr. Carney because GFANZ has withheld responsive documentary information from the Committee.

[185] Aviva Invs., Our Global Responsible Investment Approach: Annual Review 2018 46–47 (2018), AV169 at AV214–15.

[186] E-mail from Adam Seitchik to Farnum Brown & Natasha Lamb (Dec. 29, 2021), ARJUNA16161 at ARJUNA16161.

[187] Transcribed Interview of Mary Schapiro, *supra* note 184, at 156:19–157:8; *see id.* at 132:2–7.

Furthermore, substantial shifts in the global economy are required for market based indexes to achieve net zero emissions by 2050 or sooner.[188]

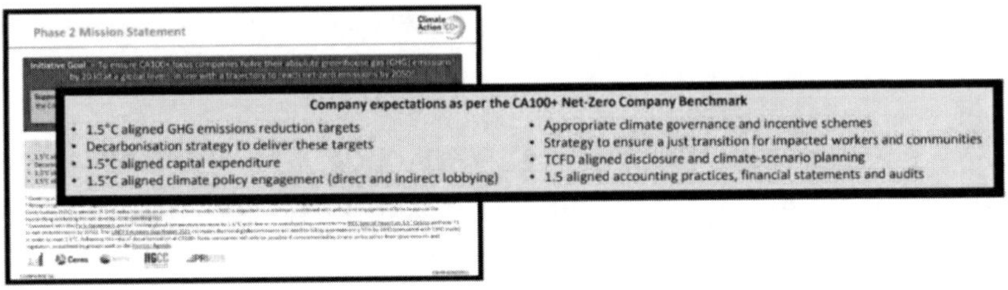

Climate Action 100+'s "expectations" include various demands that companies disclose, reduce, and enforce carbon commitments.[189]

The climate cartel's collusive efforts to impose decarbonization on the American economy generally can be described as seeking (1) "[c]limate [r]isk [d]isclosure," (2) "[a]ctions to [r]educe GHG emissions," and (3) enforcement (and reinforcement) of these disclosure and reduction commitments from corporations.[190] Significantly, the climate cartel is escalating its substantive demands of corporations along this disclose-reduce-enforce axis. Climate Action 100+ has said that it is "moving beyond simple disclosure requests and now . . . making more action-oriented requests" and "more ambitious asks" of companies.[191] In other words, Climate Action 100+ engagements are "about action at this point, not just words/commitments/ disclosure."[192] Netherlands-based stockholder engagement service provider Follow This, which expressly "buy[s] shares in order to work on [its] mission to stop climate change, not to make a financial profit,"[193] has framed the climate cartel's demand escalation even more bluntly as a "Trojan horse":

> The [Paris-compliant targets] resolution asks for something that nobody can be against. This will ultimately result in the fulfilment [*sic*] of our mission: as soon as a company aligns its targets with Paris, it will

---

[188] E-mail from Vanguard employee to Vanguard employee et al. (Sept. 27, 2021), VAN_HJC_30030 at VAN_HJC30032.

[189] Climate Action 100+, *Strategy Summary for Funders* 6 (Jan. 4, 2022), CERES3848 at CERES3853.

[190] Climate Action 100+, *Steering Committee Agenda* 29 (Sept. 27, 2018), CERES31773 at CERES31801.

[191] *KPI Summary and Rationale*, *supra* note 25, at CERES62709.

[192] *Long Term Strategy Meeting 14.10.21*, *supra* note 24, at CERES59160.

[193] Follow This, *Buying a Share*, https://www. follow-this.org/how-it-works/.

> conclude that there is no room for further investments in exploring for more oil and gas. The company will therefore stop exploring for more oil and gas and start exploring for new business models. Therefore: Trojan horse.[194]

Thus, each of the climate cartel's escalating asks—disclosure, reduction, and enforcement—is intended to decarbonize. Moreover, each necessarily reduces output and increases prices for American consumers.[195]

A. First, the Climate Cartel Seeks Immaterial Disclosure of Carbon Emissions

The climate cartel pressures corporations to make immaterial "climate-related financial disclosures."[196] Generally, these demands "seek information about how companies plan to address carbon asset risks and disclose what they are doing to retool for a low-carbon economy."[197] "[M]ost common is a request that the company assess and disclose its business model response to global climate regulations aimed at limited warming to 2°C, the goal of the Paris Agreement."[198] Another frequent demand is that corporations make more exhaustive disclosures of climate governance, strategy, risk management, and metrics and targets.[199]

Disclosing emissions is likely to lead, both directly and indirectly, to reduced output of disfavored, carbon-intensive products. Directly, disclosure requirements may cause fossil fuel companies to "limit[] the amount of capital that is allocated to the exploration and development of fossil fuel reserves," which in turn will reduce their output.[200] Indirectly, climate disclosures may subject all companies to increased attack by government regulators and activists alike. "Corporate behavior can be influenced by consumer reaction

---

194 Follow This, *For Investors*, https://www.follow-this.org/for-investors/.

195 *See* discussion *infra* Part IV.

196 Climate Action 100+, *2023 Proxy Season: An Introduction to Flagged Votes* (Mar. 8, 2023), https://www.climateaction100.org/news/flagged-votes-and-proxy-season-an-introduction/.

197 Heidi Welsh & Michael Passoff, As You Sow et al., *Proxy Preview 2020* 6 (Apr. 3, 2020).

198 Madison Condon, *Externalities and the Common Owner*, 95 Wash. L. Rev. 1, 24 (2020).

199 *Steering Committee Agenda*, *supra* note 190, at CERES31794; *see* Task Force on Climate-related Financial Disclosures, *Recommendations of the Task Force on Climate-related Financial Disclosures* 14 (June 2017).

200 Condon, *supra* note 198, at 40.

and activist targeting, but knowledge of those practices is a prerequisite."[201] As As You Sow President and Chief Counsel Danielle Fugere explained to the Committee in her transcribed interview, "they first need to have the full information before they set a target."[202] In other words, activists "want to use the information to prod companies to change policies in socially-motivated directions," and may use emissions disclosures "to organize boycotts, demonstrations, and social media campaigns against 'brown' companies."[203]

There is no legitimate procompetitive justification for requiring additional emissions disclosures, as they are immaterial and would harm the disclosing company. Even before the SEC's recent adoption of rules mandating specific climate-related disclosures,[204] longstanding federal securities law required "compan[ies] to disclose known risks that are material to [their] future operations and financial position[s]."[205] Information "is material if there is a substantial likelihood that a reasonable shareholder would consider it important in deciding how to vote" or invest, and would view it as "significantly alter[ing] the 'total mix' of information made available."[206] This means that investors already have been provided with all of the information that matters—and, conversely, that anything that has not been disclosed is "trivial information."[207] Thus, the climate cartel's disclosure demands seek immaterial information that is not relevant to the decision of whether and how to invest.

Absent collusion, it is unclear why a company voluntarily would disclose information about its carbon emissions. Companies already "have the best information about their [own] exposure to climate risk."[208] Making disclosures shares this information with "the firm's industry competitors, suppliers, and customers [and] weakens the firm's competitive advantage and bargaining

---

[201] *Id.*

[202] Transcribed Interview of Danielle Fugere, *supra* note 20, at 126:7.

[203] Paul G. Mahoney & Julia D. Mahoney, *The New Separation of Ownership and Control: Institutional Investors and ESG*, 2021 Colum. Bus. L. Rev. 840, 851–52 (2021).

[204] The Enhancement and Standardization of Climate-Related Disclosures for Investors, 89 Fed. Reg. 21,668 (Mar. 28, 2024). The effective date of the SEC's rule has been "delayed indefinitely" due to legal challenge. The Enhancement and Standardization of Climate-Related Disclosures for Investors; Delay of Effective Date, 89 Fed. Reg. 25,804, 25,804 (Apr. 12, 2024).

[205] Mahoney & Mahoney, *supra* note 203, at 851; *see, e.g.*, 17 C.F.R. § 229.105(a) (requiring "discussion of the material factors that make an investment in the registrant or offering speculative or risky").

[206] *Basic Inc. v. Levinson*, 485 U.S. 224, 231–32 (1988) (quoting *TSC Indus., Inc. v. Northway, Inc.*, 426 U.S. 438, 449 (1976)).

[207] *Id.* at 233 (quoting *TSC Indus. Inc.*, 426 U.S. at 448).

[208] Condon, *supra* note 198, at 42.

position."[209] Conversely, by keeping immaterial emissions information confidential, a company may be able to avoid harm from "both regulatory action and reputational damage."[210] Indeed, voluntarily making such disclosures is exactly the sort of "act[ion] contrary to [one's] own independent interest" that may give rise to an inference of conspiracy.[211]

B. Second, the Climate Cartel Seeks Reduction of Carbon Emissions that Require Output Reductions

The climate cartel also pressures corporations to reduce their emissions.[212] These demands often seek the adoption of "GHG reduction targets aligned with the Paris Agreement's ambition of maintaining global temperature rise to 1.5 degrees Celsius."[213] Another frequent demand is for corporations to commit to specific "[t]ransition plans" for how they will effect these emissions reductions.[214] Notably, Climate Action 100+ is now "ask[ing] companies to not only disclose but to implement robust transition plans."[215]

---

[209] *Id.* at 78 n.381.

[210] *Id.* at 39.

[211] *Kreuzer v. Am. Acad. of Periodontology*, 735 F.2d 1479, 1488 (D.C. Cir. 1984); *see Interstate Cir. v. United States*, 306 U.S. 208, 221 (1939) (inferring agreement "from the course of conduct of the alleged conspirators").

[212] *See 2023 Proxy Season: An Introduction to Flagged Votes*, *supra* note 196.

[213] Heidi Welsh & Michael Passoff, As You Sow et al., *Proxy Preview 2023* 22 (Mar. 27, 2023); *see* Condon, *supra* note 198, at 27 ("Most reduction commitments ask firms to reduce emissions in line with the goals of the Paris Agreement, enough to keep warming below 2°C.").

[214] *Steering Committee Agenda*, *supra* note 190, at CERES31891.

[215] Climate Action 100+, *Climate Action 100+ Phase 2: Summary of Changes* 6, https://www.climateaction100.org/wp-content/uploads/2023/06/CA100-Phase-2-Summary-of-Changes.pdf.

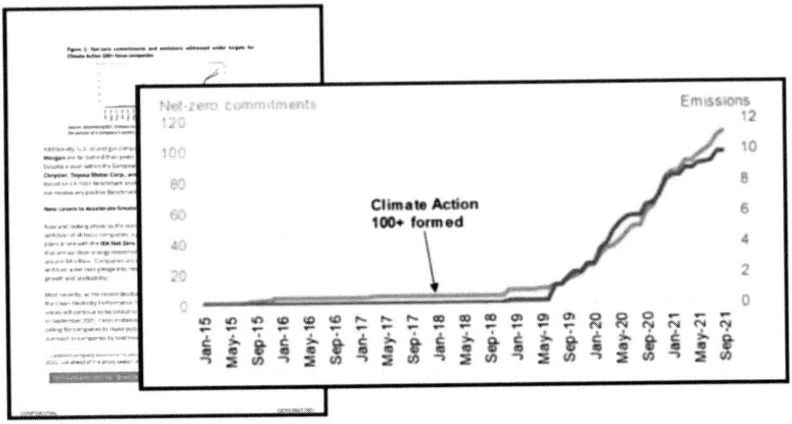

Since the formation of Climate Action 100+, the number of its focus companies making net zero commitments and setting emissions targets increased dramatically.[216]

The effect—and intent—of such proposals is to reduce output, which increases prices for American consumers. "[E]missions reductions proposals at their core seek" to "reduce supply."[217] Indeed, reducing emissions necessarily requires reduced output in disfavored, carbon- intensive industries like fossil fuels, aviation, and agriculture.[218] For example, as ExxonMobil explained in its lawsuit against Arjuna, reducing its emissions would force ExxonMobil "to reduce or eliminate production and sell fewer of certain products."[219]

There is no legitimate procompetitive justification for emissions reduction targets. "The social justifications proffered for [a] restraint of trade . . . do not make it any less unlawful."[220] Unsurprisingly, "companies themselves argue that their self-interest points sharply away from" voluntarily reducing their emissions.[221] Further, in demanding carbon reduction commitments, the members of the climate cartel fundamentally "are arguing that they themselves have a better understanding of the growth that will be needed to meet expected

---

216 Ceres, Climate Action 100+: Global Investors Driving Business Transition 3 (Oct. 2021), CERES17955 at CERES17957.

217 Condon, *supra* note 198, at 55.

218 *See* discussion *infra* Part IV.

219 Compl., *supra* note 177, ¶ 84; *see* discussion *supra* Section III.A.

220 *Superior Ct. Trial Laws. Ass'n*, 493 U.S. at 424; *see* discussion *supra*.

221 Condon, *supra* note 198, at 31.

demand than the executives who work within the energy industry."[222] As ExxonMobil explained in its lawsuit, Arjuna's emissions reduction proposal "seeks to directly interfere with management's business judgment and micromanage ExxonMobil's core business—the energy and petrochemical products and services that ExxonMobil offers."[223]

C. Finally, the Climate Cartel Seeks to Enforce and Reinforce Decarbonization by Handcuffing Corporate Management and Muzzling Free Speech and Petitioning

The climate cartel further pressures corporations to enforce—and reinforce—their carbon disclosure and reduction commitments, including by handcuffing corporate management and muzzling corporate free speech and petitioning.[224] Each of these demands is intended "to detect and deter defections from [the climate cartel's] collusive strategies."[225]

1. The Climate Cartel Seeks to Restrain Corporate Executives and Directors

At the executive level, demands to tie corporate compensation to climate "progress" seek to force companies to "incorporate climate change performance" and "progress towards achieving the company's GHG reduction targets" in "senior executive[] remuneration arrangements."[226] Climate Action 100+ has indicated that it intends to "focus[] on executive compensation to ensure targets get actually achieved."[227] At the board level, demands for board oversight of climate issues seek to require "Board or Board committee oversight of the management of climate change risks," including "a position at the Board level with responsibility for climate change."[228] Both types of demands infringe upon the board's freedom to manage the corporation for the benefit and in the best interests of its stockholders.[229]

---

[222] *Id.* at 27.
[223] Compl., *supra* note 177, ¶ 73; *see* discussion *supra* Section I.D.
[224] *See Steering Committee Agenda*, *supra* note 190, at CERES31801.
[225] Levenstein & Suslow, *supra* note 75, at 44.
[226] Climate Action 100+, *Net Zero Company Benchmark 2.0* 33 (Mar. 2023).
[227] *Long Term Strategy Meeting 14.10.21*, *supra* note 24, at CERES59159.
[228] *Net Zero Company Benchmark 2.0*, *supra* note 226, at 33.
[229] *See* 8 Del. Code § 141(a) ("The business and affairs of every corporation . . . shall be managed by or under the direction of a board of directors").

2. The Climate Cartel Seeks to Silence Corporate Speech and Petitioning

With regard to limits on corporate speech and petitioning, the snake is eating its own tail: "[i]nstitutional investors are simultaneously arguing both that fossil fuel companies are failing to respond to imminent climate regulation, and also requesting that they stop thwarting this regulation, so as to hasten its imminence."[230] Demands to silence corporate speech and petitioning "ask[] companies to provide enhanced disclosure to ensure that climate-related lobbying activities are consistent with the goals of the Paris Agreement and/or with the respective company's own climate strategies and targets."[231] Thus, the climate cartel seeks to limit companies' speech and petitioning to only "activities in accordance with the goals of the Paris Agreement."[232]

In addition to reinforcing anticompetitive emissions disclosure and reduction commitments, limiting free speech and petitioning is likely to lead to reduced output of disfavored products because of its potential impact on public policy. Restricting corporate speech and petitioning "can only serve to help the implementation of regulatory measures," which "will in turn lead to actual emissions reductions."[233] As Climate Action 100+ has admitted, "decarbonization and lobbying activities are intrinsically linked" because "the speed of decarbonization required to reach goals of the Paris Agreement is contingent on an enabling policy environment."[234]

There is no legitimate procompetitive justification for restrictions on corporate speech and petitioning. Such "proposals do not serve the best interests of the target companies."[235] Rather, these demands seek to limit the output of ideas, just as their substantive effect is to limit the output of disfavored products. That censorship stands against not just antitrust law but fundamental principles of American liberty: "[t]he remedy for speech that is false is speech that is trueThe theory of our Constitution is that the best test of truth is the power of the thought to get itself accepted in the competition of the market."[236]

---

[230] Condon, *supra* note 198, at 32.

[231] Climate Action 100+, *2023 Proxy Season: An Introduction to Climate Lobbying* (Mar. 29, 2023), https://www.climateaction100.org/news/2023-proxy-season-an-introduction-to-climate-lobbying/.

[232] *Net Zero Company Benchmark 2.0*, *supra* note 226, at 30.

[233] Condon, *supra* note 198, at 38–39.

[234] *2023 Proxy Season: An Introduction to Climate Lobbying*, *supra* note 231.

[235] Condon, *supra* note 198, at 32.

[236] *United States v. Alvarez*, 567 U.S. 709, 727–28 (2012) (cleaned up).

III. The Climate Cartel Applies Escalating "Engagement" Pressure on Corporations, from Negotiating with Management to Filing and Flagging Resolutions to Taking Out Board Directors

The climate cartel has made this clear: it will escalate its tactics against corporations to ensure that they adopt radical, output-reducing decarbonization policies. Internal documents produced to the Committee in this investigation have revealed Climate Action 100+'s plan to "[r]amp up" and "[e]scalate engagements with laggard focus companies."[237] Ceres has suggested that "pressuring boards remains one of the few avenues for investors to force companies to act,"[238] and Climate Action 100+ has indicated that it intends "to increase engagement with boards to put more pressure on management."[239] Lest there be any doubt about the climate cartel's intentions, Climate Action 100+ has emphasized that "it is important to demonstrate that investors are willing to go to the top rung" in order "to generate bold action."[240]

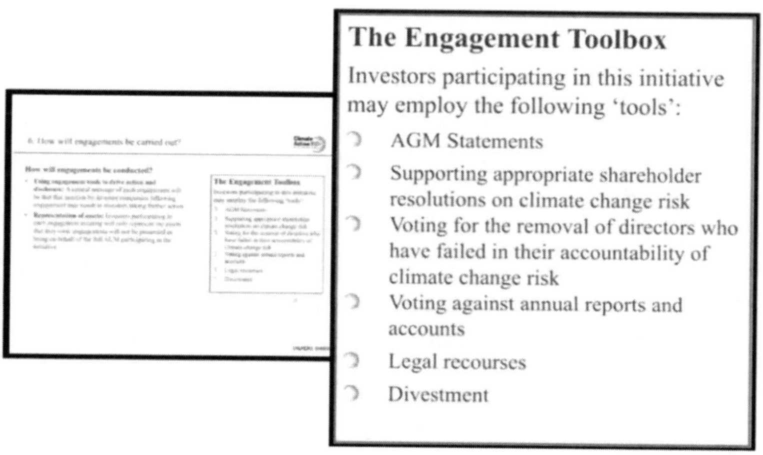

[237] *Work Plan Prepared for CIFF*, *supra* note 7, at CERES66963.
[238] Memorandum from Kirsten Spalding to PMT, *supra* note 55, at CERES13571.
[239] *Long Term Strategy Meeting 14.10.21*, *supra* note 24, at CERES59159.
[240] *Work Plan Prepared for CIFF*, *supra* note 7, at CERES66964.

The Climate Action 100+ "engagement toolbox" includes shareholder resolutions and the removal of corporate directors.[241]

Generally, this escalation proceeds in three steps: first, the climate cartel negotiates with corporate management; second, the climate cartel files and flags shareholder resolutions; and third, the climate cartel votes against and replaces members of the board of directors.

A. First, the Climate Cartel Negotiates with and Threatens Management

First, members of the climate cartel leverage their stock holdings to demand meetings with senior corporate leadership. Dominant stockholders like the "Big Three" asset managers, who each held an average of between 4.5% and 9.7% of every S&P 500 company as of the end of 2021, have the power to command meetings with company executives and directors on their own.[242] As You Sow Chief Executive Officer Andrew Behar explained this to the Committee in his deposition: "BlackRock owns about 7 percent of every company. And so as a shareholder, they have, you know, a certain amount of influence when they tell the company they'd like to meet and talk about material risks BlackRock writes a letter, they get a meeting."[243] Indeed,

the "Big Three" appears to hold hundreds and hundreds of such meetings each year: BlackRock conducted more than 3,700 engagements with companies in 2023, 1,402 of which concerned "[c]limate and natural capital" matters;[244] State Street conducted 940 engagements with companies in 2023, more than 160 of which concerned "climate-related risk management";[245] and Vanguard conducted 1,659 engagements with 1,334 companies in 2023.[246] Conversely, activist gadfly investors, who often "acquire a minimal ownership stake . . . to work on [their] mission to stop climate change, not to make a

---

241 *Investor Briefing Pack: Overview of the Climate Action 100+ and How to Join*, *supra* note 108.

242 Hirst & Bebchuk, *supra* note 10, at 1556.

243 Deposition of Andrew Behar, *supra* note 8, at 108:25–109:25.

244 BlackRock, *Investment Stewardship Annual Report* 12 (2024), https://www.blackrock.com/corporate/literature/publication/annual-stewardship-report-2023-summary.pdf.

245 State Street Global Advisors, *Stewardship Report 2023* 15, 39 (May 2024), https://www.ssga.com/us/en/institutional/ic/library-content/assets/pdf/global/asset-steward ship/2024/asset-stewardship-report-2023.pdf.

246 Vanguard, *Investment Stewardship 2023 Annual Report* 10 (Feb. 2024), https://corporate.vanguard.com/content/dam/corp/advocate/investment-stewardship/ pdf/policies-and-reports/investment_stewardship_2023_annual_report. pdf.

financial profit," may lack the influence required to obtain such meetings on their own.[247] Accordingly, small investors band together and aggregate their holdings through initiatives like Climate Action 100+ and stockholder engagement service providers like As You Sow to obtain such meetings. For example, as Mr. Behar euphemistically explained to the Committee, Climate Action 100+ "was created . . . [s]o shareholders could convene and . . . do it in joint . . . meeting[s] with ten shareholders [rather] than ten separate meetings."[248]

These meetings—and the lurking threat of escalation to shareholder proposals and director votes—have proven tremendously successful in getting the climate cartel what it wants at the expense of corporations and their stockholders. "Many times [the climate cartel's] questions are answered during an engagement and the company agrees with [its] terms"[249]

Such an outcome—a bloodless victory for the climate cartel, if not for American corporations and consumers—is the climate cartel's preference. As Mr. Behar explained to the Committee during his deposition, "we hope that 100 percent of the companies we engage would say, great idea, let's go do it and we'd never have to escalate. It's expensive for us and takes more resources than having a conversation."[250] Correspondingly, as As You Sow President and Chief Counsel Danielle Fugere understatedly has acknowledged, "[c]ompanies don't like to necessarily have proposals filed."[251] That is unsurprising: corporations may spend as much as $150,000 to consider a single shareholder resolution, in addition to diverting time and resources that could be spent elsewhere.[252]

---

[247] Mar. 10, 2023, Letter, *supra* note 9, at ARJUNA12844.

[248] Deposition of Andrew Behar, *supra* note 8, at 22:19–24.

[249] As You Sow, *2022 Shareholder Impact Review: Changing Corporations for Good* 4 (Sept. 20, 2022), https:// www.asyousow.org/s/AsYouSow2022_Shareholder-Impact-Review-Report_ v7_FIN_20220920.pdf.

[250] Deposition of Andrew Behar, *supra* note 8, at 71:3–6.

[251] Transcribed Interview of Danielle Fugere, *supra* note 20, at 89:21.

[252] Procedural Requirements and Resubmission Thresholds under Exchange Act Rule 14a-8, 85 Fed. Reg. 70,240, 70,274 (Nov. 4, 2020).

B. Second, the Climate Cartel Challenges Management with Shareholder Resolutions

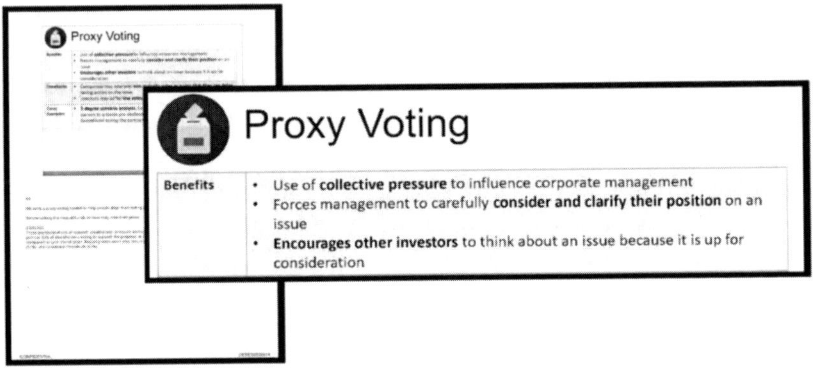

According to Ceres, a benefit of proxy voting is the "[u]se of collective pressure to influence corporate management."[253]

Where discussions with corporate management do not yield the results that the climate cartel wants, its shareholder members will file resolutions seeking to impose output-reducing decarbonization policies upon corporations, and its initiative members will "flag" these resolutions for support by other members of the climate cartel. As Ms. Fugere explained to the Committee during her transcribed interview, when corporations are "either unwilling to meet or unwilling to take the actions that [it] want[s]," the climate cartel will "escalate or . . . push the issues further" by "fil[ing] shareholder resolutions Where a company is not providing information requested by a shareholder or maybe where they are not taking action that investors think are necessary to reduce risk and to protect shareholder value, they can file a proposal."[254] Her colleague Mr. Behar testified more bluntly: "In the case where [companies] are more reticent, then we use our legal rights as shareholders to file a shareholder resolution."[255] Such resolutions may be filed by investors who hold as little as $2,000 of stock in a company.[256] Their numbers have increased dramatically in recent years. According to the Harvard Law School Forum on Corporate Governance, the number of filed

---

[253] Ceres, Ceres' Dominant Strategic Driver: Moving Companies Through Investor Engagement 5 (2018), CERES39910 at CERES39914.
[254] Transcribed Interview of Danielle Fugere, *supra* note 20, at 19:9–12, 114:7–10.
[255] Deposition of Andrew Behar, *supra* note 8, at 14:10–11.
[256] *See* 17 C.F.R. § 240.14a-8 (2022).

shareholder resolutions increased from 447 in 2020 and 449 in 2021, to 522 in 2022, to 616 in 2023.[257]

Documents reviewed by the Committee in this investigation have confirmed that the climate cartel will threaten and use shareholder resolutions until corporations bow. Climate Action 100+'s stated plan is to "[r]amp up escalations using a set of tactics . . . including . . . [s]hareholder resolutions."[258] Members across the climate cartel have embraced this escalation tactic. For example, State Street takes the position that, "[w]here initial engagement attempts with individual portfolio companies do not achieve the desired outcome, . . . [it] may escalate concerns by . . . [s]upporting relevant shareholder resolutions."[259] Similarly, Arjuna has explained that it "engage[s] companies . . . and attempt[s] to provide education If [it] finds a company is reluctant to provide this transparency to investors, [it]'ll take the issue to the annual meeting to allow other investors to weigh in."[260]

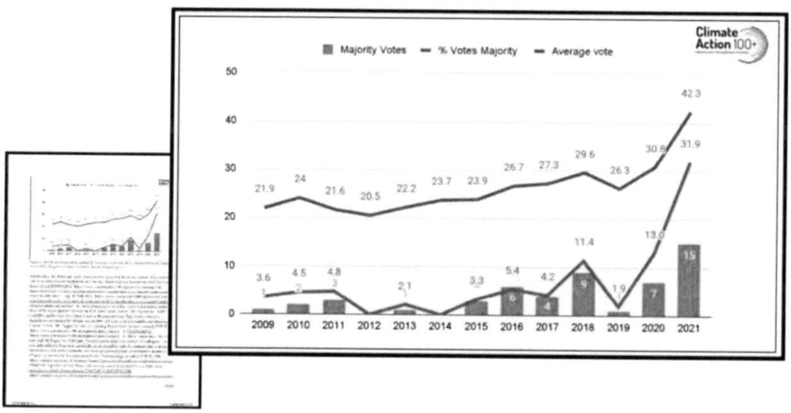

Climate Action 100+ has boasted that its flagging process increased shareholder votes.[261]

The efficacy and impact of these resolutions is enhanced by their being "flagged" by members of the climate cartel. Climate Action 100+ flags

[257] Lindsey Stewart, *Proxy Voting Insights: Key ESG Resolutions* (Oct. 4, 2023), https://corpgov.law.harvard.edu/2023/10/04/proxy-voting-insights-key-esg-resolutions/.

[258] *Work Plan Prepared for CIFF*, *supra* note 7, at CERES66963.

[259] State Street Global Advisors, *Stewardship Report 2023*, *supra* note 245, at 20.

[260] Antoinette Giblin, *In-Depth: Q&A with Arjuna Capital* (Apr. 3, 2024), https://www.diligent.com/en-gb/resources/blog/in-depth-q-and-a-with-arjuna-capital.

[261] *Narrative Report to Yajilarra Trust*, *supra* note 154, at CERES29337.

stockholder proposals so that its "signatories are informed of votes with potential to advance the goals of the initiative."[262] Documents produced to the Committee have revealed that Climate Action 100+ viewed "[c]reat[ing] a sub-set of 'Climate Action 100+ flagged resolutions' in order to inform investor voting priorities" and "establish[] discipline" as a "[k]ey activit[y]" to "[s]trengthen [its] ability to win key votes."[263] Likewise, Ceres has boasted of "how powerful [this] flagging process is": because investors "know [they]'re being scrutinized on how [they] vote," it creates "accountability for investors."[264] As Ceres has explained:

> [F]lagging votes was a crucial process in creating additional accountability for investors during the 2021 proxy season, as signatories were made aware that their votes towards flagged resolutions would be under scrutiny. It also provided a platform to educate investors as well as leading proxy advisors on voting— particularly focusing on [asset managers] with low votes in 2020— *to ultimately be able to coordinate investor signatories in public support of Climate Action 100+ flagged votes*.[265]

Resolutions do not have to succeed at the stockholder vote for them to be successes for the climate cartel. "[S]hareholder proposals," after all, "typically are non-binding on the company, even if they are approved by a shareholder vote."[266] Nevertheless, As You Sow Chief Executive Officer Andrew Behar testified in his deposition that, even where just "30 percent of [corporate] shareholders think this is a good idea," As You Sow will "sit down with the company" for it to "look at [the proposal] a little more closely."[267] Similarly, from 2018 through last year, Glass Lewis's expectation was "that boards should engage with shareholders and demonstrate some initial level of responsiveness" when as few as "20% or more of shareholders vote contrary to management" because even "a 20% threshold is significant enough to warrant a close examination of the underlying issues and an evaluation of

---

262 Climate Action 100+, *Climate Action 100+ Vote Flagging Process* 1, CALPERS_50243 at CALPERS_50243.
263 *Work Plan Prepared for CIFF*, *supra* note 7, at CERES66958–59.
264 E-mail from Ceres employee to Morgan LaManna, *supra* note 58, at CERES9645.
265 *Narrative Report to Yajilarra Trust*, *supra* note 154, at CERES29336 (emphasis added).
266 Substantial Implementation, Duplication, and Resubmission of Shareholder Proposals Under Exchange Act Rule 14a–8, 87 Fed. Reg. 45,052, 45,067 (July 27, 2022).
267 Deposition of Andrew Behar, *supra* note 8, at 56:10–12.

whether the board responded appropriately following the vote."[268] Ceres has recognized as much, asserting that "20% or more support has been considered the threshold by which company boards should demonstrate some level of responsiveness to address the concerns of shareholders."[269]

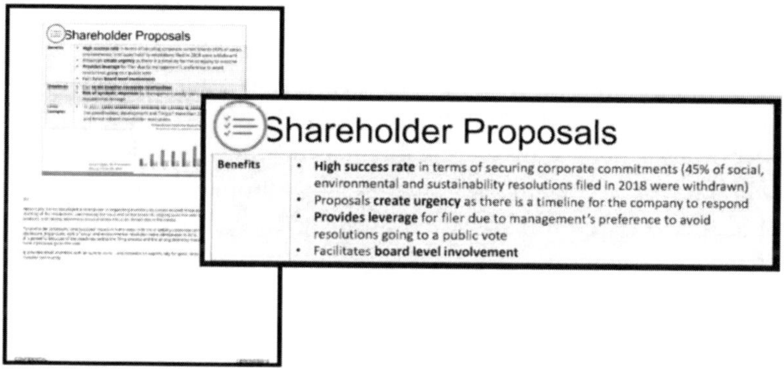

Ceres has emphasized the "leverage" and "urgency" that it derives from resolutions.[270]

Moreover, the climate cartel often will withdraw resolutions upon reaching agreement with—that is, extracting a concession from—corporate management. As You Sow President and Chief Counsel Danielle Fugere explained that if a corporation "were to agree on actions, [As You Sow] could withdraw the proposal . . . kind of like reaching a settlement in a lawsuit."[271] When climate cartel members like As You Sow do so, "it is always as part of an agreement with company management."[272] By way of example, Ms. Fugere explained:

> So let's say we have asked a company to set greenhouse gas emissions targets because they've—they have disclosed emissions, and then we begin talking with them and we—through those discussions find out that they actually haven't covered all of the emission scopes. And maybe they

---

[268] Glass Lewis, *2023 Policy Guidelines* 10, https://www.glasslewis.com/wp-content/uploads/2022/11/US-Voting- Guidelines-2023-GL.pdf; *see* Glass Lewis, *2018 Policy Guidelines* 7, https://www.glasslewis.com/wp-content/ uploads/2017/11/US_Guidelines_2018.pdf.

[269] Ceres, Narrative Report to the Children's Investment Fund Foundation (CIFF) 8 (July 29, 2022), CERES62685 at CERES62693.

[270] Ceres' Dominant Strategic Driver: Moving Companies Through Investor Engagement, supra note 253, at CERES39913.

[271] Transcribed Interview of Danielle Fugere, supra note 20, at 90:14–19.

[272] Id. at 125:18–20.

> say that they have X amount of scope [three] emissions, but if they had provided more detail to shareholders, we might find out that that was just company travel. Or, for banks, it might be the buildings. So a very small part of their emissions. In that case, what we might agree with the company is, "Okay, agree to fully disclose your emissions because we now found out that you did not," and they would agree to do that.[273]

A great number of shareholder resolutions are in fact withdrawn in exchange for extracting an agreement with corporate management. Climate Action 100+ has explained that "[t]he threat of flagging the resolutions proved successful in pushing companies to make commitments ahead of [annual general meetings] in return for a withdrawal" and that, "[i]f withdrawals were counted in the overall figure of the number of flagged resolutions, then [Climate Action 100+] would be vastly exceeding [its] Targets."[274] Likewise, Ms. Fugere testified that for "a significant portion"—"either 40 or 60 percent"—of As You Sow's proposals, it is "able to reach resolutions with companies and withdraw."[275]

C. Finally, the Climate Cartel Seeks to Change the Board

When corporate management does not yield to negotiations and resolutions, the climate cartel seeks to change the board of directors. Climate Action 100+ has explained that its escalation tactics include "[v]otes against one or more board members."[276] Ceres has confirmed that a condition on $3.7 million of funding to Climate Action 100+ was "[r]apid escalation of engagement to fire directors who fail to deliver transition plans aligned with Paris, with a vanguard of activist investors taking the lead."[277] Likewise, State Street has indicated that it "may escalate [its] concerns by . . . [v]oting against relevant board members."[278] Such "'[v]ote no' campaigns essentially seek to withhold as many votes as possible from the board nominees who have been targeted. By achieving a compelling 'withhold' vote . . . the campaign seeks to send a

---

273 *Id.* at 125:23–126:6.
274 *KPI Summary and Rationale*, *supra* note 25, at CERES62709.
275 Transcribed Interview of Danielle Fugere, *supra* note 20, at 126:13–15.
276 *Work Plan Prepared for CIFF*, *supra* note 7, at CERES66963.
277 E-mail from David Ziv-Kreger to Kirsten Spalding et al. (Mar. 16, 2020), CERES62751 at CERES62752.
278 *Stewardship Report 2023*, *supra* note 245, at 29.

strong message to the company's board of directors that shareholders are dissatisfied."[279]

"However, a 'vote no' campaign does not propose alternative candidates for the board"— and the climate cartel has revealed a willingness and the ability to go even further by replacing corporate directors with those of its own choosing.[280] In 2020, Climate Action 100+ plotted to "[e]stablish a credible threat of board member refreshment, by implementing an unprecedented effort to replace board members at one of the world's very largest companies," ExxonMobil.[281] "[G]oing after Exxon" in such an aggressive fashion would "show [Climate Action 100+] has teeth," according to one internal e-mail produced to the Committee.[282] That effort to "refresh" the board at ExxonMobil was a tremendous success for the climate cartel, resulting in the replacement of three of the company's directors with "climate activists . . . backed publicly by . . . Climate Action 100+ signatories."[283] Now, companies "cannot ignore" the demands of the climate cartel "without subjecting their board members to possible replacement."[284] "When recalcitrant companies demonstrate that other escalation tactics are not working," the climate cartel may "take concerted action to refresh the board of directors."[285]

IV. The Climate Cartel Restrains Trade by Reducing Output of Fossil Fuels, Flights, and Food

The climate cartel's agreements to decarbonize and reach net zero necessarily mean decreased output and increased prices for American consumers. The implications of this anticompetitive collusion are particularly stark in key sectors such as fossil fuels, aviation, and farming—the very industries that allow Americans to drive, fly, and eat.

---

279 E-mail from Cynthia McHale to Mindy Lubber et al. (Feb. 8, 2020), CERES54034 at CERES54034.

280 *Id.* at CERES54034.

281 *Work Plan Prepared for CIFF*, *supra* note 7, at CERES66963.

282 E-mail from David Ziv-Kreger to Kirsten Spalding et al., *supra* note 277, at CERES62752.

283 *Narrative Report to Yajilarra Trust*, *supra* note 154, at CERES29337; *see* discussion *supra* Section I.D.

284 *Narrative Report to Yajilarra Trust*, *supra* note 154, at CERES29338.

285 *Work Plan Prepared for CIFF*, *supra* note 7, at CERES66964.

A. Keep It "in the Ground": Fossil Fuels

Demand for energy is growing and will continue to grow. By 2022, "total primary energy consumption" was "around 3% above the 2019 pre-COVID level," and both oil and coal "consumption continued to increase."[286] The Organization of the Petroleum Exporting Countries (OPEC) has predicted that "[g]lobal primary energy demand" will increase 23% by 2045.[287] Similarly, the U.S. Energy Information Administration predicts that "[g]lobal energy consumption" will increase 34% by 2050.[288] Fossil fuels will remain a key part of meeting the world's increasing energy needs: in 2045, "oil will remain the fuel with the largest share," and "the combined share of oil and gas" is projected to be 54%—i.e., continuing to represent the majority of energy use.[289]

However, despite civilization's basic need for energy, the climate cartel wants fossil fuels to "stay in the ground" because "carbon emissions would be lower [if] that coal or that gas or that oil wouldn't be dug out or excavated and burned."[290] According to Climate Action 100+ "research partner" Carbon Tracker,[291] "a warming of 1.5°C is already effectively locked in" and "no new oil & gas project would be compliant" with net zero.[292] "Emissions from existing and planned energy infrastructure would alone exceed the carbon budget by 66%."[293] In other words, continued fossil fuel consumption and production are incompatible with the decarbonization agenda—and the climate cartel loudly has called for fossil fuel output to be reduced.

---

286 Energy Inst., *Statistical Review of World Energy* 3 (2023), https://www.energyinst.org/data/assets/pdf_file/0004/1055542/EI_Stat_Review_PDF_single_3.pdf.

287 Org. of the Petrol. Exporting Countries, *Executive Summary 2023* 6 (2023), https://vert.eco/wp-content/uploads/2023/10/ES_WOO_2023.pdf.

288 U.S. Energy Info. Admin., *International Energy Outlook 2023* 8 (Oct. 2023), https://www.eia.gov/outlooks/ieo/ pdf/IEO2023_Narrative.pdf.

289 Org. of the Petrol., *supra* note 287, at 8–9.

290 Transcribed Interview of Mary Schapiro, *supra* note 184, at 134:18–135:3; *see* Transcribed Interview of Mark Carney, *supra* note 184, at 88:3–11.

291 Carbon Tracker Initiative, *Climate Action 100+ Alignment Assessments Methodology* 1 (Mar. 2022), https://www.climateaction100.org/wp-content/uploads/2021/11/CTI-CA100-Benchmark-Alignment-Indicators-Methodology_ Nov21.pdf.

292 Carbon Tracker Initiative, *Measuring Commitment to Climate Goals* 1 (2019), AV18990 at AV18990.

293 GFANZ, Net-Zero Transition Plan (NZTP) Workshop: The Four Key Financing Strategies 30, GFANZ2634 at GFANZ2663.

Climate Action 100+ "research partner" Carbon Tracker has said that net zero does not allow for any new oil and gas projects—and that, without carbon capture and storage (CCS), existing fossil fuel projects alone would cause 1.5°C of global warming.[294]

On the consumption side, reaching net zero would require draconian "declines in the use of coal, oil and gas"[295]: as much as 98% for coal,[296] 94% for oil, and 86% for fossil fuels overall.[297] Thus, As You Sow President and Chief Counsel Danielle Fugere testified that "ultimately fossil fuel use has to be reduced."[298] Likewise, Carbon Tracker has stated that "the use of oil, gas and coal will need to peak and fall in absolute terms, and soon."[299] GFANZ has said that global oil supplies must fall between 55% to 79% and gas supplies between 54% to 93% by 2050.[300] Further, GFANZ Co-Chair Mark Carney testified to the Committee that "more than half of the world's coal

---

[294] *Measuring Commitment to Climate Goals*, *supra* note 292, at AV18990.

[295] Int'l Energy Agency, *Net Zero by 2050*, https://www.iea.org/reports/net-zero-by-2050.

[296] Int'l Energy Agency, *Net Zero By 2050: A Roadmap for the Global Energy Sector* 21 (May 2021), https://iea. blob.core.windows.net/assets/deebef5d-0c34-4539-9d0c-10b13d840 027/NetZeroby2050-ARoadmapfortheGlobal EnergySector_CORR.pdf.

[297] *See* State of Cal., *California Releases World's First Plan to Achieve Net Zero Carbon Pollution* (Nov. 16, 2022), https://www.gov.ca.gov/2022/11/16/california-releases-worlds-first-plan-to-achieve-net-zero-carbon-pollution/; *see also Net Zero by 2050: A Roadmap for the Global Energy Sector*, *supra* note 296 (Fossil fuels must "fall from almost four-fifths of total energy supply today to slightly over one-fifth by 2050.").

[298] Transcribed Interview of Danielle Fugere, *supra* note 20, at 163:4–6.

[299] Carbon Tracker Initiative, *Comment on Chevron and Scope 3 Emissions Considerations* 1 (Feb. 2019), CALPERS_40605 at CALPERS_40605.

[300] GFANZ, Net-Zero Pathways Analysis and Expectations for Transition Plans: Oil and Gas 30, GFANZ54611 at GFANZ54654.

reserves need to stay in the ground in order for the world to be in line with Paris."[301]

On the production side, the climate cartel has said that "most oil and gas companies will need to substantially lower their production of fossil fuels."[302] Trillium has explained that "continuing to finance fossil fuel expansion is incompatible with a net-zero by 2050 scenario."[303]

"No new oil and natural gas fields are needed in the net zero pathway,"[304] and thus "no new oil and gas fields must be developed."[305] One Climate Action 100+ member succinctly stated: "there is no need for any new oil."[306] Similarly, GFANZ has said that "there is no rationale for financing new coal projects."[307]

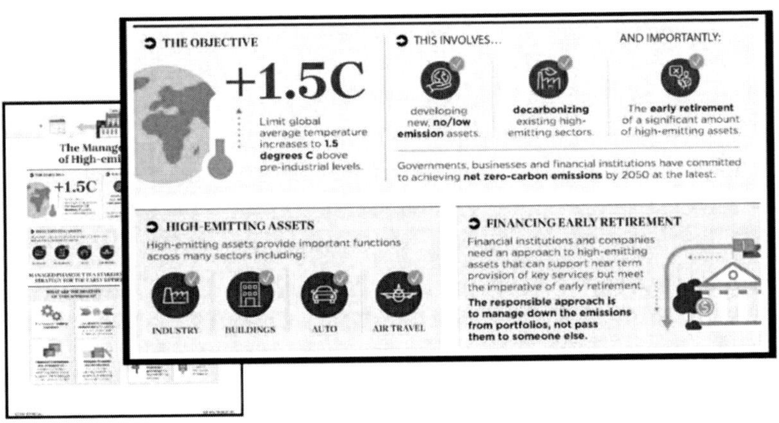

[301] Transcribed Interview of Mark Carney, *supra* note 184, at 100:23–25.

[302] TPI employee et al., *Establishing a "Net Zero Standard" for the Oil and Gas Sector: Proposed Final Draft* 7, 15 (Feb. 9, 2021), CALPERS_7103 at CALPERS_7109, CALPERS_7117.

[303] Trillium, 2021 Impact Report 27 (2021), https://web.archive.org/web/20221002 061031/ https://www.trilliuminvest.com/sustainability-related-disclosures/firm-impact-report-2021.

[304] Majority Action, Presentation to Glass Lewis Follow This, Arjuna, Majority Action 3 (Apr. 11, 2022), ARJUNA5707 at ARJUNA5709.

[305] UN Env't Programme Fin. Initiative, Net-Zero Asset Owner Alliance Sets Expectations for Oil and Gas Investments and Calls on Companies and Policymakers to Align With 1.5C Pathways (Mar. 29, 2023), https://www. unepfi.org/industries/net-zero-asset-owner-alliance-outlines-new-guidance-for-oil-and-gas-investments-while-calling-on-companies-policymakers-and-investors-to-align-with-1-5c-pathways/.

[306] E-mail from BNP Paribas Asset Management employee to UBS employee et al. (Nov. 10, 2022), CALPERS_37025 at CALPERS_37025.

[307] GFANZ, Statement on "No New Coal" from Michael Bloomberg, Mark Carney and Mary Schapiro 1, GFANZ41799 at GFANZ41799.

GFANZ admits that "Managed Phaseout" means the "early retirement" of "assets provid[ing] important functions across many sectors."[308]

Even worse, the climate cartel has called for the premature retirement of existing, productive fossil fuel assets. These early facility retirements would occur "[b]efore the end of their technically useful life"[309] and while they are "still economically profitable."[310] GFANZ has emphasized that "[t]he early retirement of many physical assets in high-emitting sectors before the end of their operational lifespan is essential to reducing global emissions."[311] Such high- emitting assets include "coal mines, fossil-fuel power stations, oil fields, and gas pipelines."[312]

Likewise, Carbon Tracker has said that the "premature[] clos[ure of] existing projects" is necessary to avoid "a warming of 1.5°C."[313]

As You Sow Chief Executive Officer Andrew Behar testified in his deposition that "an oil and gas company [could not] reach net zero while continuing to produce fossil fuels."[314] Thus, the climate cartel has acknowledged that "reaching net zero demands a comprehensive strategic commitment from an oil and gas company to transform its business."[315] GFANZ estimates that there would be "$10.5 [trillion in] forgone revenue from fossil fuel extraction in 1.5C pathway relative to business as usual"—including more than $4 trillion in North America alone:[316]

---

308 GFANZ, *The Managed Phaseout of High-Emitting Assets* 7 (2022), GFANZ186 at GFANZ193.

309 Transcribed Interview of Mark Carney, *supra* note 184, at 98:17–21; *see* Transcribed Interview of Mary Schapiro, *supra* note 184, at 133:21–23.

310 Transcribed Interview of Mary Schapiro, *supra* note 184, at 133:24–134:1.

311 *Net-Zero Transition Plan (NZTP) Workshop: The Four Key Financing Strategies*, *supra* note 293, at GFANZ2663.

312 *The Managed Phaseout of High-Emitting Assets*, *supra* note 308, at GFANZ195–96.

313 *Measuring Commitment to Climate Goals*, *supra* note 292, at AV18990.

314 Deposition of Andrew Behar, *supra* note 8, at 27:9–11.

315 TPI employee et al., *supra* note 302, at CALPERS_7109, CALPERS_7117.

316 GFANZ, *The Managed Phaseout of High Emitting Assets: Exhibits* (May 2022), GFANZ47120 at GFANZ47136.

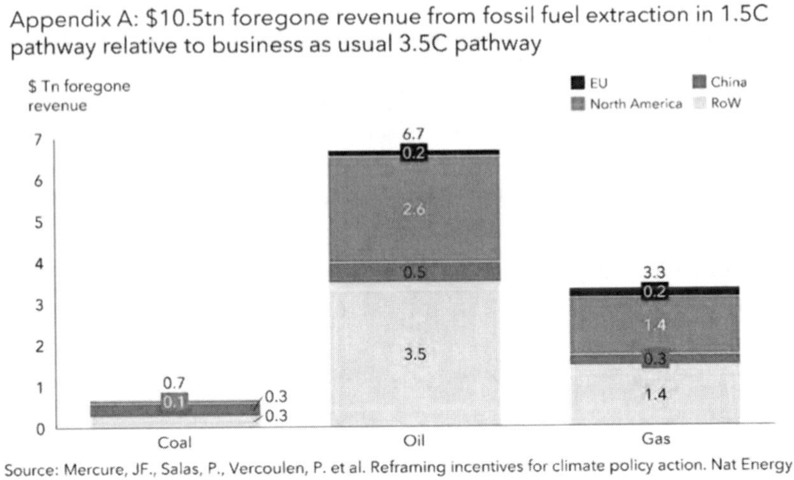

CONFIDENTIAL GFANZ00047136

The climate cartel's quest for net zero would cost North American fossil fuel producers more than $4 trillion in revenue.[317]

The impact on American producers, and the jobs they create and support, would be profound. ExxonMobil, the United States' largest oil company, would need to cut production by 55%.[318] Chevron, America's second-largest oil producer, would need to reduce output by 57%.[319] At ConocoPhillips, the nation's third-largest oil company, production would need to fall by 85%.[320]

---

317 *Id.*

318 E-mail from PRI employee to AIR Capital employee et al. (Dec. 2, 2019), BLK-HJC-62577 at BLK-HJC-62583.

319 *Presentation to Glass Lewis, Follow This, Arjuna, Majority Action*, *supra* note 304, at ARJUNA5712; *see* Chevron, *Our History: Market Expansion 1980–2001*, https://www.chevron.com/who-we-are/history; *see also Largest Oil and Gas Companies by Market Cap*, *supra* note 146.

320 E-mail from PRI employee to AIR Capital employee et al., *supra* note 318, at BLK-HJC-62583.

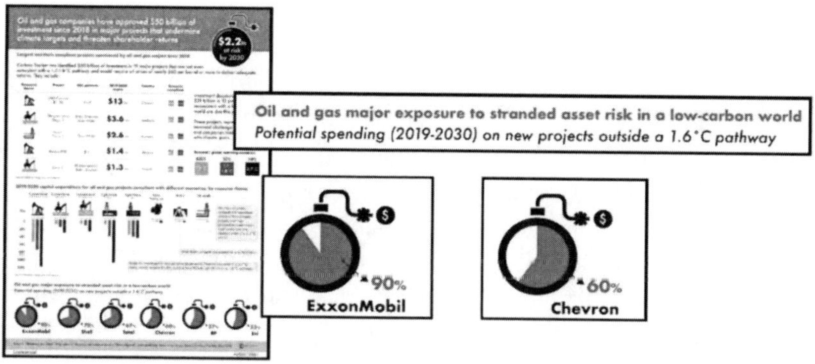

According to Climate Action 100+ "research partner" Carbon Tracker, 90% of ExxonMobil's new project spending and 60% of Chevron's is incompatible with net zero.[321]

As one Climate Action 100+ member summed it up: "Ignoring decarbonisation & energy efficiency" leads to "[h]igher profits & [h]igher capital" and "[m]ore reinvestment"; "Paris- aligned" investing leads to "[l]ower / no profits & impaired capital" and "[n]o reinvestment":[322]

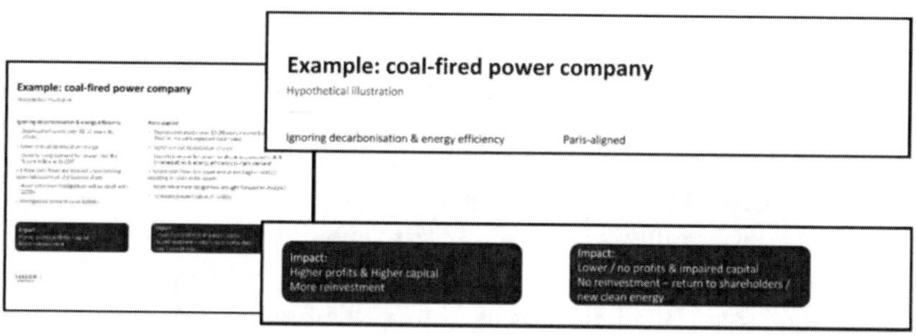

A Climate Action 100+ member set forth the costs of "Paris-aligned" investing.[323]

The fossil fuel output reductions demanded by the climate cartel would cause significant pain at the pump. Senate Democrats have acknowledged that collusion in oil production "may have increased gasoline, diesel fuel, heating oil, and jet fuel costs in a way that has materially harmed virtually every

---

[321] *Measuring Commitment to Climate Goals*, *supra* note 292, at AV18991.

[322] Sarasin & Partners, *Paris-aligned Accounting* 4 (July 2020), CALPERS_40079 at CALPERS 40082.

[323] *See id.*

American household and business," as "hardworking Americans end up paying the price through higher costs for gas, fuel, and related consumer products."[324] Even worse, fossil fuel output reductions would require radical changes in Americans' daily lives and to American industry, such as "end[ing] sales of new internal combustion engine cars by 2035."[325] Indeed, Climate Action 100+ has indicated that it intends to engage American automakers to force them "to significantly scale deployment of electric vehicles and phase out production of vehicles with internal combustion engines."[326] Likewise, Ceres boasts that it "has made important contributions" in transitioning the automotive industry, which has "decrease[d] demand for oil and discourage[d] investment in new sources of supply—helping to keep fossil fuels in the ground."[327]

B. Death to Flying Things: Aviation and Air Travel

Aviation demand is expected to continue to grow. From 2010 to 2019, passenger air travel increased by "around 6%" per year.[328] PRI has predicted that "[t]he aviation industry [will] grow 5% per year for the foreseeable future."[329] Similarly, the International Energy Agency (IEA) predicts that passenger air travel "[d]emand would grow more than threefold globally between 2020 and 2050," with "[a]bout 60% of this growth . . . in emerging market[s] and developing economies."[330] Even GFANZ concedes that "global air passenger demand is expected to grow by 3%–4% annually up to 2040, despite the impacts of COVID-19."[331]

However, despite the importance of air travel to exercising Americans' "fundamental right . . . to travel" across a vast country,[332] the climate cartel views aviation as an impediment to its net zero ambitions.

---

324 Letter from Sen. Charles Schumer et al. to Merrick Garland, Attorney General, & Jonathan Kanter, Assistant Attorney General 3 (May 30, 2024).

325 *Net Zero by 2050: A Roadmap for the Global Energy Sector*, *supra* note 296, at 19.

326 Climate Action 100+, *The Climate Action 100+: Investors Driving Corporate Action Proposal* 13 (Apr. 2018), CERES43806 at CERES43819.

327 *Draft Ceres Organizational Profile for the Skoll Foundation*, *supra* note 19, at CERES59903.

328 *Net Zero by 2050: A Roadmap for the Global Energy Sector*, *supra* note 296, at 135.

329 Principles for Responsible Inv., *Aviation and Climate Change: An Essential Sector Overview for Investors* 12 (Mar. 21, 2020), CALPERS_10730 at CALPERS_10741.

330 Net Zero by 2050: A Roadmap for the Global Energy Sector, supra note 296, at 84–85.

331 GFANZ, Net-Zero Pathways Analysis and Expectations for Transition Plans: Aviation 14, GFANZ54989 at GFANZ55014.

332 *Jones v. Helms*, 452 U.S. 412, 417 (1981).

As PRI has explained, while "the aviation industry currently consumes 3% of the global carbon budget," that amount may "increase to 20% by 2050" "[d]ue to in-sector growth and emission reductions in other industries."[333] Thus, Climate Action 100+ has suggested that, to reach net zero, aviation emissions need to have peaked by 2025 and by 2030 need to be 23% lower than in 2019 (the pre-pandemic level). Emissions in the sector will need to fall by 80% between 2019 and 2050, leaving some residual emissions from aviation in 2050 . . . to be covered by negative emissions, so that the global energy system can reach net-zero emissions by 2050.[334]

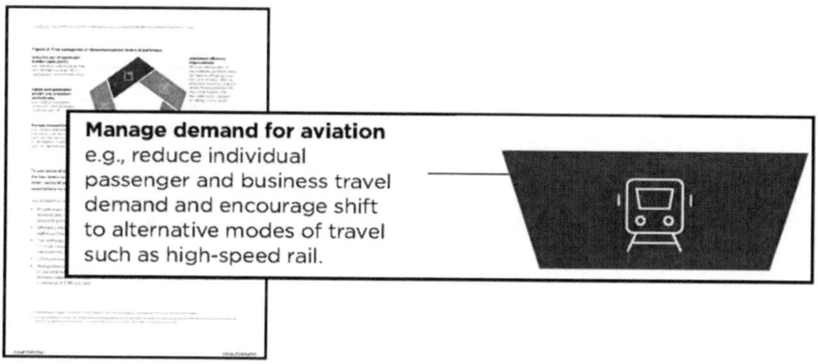

"Manag[ing] demand for aviation"—that is, reducing demand and shifting travelers away from air travel—is a primary "decarbonization lever" for the climate cartel.[335]

Such drastic emissions reductions necessarily require output reductions. Climate Action 100+ has been clear: sustainable aviation fuels "and new technologies alone are not sufficient to achieve the deep emissions reductions required."[336] Rather, "demand management is now a central part of the agenda for decarbonising the aviation sector."[337] That euphemistic term for output reduction "refers to the actions taken . . . to limit the demand for jet fuel

[333] Aviation and Climate Change: An Essential Sector Overview for Investors, supra note 329, at CALPERS_10740.

[334] Global Sector Strategies: Investor Actions to Align the Aviation Sector with the IEA's 1.5° Decarbonisation Pathway, supra note 21, at SSGA-HJC.66660.

[335] Net-Zero Pathways Analysis and Expectations for Transition Plans: Aviation, supra note 331, at GFANZ 54995.

[336] *Id.* at SSGA-HJC.66661.

[337] *Id.* at SSGA-HJC.66665.

through the curtailment of demand for air transportation."[338] More specifically:

> Demand management will require policy interventions, which may take the form of market-based measures (e.g., carbon pricing, passenger flight taxes, frequent flyer levies); regulation (e.g., banning short-haul domestic flights where there is [a high-speed rail] alternative . . . ; company disclosure requirements around corporate travel; and public awareness campaigns. In addition, aviation companies themselves can take measures to manage demand or bring about behavioural changes, for example, by ending frequent flyer reward programmes, ending advertising campaigns that target growth in developed markets with already high per-capita flights, disclosing the carbon footprint of flights at the point of ticket purchase or by entering into partnerships with rail operators to offer combined air and train tickets.[339]

Even Climate Action 100+ acknowledges that these draconian restrictions on passenger air travel "will be unwelcome for the aviation sector . . . and will present challenges for both aviation companies and investors."[340] For its part, IEA admits that the radical "types of behavioural changes" that the climate cartel would impose on Americans "would have some effect on nearly everyone's daily life."[341]

The climate cartel has been remarkably precise in setting forth the output reductions that it would effect in the aviation sector. Specifically, Climate Action 100+ would "reduce total flights by . . . 12%."[342] Identically, IEA would "reduc[e] the number of flights by . . . 12%."[343] Further, despite predicting continued growth in consumer demand for passenger aviation, the climate cartel would cap air travel at 2019 levels, raising prices and reducing the availability of flights. Specifically, the climate cartel calls for:

- Keeping business travel to 2019 levels
- Capping long-haul flights of more than 6 hours for leisure reasons at 2019 levels

[338] *Id.* at SSGA-HJC.66681.

[339] *Id.* at SSGA-HJC.66673 (cleaned up).

[340] *Id.* at SSGA-HJC.66661.

[341] *Net Zero by 2050: A Roadmap for the Global Energy Sector*, *supra* note 296, at 67, 70.

[342] Global Sector Strategies: Investor Actions to Align the Aviation Sector with the IEA's 1.5° Decarbonisation Pathway, supra note 21, at SSGA-HJC.0066673 (emphasis added).

[343] Net Zero by 2050: A Roadmap for the Global Energy Sector, supra note 296, at 85.

- Shifting demand to high-speed rail . . .[344]

C. "Cows Are the New Coal": Food and Agriculture

Food demand also will continue to grow. Climate Action 100+ predicts that consumer demand for food will increase, and that "the consumption of carbon intensive foods including red meat is expected to increase with rising incomes in emerging markets."[345] Likewise, the United Nations-backed World Resources Institute (WRI) estimates that "overall food demand is on course to increase by more than 50 percent" between 2010 and 2050, that "demand for animal- based foods" is set to increase "by nearly 70 percent," and that demand for ruminant meat— "cattle, sheep, and goats"—"is projected to grow by 88 percent between 2010 and 2050."[346]

However, despite the fundamental human need for food, the climate cartel sees agriculture as a leading source of greenhouse gas emissions. Climate Action 100+ has stated that "the food and agriculture sector has a disproportionate impact on climate change."[347] Similarly, GFANZ has identified agriculture as having a high "[m]ateriality of emissions" and as being a high-priority industry sector.[348] WRI frames the issue more starkly: "feeding the planet would . . . releas[e] enough GHG emissions to exceed the 1.5°C and 2°C warming targets enshrined in the Paris Agreement—even if emissions from all other human activities were entirely eliminated."[349]

Thus, Climate Action 100+ expressly has called for "coordinated and collaborative action" by investors to align the agricultural sector with net zero—including through output reduction and "a demand-side shift in diets away from emission intensive food like beef to a plant-rich diet."[350] WRI

---

344 Principles for Responsible Inv., *Climate Action 100+ Warns that the Aviation Industry Must Take Urgent Action to Keep 1.5°C Within Reach* (Mar. 10, 2022), https://www.unpri.org/news-and-press/climate-action-100-warns-that-the-aviation-industry-must-take-urgent-action-to-keep-15c-within-reach/9644.article.

345 Climate Action 100+, Global Sector Strategies: Recommended Investor Expectations for Food and Beverage 19 (Aug. 2021), VAN_HJC_50783 at VAN_HJC_50802.

346 World Res. Inst., Creating a Sustainable Food Future 1–2 (Dec. 2018), https://research.wri.org/sites/default/files/2019-07/WRR_Food_Full_Report_0.pdf.

347 Global Sector Strategies: Recommended Investor Expectations for Food and Beverage, supra note 345, at VAN_HJC_50796.

348 GFANZ, Additional Sector Selection 7 (Jan. 2022), GFANZ18149 at GFANZ18155.

349 *Creating a Sustainable Food Future*, *supra* note 346, at 1–2.

350 *Global Sector Strategies: Recommended Investor Expectations for Food and Beverage*, *supra* note 345, at VAN_HJC_50791, 802.

similarly has suggested that a "sustainable food future" requires "reduce[d] growth in demand for food and agricultural products" and "shifting the diets of high meat consumers toward plant-based foods."[351]

The climate cartel's demands for agricultural output reductions are perhaps loudest when it comes to beef. As the founder of an agriculture-focused ESG investor network infamously put it: "cows are the new coal."[352] Accordingly, Ceres has suggested that "global per capita meat consumption must be reduced to around 1.5 burgers per person per week"—"around a 35% reduction from current consumption levels."[353] The impact on American beef consumers would be more pronounced: such a reduction to just "50 calories a day" of ruminant meat would be only "about half of current U.S. levels."[354]

Conclusion

The Committee's ongoing investigation into collusion between left-wing activists and major financial institutions has revealed that a climate cartel is working to decarbonize the U.S. economy—with disastrous implications for American consumers. The climate cartel has declared war on our way of life, escalating its attacks on free markets and demanding that companies slash output of the critical products and services that allow Americans to drive, fly, and eat.

The Biden Administration has failed to act upon the climate cartel's apparent violations of longstanding U.S. antitrust law. The Committee, in contrast, is actively investigating their anticompetitive behavior. Following the launch of this investigation, dozens of members have withdrawn from Climate Action 100+, including three of the world's largest asset managers: BlackRock, State Street, and JPAM.

Despite the damage it has caused, the climate cartel has made clear that it intends to press for ever-more radical demands, and that it views its "job [a]s

---

351 *Creating a Sustainable Food Future*, *supra* note 346, at 1–2.

352 Planet Tracker & Changing Markets Found., *Hot Money: 40 Financial Institutions Are Funding a Climate- changing Agri-methane Footprint* 11 (Jan. 2023), SSGA-HJC.324209 at SSGA-HJC.324219.

353 Ceres, *The Investor Guide to Climate Transition Plans in the U.S. Food Sector* 20 (May 2022), https://assets.ceres.org/sites/default/files/reports/2022-05/FF_TransitionPlanin Food Sector_FINAL_LR_May22.pdf.

354 *6 Pressing Questions About Beef and Climate Change, Answered*, *supra* note 23.

. . . only just begun."[355] The Committee will continue to fulfill its duty examine the sufficiency of federal law to "[p]rotect[] trade and commerce against unlawful restraints and monopolies" such as the climate cartel's anticompetitive collusion.[356] The Committee will supplement this interim report as necessary.

[355] E-mail from Anne Simpson to Robert Eccles et al., *supra* note 26, at ENGINENO1-118HJC-PROD-6866.

[356] Rules of the House of Representatives R. X(1)(l)(16) (2023).

Chapter 4

Jordan and Massie Demand Information from Over 130 Companies Surrounding Their Involvement with Woke ESG Cartel Climate Action 100+*

Committee on the Judiciary

WASHINGTON, D.C. – Today, House Judiciary Committee Chairman Jim Jordan (R-OH) and Subcommittee on the Administrative State, Regulatory Reform, and Antitrust Chairman Thomas Massie (R-KY) demanded information from more than 130 U.S.-based companies, retirement systems, and government pension programs about their involvement with the woke ESG cartel Climate Action 100+.

In June, the Committee released an interim staff report titled, "Climate Control: Exposing the Decarbonization Collusion in Environmental, Social, and Governance (ESG) Investing," which details direct evidence of a "climate cartel" consisting of left-wing activists and major financial institutions that collude to impose radical environmental, social, and governance goals on American companies.

The Committee continues to examine whether existing civil and criminal penalties and current antitrust law enforcement efforts are sufficient to deter anticompetitive collusion to promote ESG-related goals in the investment industry. The over 130 companies, retirement systems, and government pension programs with membership in Climate Action 100+ must answer

* This is an edited, reformatted and augmented version of the Press Release of the Committee on the Judiciary, dated July 30, 2024.

In: The Climate Cartel
Editor: Gabriel A. Darrick
ISBN: 979-8-90134-148-3

for their involvement in prioritizing woke investments over their own fiduciary duties.

The Committee sent letters to the following entities, organized by state:

California

Aristotle Credit LLC
Aristotle Pacific Capital
Bailard, Inc.
California State Teachers' Retirement System
Crescent Capital Group LP
Dalton Investments
East Bay Municipal Utility District Employees Retirement System
Franklin Templeton Investments
JLens
Legato Capital Management, LLC
Los Angeles Capital Management
Los Angeles County Employees Retirement Association
Payden & Rygel
Redwood Grove Capital, LLC
San Francisco Employees' Retirement System
Sierra Club Foundation
Skoll Foundation
Strategic Global Advisors
The TCW Group, Inc.
University of California Investments Office
Loyola MaryMount University
Vert Asset Management

Connecticut

ARGA Investment Management
Axiom Investors
Connecticut Retirement Plans & Trusts
CoreCommodity Management, LLC
Calvert
SOC Investment Group
Terra Alpha Investments
World Resources Institute

District of Columbia

Sanders Capital, LLC

Hawaii

Employees' Retirement System of the State of Hawaii

Illinois

Nuveen
Builders Vision
Christian Brothers Investment Services
City of Chicago Investors
Core Capital Management LLC
Fairpointe Capital, LLC
Northern Trust Asset Management
Office of the Illinois State Treasurer
Wespath Benefits and Investments
William Blair Investment Management, LLC
Great Lakes Advisors

Kansas

Ecofin

Kentucky

Presbyterian Mission Agency

Massachusetts

Acadian Asset Management Limited
Amherst College
Baldwin Brothers LLC
Boston Common Asset Management
Boston Trust Walden
Breckinridge Capital Advisors
The Christopher Reynolds Foundation, Inc.

Easterly Investment Partners LLC
Essex Investment Management, LLC
Global Delta Capital
Grantham, Mayo, Van Otterloo & Co. LLC
Harvard Management Company
Mellon Investments Corporation
MFS Investment Management
Massachusetts Institute of Technology
SLC, Fixed Income
Stance Capital
The Sustainability Group of Loring, Wolcott & Coolidge
Unitarian Universalist Association
Wellington Management Company LLP
Zevin Asset Management
Green Century Capital Management
Reynders, McVeigh Capital Management

Maryland

Brown Advisory
Hannon Armstrong
Karner Blue Capital
Maryland State Retirement and Pension System

Missouri

Mercy Investment Services

Minnesota

Macalester College
Minnesota State Board of Investment
The McKnight Foundation

North Carolina

Barings LLC

New Hampshire

Veris Wealth Partners

New Jersey

New Jersey Department of the Treasury, Division of Investment
Investor Advocates for Social Justice
Sisters of Saint Dominic of Caldwell

New York

Epoch Investment Partners
ClearBridge Investments
Nathan Cummings Foundation
Neuberger Berman
New Alternatives Fund
New York City Office of the Comptroller
New York State Common Retirement Fund
Rockefeller Asset Management
Nomura Greentech
JCIR
Jennison Associates
Lyrical Asset Management LP
Macquarie Asset Management
Miller/Howard Investments Inc.
New York State Teachers' Retirement System
Resolution Capital
Segal Marco Advisors
Stone Harbor Investment Partners
Sustainable Insight Capital Management
The Pension Boards-United Church of Christ, Inc.
United Church Funds
United Nations Joint Staff Pension Fund
University of Rochester
Water Asset Management
WaveCrest Wealth Management
Goldman Sachs Asset Management

Ohio

Domini Impact Investments LLC
The George Gund Foundation

Oregon

Oregon State Treasurer
Progressive Investment Management

Pennsylvania

CenterSquare Investment Management
Brandywine Global Investment Management, LLC
Friends Fiduciary Corporation
Impax Asset Management LLC
SEI
SEIU Master Trust
The Board of Pensions of the Presbyterian Church (U.S.A.)

Rhode Island

Everhope Capital

Texas

Sage Advisory Services Ltd. Co.

Virginia

The Ithaka Group, LLC

Vermont

Prentiss Smith & Company
Office of the Vermont State Treasurer
Vermont Pension Investment Commission

Washington

Parametric
Seattle City Employees' Retirement System
Washington State Investment Board

Wisconsin

Dana Investment Advisors
Praxis Mutual Funds
Seventh Generation Interfaith CRI
Riverwater Partners

Chapter 5

Republicans Launch Antitrust Investigation into Climate-Obsessed Corporate 'Cartel'*

Tristan Justice

House Republicans launched an investigation Tuesday probing whether major climate groups that spearhead the "environmental, social, and governance" (ESG) movement are violating antitrust laws.

In a letter sent to executives of the Steering Committee for Climate Action 100+, Republicans led by Ohio Rep. Jim Jordan are demanding a treasure trove of documents that illustrate the coalition's network of influence. Climate Action 100+, they wrote, "seems to work like a cartel to 'ensure the world's largest corporate greenhouse gas emitters take necessary action on climate change.'"

"Woke corporations are collectively adopting and imposing progressive policy goals that American consumers do not want or do not need. An individual company's use of corporate resources for progressive aims might violate fiduciary duties or other laws, harming its viability and alienating consumers," Republicans warned. "But when companies agree to work together to punish disfavored views or industries, or to otherwise advance environmental, social, and governance (ESG) goals, this coordinated behavior may violate the antitrust laws and harm American consumers."

Jordan, the incoming chair of the House Judiciary Committee, was joined by Reps. Dan Bishop of North Carolina, Matt Gaetz of Florida, Scott Fitzgerald of Wisconsin, Cliff Bentz of Oregon, and Tom McClintock of California.

---

* This is an edited, reformatted and augmented version of the Tristan Justice, dated December 22, 2022.

In: The Climate Cartel
Editor: Gabriel A. Darrick
ISBN: 979-8-90134-148-3

In a June op-ed published in the Wall Street Journal and cited by lawmakers, Sean Fieler, the president of Equinox Partners, a Manhattan-based investment firm, outlined how "The ESG Movement Is a Ripe Target for Antitrust Action."

"Advancing the ESG agenda requires that the owners of capital collude to restrict the supply of certain goods and services," Fieler wrote, after highlighting how ESG standards have effectively crushed oil and gas production. "Regardless of the colluding parties' motivations, this is a textbook antitrust violation."

Republican Arizona Attorney General Mark Brnovich launched a separate antitrust investigation into the Climate Action 100+ network in November last year.

In his own op-ed for the Wall Street Journal published in March, Brnovich, who is being term-limited out of office next year, explained why Climate Action 100+ leading the ESG movement is an antitrust violation:

Here's what is happening: The biggest banks and money managers seek to implement a political agenda, such as compliance with the Paris Climate Accord. Then a group mobilizes: Climate Action 100+, for example, comprised of hundreds of big banks and money managers that together manage $60 trillion. The group uses its coordinated influence to compel companies to shut down coal and natural-gas plants. The activism can include pushing climate goals at shareholder meetings and voting against directors and proposals that don't comport with the agenda, even if other decisions may benefit investors.

Firms then report their plans to Climate Action 100+, Brnovich added, which "helps ensure maximum coordinated effort toward the common goal of overhauling the energy industry."

"Money managers wield influence over these companies because they represent investors who are shareholders, often through their 401(k)s or pension plans," the attorney general explained. "In other words, your retirement funds are likely helping facilitate these political campaigns to advance far-left policy goals, with consumers bearing the costs of increased energy prices."

In August, Brnovich led a coalition of 19 states in sending a letter to BlackRock, the world's largest asset management firm, warning the company about potential antitrust violations over the Wall Street behemoth's championship of ESG standards.

"BlackRock's actions appear to intentionally restrain and harm the competitiveness of the energy markets," wrote 19 attorneys general in the joint letter. "These antitrust concerns are especially acute because BlackRock and other asset managers affirmatively tout their market dominance. BlackRock is the world's largest investment management company, with $10 trillion in assets."

Some state treasurers have already begun to pull taxpayer funds from BlackRock's possession, pulling $1 billion from the company as of October, according to the New York Post.

Chapter 6

JERROLD NADLER, New York
CHAIRMAN

JIM JORDAN, Ohio
RANKING MEMBER

ONE HUNDRED SEVENTEENTH CONGRESS

Congress of the United States

House of Representatives

COMMITTEE ON THE JUDICIARY

2138 RAYBURN HOUSE OFFICE BUILDING

WASHINGTON, DC 20515-6216

(202) 225-3961
judiciary.house.gov

Letters to Ms. Mindy S. Lubber*

Dan Bishop
and Jim Jordan

December 31, 2022

Ms. Mindy S. Lubber
Ceres, Chief Executive Officer and President
Investor Network Representative, North America, Climate Action 100+
99 Chauncy Street, 6th Floor
Boston, MA 02111

Dear Ms. Lubber:

We are disappointed that your letter dated December 20, 2022, indicates that you do not intend to cooperate voluntarily with our oversight of how coordinated efforts to push environmental, social, and governance (ESG)

---

* This is an edited, reformatted and augmented version of the Congress of the United States, House of Representative, Committee of Judiciary Publication.

In: The Climate Cartel
Editor: Gabriel A. Darrick
ISBN: 979-8-90134-148-3

policies could violate antitrust laws.[1] As we explained in our initial letter, which is enclosed, Climate Action 100+ seems to function like a cartel, facilitating collusion to push ESG goals in a way that may be anticompetitive.[2] Ceres is a Climate Action 100+ cofounder that runs a regional corporate network for the group.[3] Accordingly, we believe Ceres possesses documents and information that would advance our oversight and inform any potential legislation relating to collusive ESG policies.

Your December 20 letter seems to concede that Ceres and Climate Action 100+ engage in collusive behavior to "address complex, systemic challenges"[4] Your defense, however, is to allege that this collusive behavior is not anti-competitive, and you offer several broad assertions about the positive economic effects of ESG policies without offering any evidence to support your claims. Indeed, you did not produce any of the material we requested or certify that you are preserving all responsive documents. In doing so, you provide us with no ability to verify the accuracy of your assertions or to gauge whether ESG policies—and Ceres's and Climate Action 100+'s coordination of those policies—are pro- or anti-competitive.

Accordingly, the requests in our initial letter dated December 6, 2022, remain outstanding.[5] We reiterate these requests and ask for your prompt voluntarily compliance. To the extent you believe these requests pose legitimate burdens, we are willing to engage about potential accommodations. You can be assured, however, that the Committee will continue to pursue this oversight matter into the 118th Congress. Please be advised that the Committee may be forced to resort to compulsory process in the 118th Congress if these requests remain outstanding.

The congressional oversight power, rooted in Article I of the Constitution, is "broad and indispensable."[6] This authority "encompasses inquiries into the administration of existing laws, studies of proposed laws, and surveys of defects in our social, economic or political system for the purpose of enabling

---

[1] *See generally* Letter from Rep. Jim Jordan, Ranking Member, H. Comm. on the Judiciary, et al., to Mindy S. Lubber, CEO & President, Ceres (Dec. 6, 2022).

[2] *See generally id.*

[3] *Id.* at 1.

[4] Letter from Mindy S. Lubber, President & CEO, Ceres, to Rep. Jim Jordan, Ranking Member, H. Comm. on the Judiciary, et al., at 1 (Dec. 20, 2022).

[5] In addition, your assertion that our requests were not "authorized," *id.* at 1 n.1, belies a fundamental misunderstanding of the Rules of the House of Representatives. Nothing in House Rules prevents you from voluntarily complying with our requests.

[6] *See, e.g., Trump v. Mazars USA, LLP*, 140 S. Ct. 2019, 2031 (2020) (citing *Watkins v. United States*, 354 U.S. 178, 187, 215 (1957)) (internal quotation marks and citations omitted).

the Congress to remedy them."[7] The Committee on the Judiciary is specifically authorized by Rule X of the House of Representatives to examine and consider potential legislation relating to unlawful restraints on trade.

Thank you for your prompt attention to this matter.

Sincerely,

Dan Bishop
Member of Congress

Jim Jordan
Ranking Member

cc: The Honorable Jerrold L. Nadler, Chairman Enclosure

December 6, 2022

Ms. Mindy S. Lubber
Ceres, Chief Executive Officer and President
Investor Network Representative, North America,
Climate Action 100+ 99 Chauncy Street, 6th Floor
Boston, MA 02111

Mr. Simiso Nzima
Managing Investment Director, Global Equity,
CalPERS Investor Representative, North America,
Climate Action 100+ 400 Q Street
Sacramento, CA 95811

Dear Ms. Lubber and Mr. Nzima:

We are writing to you because of your roles coordinating how some companies pursue environmental, social, and governance (ESG) policies in ways that may violate antitrust laws. Each of you is on the Steering Committee for Climate Action 100+, which seems to work like a cartel to "ensure the world's largest corporate greenhouse gas emitters take necessary action on climate change."[8]

---

[7] *Id.* (internal quotation marks omitted).

[8] *Climate Action 100+*, CERES, https://www.ceres.org/climate/climate-action- 100#:~:text= Ceres%20is%20a%20founding%20network, necessary%20action%20on%20climate% 20change (last visited Dec. 2, 2022); *About Climate Action 100+*, CLIMATE ACTION 100+, https://www.climateaction100.org/about/(last visited Dec. 2, 2022).

In addition, Ms. Lubber leads Ceres, a non-profit co-founder of Climate Action 100+. Ceres runs a regional corporate network for Climate Action 100+, advancing ESG policies by encouraging and helping drive "collective action."[9] Mr. Nzima works for the California Public Employees' Retirement System (CalPERS), the largest U.S. public pension fund. CalPERS—a board member of Ceres—also co-founded and now helps govern Climate Action 100+.[10] In short, you and your organizations appear to play major roles in efforts to advance ESG policies. We therefore write to request information about related conduct or agreements that may be unlawful under U.S. antitrust laws.

Woke corporations are collectively adopting and imposing progressive policy goals that American consumers do not want or do not need.[11] An individual company's use of corporate resources for progressive aims might violate fiduciary duties or other laws, harming its viability and alienating consumers.[12] But when companies agree to work together to punish disfavored views or industries, or to otherwise advance environmental, social, and governance (ESG) goals, this coordinated behavior may violate the antitrust laws and harm American consumers.

Many domestic corporate interests increasingly march in unison in advancing progressive policy goals.[13] Some companies and executives promote these left-wing views and policies[14] even when doing so runs counter

---

[9] *See id.*; *About Us*, CERES, https://www.ceres.org/about-us (last visited Dec. 2, 2022).

[10] *Climate Change*, CALPERS, https://www.calpers.ca.gov/page/investments/sustainable-investments-program/climate-change (last visited Dec. 2, 2022); *How We Got Here*, CLIMATE ACTION 100+, https://www.climateaction100.org/approach/how-we-got-here/ (last visited Dec. 2, 2022).

[11] See, e.g., Sean Fieler, The ESG Movement Is a Ripe Target for Antitrust Action, WALL ST. J. (June 2, 2022); see also Mike Pence, Republicans Can Stop ESG Political Bias, WALL ST. J. (May 26, 2022).

[12] See generally Jed Rubenfeld & William Barr, ESG Can't Square With Fiduciary Duty, WALL ST. J. (Sept. 6, 2022); Lydia Moynihan, BlackRock faces scrutiny from 19 state AGs over ESG investments, N.Y. POST (Aug. 16, 2022); Steven Adams, West Virginia treasurer joins with 15 other states to warn financial institutions of 'woke capitalism', WVNEWS (Nov. 28, 2021); In re Walt Disney Co. Derivative Litig., 907 A.2d 693 (Del. Ch. 2005); Todd Zywicki, Cancel Culture Comes to Banking, NEWSWEEK (Jan. 13, 2022); STEPHEN SOUKUP, THE DICTATORSHIP OF WOKE CAPITAL 9 (2021); Brian Morgenstern, 5 Ways American Corporations Can Avoid Becoming The Next Disney, THE FEDERALIST (May 6, 2022); Liz Peek, Message to woke corporate America: Butt out of politics, THE HILL (Apr. 26, 2022).

[13] See, e.g., Holman W. Jenkins, Inflation and the Trump Factor, WALL ST. J. (June 14, 2022) (describing "Larry Finkism").

[14] See, e.g., Matthew Impelli, A Full List of Companies That Have Advocated Against Georgia's New Voting Law, NEWSWEEK (Apr. 1, 2021); David Kihara, DeSantis says Disney 'crossed the line' in calling for 'Don't Say Gay' repeal, POLITICO (Mar. 29, 2022).

to consumer sentiment[15] or robs Americans of hard-earned income.[16] Certain large companies—some of which are involved in the work of Climate Action 100+ or Ceres, or may have connections to CalPERS—appear to be important players in these efforts.

For example, Larry Fink, who chairs one of the world's largest asset managers, BlackRock, is infamous "for his annual letters to America's CEOs chiding them to adopt the latest MSNBC- approved wisdom on politics and policy."[17]

At its core, ESG is merely partisan politics masquerading as responsible corporate governance. A major ESG "policy centerpiece" is stifling investments in oil and gas,[18] and Wall Street firms have "bragg[ed] about their coordinated efforts to choke off investment in energy."[19] Boycotting certain energy investment, however, is just a subset of the types of ESG-related goals.[20] The list includes, for example: "climate change (e.g., reporting on climate change, risks of climate change, greenhouse gas emissions goals)," "sustainability reporting," and other "energy-related" issues.[21] ESG goals can also include other policy concerns, such as "fake news dissemination" or "gun control."[22] Access to abortion has even become part of ESG.[23]

---

[15] James Varney, One thing partisan voters agree on: Woke CEOs miss the mark, WASH. TIMES (Dec. 1, 2021).

[16] See, e.g., Mark Brnovich, ESG May Be an Antitrust Violation: I'm investigating a coordinated effort to allocate markets, WALL ST. J. (Mar. 6, 2022) (describing how Americans' "retirement funds are likely helping facilitate . . . campaigns to advance far-left policy goals, with consumers bearing the costs of increased energy prices," and describing harm to "the pocketbook of all Americans, especially lower-wage workers").

[17] Inflation and the Trump Factor, supra n.6; cf. id. (identifying "the rise of the 'woke' corporation" and explaining "if you remember the 1970s [Larry Fink's] missives might strike a familiar bell. They are updated expressions of the three-martini lunch—i.e., a business honcho indulging himself with on-the-job consumption, aka an untaxed perk."). [11] The ESG Movement Is a Ripe Target for Antitrust Action, supra n.4; see also Mark Hendrickson, ESG Is Evil, THE AMERICAN SPECTATOR (Oct. 17, 2022).

[18] The ESG Movement Is a Ripe Target for Antitrust Action, supra n.4; see also Mark Hendrickson, ESG Is Evil, THE AMERICAN SPECTATOR (Oct. 17, 2022).

[19] Mark Brnovich, @GeneralBrnovich, TWITTER (Mar. 7, 2022), https://twitter.com/GeneralBrnovich/status/1500878845704118274?s=20&t=9nWxZMzzuqbN4HVx86N28g.

[20] Cf. Peter Atkins et al., Social Responsibility and Enlightened Shareholder Primacy: Views from the Courtroom and Boardroom, HARVARD LAW SCHOOL FORUM ON SOCIAL GOVERNANCE (Feb. 21, 2019), https://corpgov.law.harvard.edu/2019/02/21/social-responsibility-and-enlightened-shareholder-primacy-views-from-the-courtroom-and-boardroom.

[21] *Id.* at n.6.

[22] Cf. id.

[23] *See* Shelley Alpern, *The Newest ESG Frontier: Reproductive Rights at the Corporate Level,* CONFLUENCE PHILANTHROPY (June 16, 2022).

Corporate America's collusion in pursuit of ESG goals may violate federal or state antitrust laws.[24] Antitrust law is generally "skeptical of cooperation among competitors" over certain matters, and that includes coordination over ESG goals.[25] The "traditional principles that prohibit cooperation among competitors in ways that restrict price, output, or quality" apply "regardless of their values-based intent."[26] As one antitrust expert has explained, "[t]he loftiest of purported motivations do not excuse anti-competitive collusion among rivals. That's long- standing antitrust law."[27] Accordingly, when competitors agree with each other on how they should act in the marketplace, antitrust law enforcers have stepped in and taken a good, hard look. Anti-competitive agreements among competitors . . . are outlawed because they reduce the incentives for companies to compete vigorously, which in turn can raise prices, reduce innovation and . . . harm consumers.[28]

Ultimately, agreements not to compete can have disastrous results in relevant markets,[29] hurting both the economy and the American people.[30]

When enterprises like Climate Action 100+ or Ceres invite or facilitate collusion to achieve progressive policy goals, that activity can aid anticompetitive and unlawful agreements and behavior.[31] The actions of such organizations may enable prohibited conduct on a large scale,[32] and may even

---

24 *See, e.g.*, *ESG May Be an Antitrust Violation*, *supra* n.9; C. Boyden Gray, *Corporate Collusion: Liability Risks for the ESG Agenda to Charge Higher Fees and Rig the Market*, 4-7, TEXAS PUBLIC POLICY FOUNDATION (June 2021); Letter from Mark Brnovich, Arizona Attorney General, et al., to Mr. Lawrence Fink, BlackRock, Inc., 5 (Aug. 4, 2022), https://www.texasattorneygeneral.gov/sites/default/files/images/executive-management/BlackRock%20Letter.pdf.

25 *See* Michael Murray & Tara Giunta, *How To Mitigate Antitrust Risk In ESG Efforts*, LAW360 (Oct. 19, 2021).

26 *Id.*

27 Makan Delrahim, *Popular ends should not justify anti-competitive collusion*, USATODAY (Sept. 12, 2019).

28 *Id.*

29 *See, e.g.*, *ESG May Be an Antitrust Violation*, *supra* n.9 (offering anecdote of how "trying to raise wide-scale capital for drilling oil" has been "almost impossible").

30 *Id.*; *see also* Terrence Keeley, *ESG Does Neither Much Good nor Very Well*, WALL ST. J. (Sept. 12, 2022).

31 See, e.g., Corporate Collusion, supra n.17, at 6.

32 *See, e.g.*, *ESG May Be an Antitrust Violation*, *supra* n.9; Letter from Senator Tom Cotton to Mr. Larry Fink, Chairman & CEO, BlackRock, Inc. (July 13, 2022); *see also About Climate Action 100+*, CLIMATE ACTION 100+ (describing how Climate Action 100+ functions to affect corporate change), https://www.climateaction100.org/about/ (last visited Dec. 2, 2022); Vivek Ramaswamy, @VivekGRamaswamy, TWITTER (June 7, 2022), https://twitter.com/VivekGRamaswamy/status/1534285301773910017; Vivek Ramas wamy, @VivekGRamaswamy, TWITTER (May 10, 2022), https://twitter.com/VivekGRamaswamy/status/1524186401394368514.

lead to liability for such organizations under antitrust laws.[33] Ultimately, "[a]dvancing the ESG agenda requires that the owners of capital collude to restrict the supply of certain goods and services" and—regardless of motivations—that is a "textbook antitrust violation."[34] This is the type of prohibited conduct that Climate Action 100+ and Ceres appear to be facilitating.

No matter how firmly a company or its executives believe in the goals of ESG, that belief does not excuse anticompetitive agreements or unlawful conduct to advance progressive policies. The Committee on the Judiciary has jurisdiction to examine unlawful restraints of trade and commerce.[35] Accordingly, to help us better understand the roles you and your organizations play in facilitating and coordinating companies' efforts to achieve ESG-related goals, we request that you produce the following documents and information, for the period December 1, 2016, to the present:

1) All documents and communications referring or relating to the various markets, sectors, or industries, in which Climate Action 100+ or Ceres help investors, members, or other companies advance ESG-related goals.
2) All documents and communications referring or relating to guidance from Climate Action 100+ (including from any of its investor networks, any of its working groups, or its Steering Committee) or Ceres on how investors, members, or other companies can or should advance ESG-related goals, including but not limited to how they can or should do so with so-called "focus companies."
3) All documents and communications referring or relating to any efforts by Climate Action 100+ (including by any of its investor networks, any of its working groups, or its Steering Committee) or Ceres to obtain or solicit agreements, commitments, or other types of

---

33 *See, e.g.*, *Corporate Collusion*, *supra* n.17, at 6-7; *United States v. MMR Corp. (LA)*, 907 F.2d 489, 498 (5th Cir. 1990); *Linens of Eur., Inc. v. Best Mfg., Inc.*, No. 03 CIV. 9612 (GEL), 2004 WL 2071689, at *13 (S.D.N.Y. Sept. 16, 2004); *Spanish Broad. Sys., Inc. v. Clear Channel Commc'ns, Inc.*, 242 F. Supp. 2d 1350, 1361 (S.D. Fla. 2003); *Smithkline Beecham Corp. v. E. Applicators, Inc.*, No. CIV.A. 99-CV-6552, 2002 WL 1197763, at *8 (E.D. Pa. May 24, 2002); *Tondas v. Amateur Hockey Ass'n of U. S.*, 438 F. Supp. 310, 315 (W.D.N.Y. 1977); *Ozdoba v. Verney Brunswick Mills Inc*, 152 F. Supp. 136, 138 (S.D.N.Y. 1946); *Matter of Toys R Us, Inc.*, 126 F.T.C. 415, 584-85 (1998) (listing the elements for a hub and spoke conspiracy); *Butler v. Jimmy John's Franchise, LLC*, 331 F. Supp. 3d 786, 795 (S.D. Ill. 2018).

34 *The ESG Movement Is a Ripe Target for Antitrust Action*, *supra* n.4.

35 Rules of the House of Representatives, R. X, 117th Cong. (2021).

participation from any investors, members, or other companies, including but not limited to BlackRock, State Street, or Vanguard, to advance ESG-related goals. Please understand this request to include, but not be limited to, any documents and communications referring or relating to any investor's, member's, or other company's knowledge or awareness of a different investor's, member's, or other company's coordination or work with, or agreements to support efforts relating to, Climate Action 100+ or Ceres.

4) All documents and communications between or among investors, members, or other companies referring or relating to investors', members', or other companies' joint or collective efforts to advance ESG-related goals, including any documents and communications reflecting or suggesting agreement over specific steps, policies, or best practices.
5) All documents and communications referring or relating to the circumstances of the founding of Climate Action 100+, including any documents and communications about the need for Climate Action 100+ to facilitate advancing ESG-related goals, and about the roles of Ceres and CalPERS.
6) All documents and communications between or among proxy advisory firms, including Institutional Shareholder Services and Glass Lewis, or financial services companies, including PayPal, referring or relating to ESG-related goals.

Please produce this information as soon as possible but no later than 5:00 p.m. on December 20, 2022.

Furthermore, this letter serves as a formal request to preserve all existing and future records and materials relating to the topics addressed in this letter. You should construe this preservation notice as an instruction to take all reasonable steps to prevent the destruction or alteration, whether intentionally or negligently, of all documents, communications, and other information, including electronic information and metadata, that are or may be responsive to this congressional inquiry. This instruction includes all electronic messages sent using your official and personal accounts or devices, including records created using text messages, phone-based message applications, or encryption software.

If you have any questions about this request, please contact Committee staff at (202) 225- 6906. Thank you for your prompt attention to this matter.

Sincerely,

Dan Bishop
Member of Congress

Jim Jordan
Ranking Member

Matt Gaetz
Member of Congress

Tom McClintock
Ranking Member
Subcommittee on Immigration
and Citizenship

Scott Fitzgerald
Member of Congress

Cliff Bentz
Member of Congress

cc: The Honorable Jerrold L. Nadler, Chairman

Index

S

T

U

V

W

Y